W9-AAO-532

The History of the RCMP Marine Services

Courtesy Constable David Johns (Retd). Illustrated by Ken Burton

Previously published by the Office of the Deputy Commissioner RCMP Pacific Region

Design by Peter Vassilopoulos
Production by Pacific Marine Publishing, Canada

Printed and bound in China

Library and Archives Canada Cataloguing in Publication

Haycock, Kenneth John, 1951-
The history of the RCMP Marine Services / Kenneth John Haycock ; edited by Peter Vassilopoulos.

Includes bibliographical references and index.
ISBN 978-0-919317-47-5

1. Royal Canadian Mounted Police. Marine Services--History. 2. Government vessels--Canada--History. 3. Government vessels--Canada--History--Pictorial works. 4. Police patrol--Canada--Surveillance operations--History. I. Vassilopoulos, Peter, 1940- II. Title.

VM397.H39 2012 623.826'30971 C2012-901385-4

The History of the RCMP Marine Services

Kenneth John Haycock
Edited by Marine Author Peter Vassilopoulos

Preface

This preface was written by Cst Kenneth John Haycock several months prior to his untimely death after a courageous battle with cancer in 2009.

I am a member of the Royal Canadian Mounted Police and am privileged to serve in the 'E' Division Marine Services on the coast of British Columbia. One day I discovered in our detachment office in Nanaimo several photographs of what appeared to be naval vessels. Upon further investigation I found that they were in fact RCMP vessels which were in service during and shortly after the Second World War. I had hoped to display these photographs in our detachment office, and so began to investigate them. I wanted to know their names, where they operated, who operated them, when they were in service of the RCMP and why the RCMP lost possession of them. I was following a thought process that I know other police officers will recognize.

It was not long before this little investigation got out of control. Soon I had in my possession numerous documents identifying more than 200 vessels that served the RCMP from 1890 to 2000 and beyond. Many historical articles, written mostly by former members, were found in the National Archives and the RCMP Quarterly magazine. When it came to looking for a reference book on the subject of the RCMP Marine Services or vessels, I could not locate one. It appeared there were countless references to the RCMP Marine Services, but not in many books. References were sporadic, very limited in detail and spread over countless similar and related subjects.

Many excellent books have been written regarding the Canadian Marine Service vessels of the Canadian Coast Guard, Canadian Fisheries, and the Royal Canadian Navy and Auxiliary Ships. It was not my purpose to repeat information found in those publications, but I have used many of their references to establish correct historical data regarding government offices, names of ships and time lines of events. It is my hope that this book will enlighten others, emphasise the role of the RCMP Marine Services in Canada, and the role played by its stalwart 'maritime horsemen.'

—Kenneth John Haycock

CONTENTS

A Rigid Hulled Inflatable Boat in rough seas. RCMP members are trained to handle such craft for the conditions in which they have to operate at times.

Courtesy Frank Lalear

Foreword

The winds of disaster blew angrily across the waves and whipped up a storm that smashed the disabled vessel on the shores of Lake Winnipeg. When the storm abated its ferocity was revealed. Two policemen were missing and the captain was lying in grave condition on a bed in a Winnipeg hospital. Their immediate supervisor launched a search and investigation that was an incredible feat that involved travelling some 1,300 miles in a canoe.

This was the story of the *Keewatin* and the first marine tragedy of the North West Mounted Police. How many RCMP members today could relate to this story of adventure and misfortune? How many Canadians are aware of this marine element of the Royal Canadian Mounted Police? It is my hope that this book will demonstrate the important role played by the marine members of the RCMP and make Canadians aware of the magnitude of the RCMP marine resources. Today the RCMP marine resources are still relatively few in number and are sparsely located along Canada's shorelines, but to the communities they serve and the detachments they support they are a vital part of the police service. Because they are seldom seen by the general non-boating public, people often wonder what the police do out there. How many people work in the RCMP Marine Services? Where do they go? What are their goals?

Here are some examples of the work done by the RCMP Marine Services:

• *People in the small isolated coastal community are visibly upset as one of their neighbours lies dead. The local detachment consisting of three members is tied up in the office with the investigation. Members of the RCMP Marine Service are in attendance to take over general policing duties and to conduct an interview of a possible eye witness among the increasingly angry crowd. They will be here for a few days...*

• *RCMP Marine members have beached their small inflatable boat on the shore of an island and are cold and wet after a long and very dark night running through the straits. With them is a specialist in the use of Forward Looking Infrared equipment known as FLIR. They will now crawl through the bush and woods to get a look from afar at a possible marijuana grow site inside a secluded building...*

• *The scene has been secured and members of the RCMP Marine Services are seizing and marking exhibits and examining the murder scene in a house on the isolated shores of a coastal inlet. The responsible detachment does not have enough resources to do this, so the Marine Service has attended to assist with the investigation and to take the victim to a morgue for an autopsy...*

• *There is a huge smile on the face of the forestry official as he peers back over the stern of the RCMP vessel at a seized log barge carrying over $200,000 worth of stolen logs. He had been tracking this suspect for months and now has the evidence for which he is looking. All that remains is to match the logs with stumps in the forest from which they came and his case will be solid. He knows the RCMP Marine Services will be there to provide transportation and assistance with his investigation...*

• *Word has come in that some unidentified vessels are heading for the coast of Canada and may be carrying an illegal human cargo. Quickly an Emergency Response Team is assembled and placed aboard one of the RCMP police craft. They will run out to the edge of Canadian authority waters with National Defence Ships to intervene and take into custody the vessels and the skippers involved in this human trade...*

Just like their partners on land, the RCMP Marine Services members conduct a wide range of investigations and carry out numerous duties on a day to day basis. These could involve criminal code, customs and excise, Canada shipping, search and rescue, forestry, fisheries, commercial vessels, or simply public safety inspections. The RCMP Marine Services are always busy and on call, but when things slow down members can usually be found close at hand, such as in a ship's galley preparing their own meals. —*Kenneth John Haycock*

R.C.M. POLICE ST. ROCH

Introduction

Since the inception of the RCMP, its members have had to be mobile in order to conduct their duties. Historically this has involved horses, boats, aircraft and automobiles, with the mode of transport evolving to meet the changing needs. The Force operated under the name North West Mounted Police (NWMP) from 1873 to June 24, 1904, when in recognition of exemplary service, the title 'Royal' was granted and the name changed to Royal North West Mounted Police (RNWMP). On February 1, 1920, following the amalgamation of the Dominion Police and the RNWMP, the name changed again to Royal Canadian Mounted Police (RCMP).

For over 100 years the RCMP has used boats of all sizes to perform patrols and carry out marine duties which, like their other modes of transportation, have changed over time. In the 1890s their patrol area consisted mainly of the prairies of Central and Western Canada. Lake Winnipeg was their main waterway. In the late 1890s and early 1900s the RCMP became responsible for law and order in the Yukon, hence some smaller launches were obtained for patrols on its lakes and rivers. Sovereignty issues then arose and RCMP posts were needed in the Arctic and the Hudson Bay area. Schooners were obtained and deployed to those areas for supplies and patrols. One schooner was specifically built by the RCMP and was a floating detachment. Differing geography and social change dictated the delivery method of law enforcement.

The beginning of a much larger, professional, and marine specific part of the RCMP called the RCMP Marine Section took place in 1932 when the RCMP took over the Preventive Services of the Department of National Revenue, and control of many larger ocean-going vessels. In 1939 most of their members were transferred to the military and became instrumental in the development of the Canadian War effort. When hostilities ended in 1945 the RCMP Marine Section was re-established with ex-Royal Canadian Navy vessels and in 1947 it became the RCMP Marine Division. This continued to 1970 when the Division was terminated and control and all marine assets were turned over to their home divisions. Marine assets became known as RCMP Marine Services.

Responsibilities for marine assets changed over the years. Local detachments needed smaller craft to facilitate their special needs. Provincial divisions that fronted the oceans or lakes also needed marine assets and often coincided with federal government needs. This explains why over the years the size of vessels, number of vessels and responsible bodies have changed dramatically. They have gone from a few local detachment launches of five or six, to a floating detachment, to a Marine Section with ocean-going vessels, to a Marine Division of up to 73 ocean-going and smaller lake and river vessels, and then back to a few vessels of the Marine Services.

Long periods on patrol cause RCMP members to develop a trusting relationship with their mode of transportation. In all probability the NWMP member who marched west in 1873 had a similar relationship with his horse as a marine member has with his vessel. The naming of the horse or the vessel helps to make it an integral part of a team.

When one's life depends on transportation, such as a ship, and continuous periods are spent aboard, the particular vessel in use can become very special. This book is dedicated to recording for posterity the history of some of the special vessels of the RCMP.

Opposite: An artist's rendering of the RCMP St Roch *and her historic route through the North West Passage.*

Acknowledgements

The history of the Royal Canadian Mounted Police is punctuated by stories of ordinary men and women rendered heroic in far off and deserted corners of this country. Canadian culture, identity and indeed the very fabric of our modern society is imbued with the history and evolution of the RCMP.

Until the rise of the modern Canadian Navy and Coast Guard services, the RCMP provided the primary maritime federal representation of ships on the coast and inland waters of Canada. Many of these vessels were impressive ocean-going ships that featured modern (for that era) armaments, dedicated RCMP Marine Division crews and a complex mandate to serve the interests of Canada. These vessels served in the high Arctic, on the Great Lakes, all three oceans and virtually all the navigable inland waters of Canada. The total number of vessels utilized within the RCMP from the establishment of the Force until modern times exceeded 200.

Constable Kenneth Haycock, a Marine Services member, came to the unsettling conclusion in early 2005 that no one had ever documented or chronicled the complete history of the RCMP Marine Services. While fighting off a debilitating and ultimately fatal medical condition, Cst Haycock set out to chronicle this history.

Constable Haycock ultimately produced a substantial manuscript with the assistance of a number of people. This manuscript is a testament not only to Cst Haycock's determination, but also to the history, resolve and dedication of members of the NWMP, RNWMP and the RCMP who served at various times on Force-owned vessels.

—Inspector Kenneth Burton, RCMP Pacific Region

With much gratitude, the publishers and archivists participating in the production of this book wish to thank the following for their assistance, time and effort in providing and assembling the material contained in its pages: RCMP members, staff and supporters, including Deputy Commissioner Gary Bass, Assistant Commissioner Bernard Corrigan, CMO Robert Jorssen, Regional Sergeant Major Glen McRae, L/Cmdr Bryon Taylor, Benjamin Dunn, Sophie Chevalier-Forget and Amanda Deevy. Also the Vancouver Maritime Museum, Libraries and Archives Canada, the Glenbow Museum and Archives, the Yukon Archives, the Northwest Territories Museum and Archives, the MacBride Museum, the British Columbia Maritime Museum, the Royal Canadian Navy, the RCMP Historical Collections Unit, the RCMP Heritage Centre, the RCMP Veterans' Association and the West Coast Marine Detachment.

Thanks also to the Haycock family, Don Van Dusen, Insp Don Saigle, Cst John May, Sgt Frank Lalear, Don Klancher, Gilles Gagne, Robert F. Holtom, Roy Holtom, Pat King, Gary Dalton, Bonnie Jarvis Lowe, John Kerster, Peter Caron, Doug Scattergood, Spud Roscoe, Harry Carmen, James J. Boulton, John Horton, Peter and Carla Vassilopoulos and others whose invaluable input contributed to the completion of the work.

The listing of vessels in this book has been compiled from data extensively researched by the author and work associates involved in the final production.
A surprisingly large number of photographs of vessels became available from several sources as did technical specification of the craft included. While data from the early days was sparse and in most cases difficult to recover, that of more recent vessels of the RCMP was more forthcoming. The data published, therefore, may be incomplete, especially in the early years. The collaborators on the production of this book decided to show a listing of specifications, even though some of the details were not available for all vessels. The spaces left blank may be filled in by individuals for their own purposes in future, if they happen to know such details. In some cases photographs are missing but the available details have been included to keep the collection and history as complete as possible.
Where (1) or (2) is shown after the name of a vessel, they were the first or second craft with the same name. Some vessels carried the Roman numeral II or III which usually indicates the vessel was named while another still carried the same name.

Dedication

On May 14, 2009, eight days before he entered hospital for the last time, Kenn received a commendation from RCMP Deputy Commissioner Gary Bass in recognition of his work on this book. At that time he also received a promise that his work would be published. Even though Kenn would not live to see it, his dream of documenting the history of the RCMP Marine Services in Canada did come true, thanks to the dedication and commitment of Deputy Commissioner Bass, Inspector Ken Burton and Sergeant Major Glen McRae. They have my eternal admiration and gratitude, and I will be forever indebted to them and all others who have been involved in this project. I also wish to express my deepest gratitude to Sergeant Kathy Dickson and Superintendent Maria Nickel whose visits to our home during Kenn's illness ultimately led to the publication of this book.

During the difficult days of his treatment for lymphoma, this work provided a focus and a goal for him. As his illness progressed he felt an urgency to complete his work and tried to wrap up his research, even though it was not complete. This is where the RCMP's assistance proved invaluable, as they were able to collect information and photographs that Kenn could not, and compile them into this beautiful book.

I dedicate this book to the members of the RCMP whose friendship and support were so important to Kenn.

—Jacqueline Haycock

Commendation

Constable Kenneth Haycock, Regimental No. 42712, is officially commended for outstanding service with respect to his research into the history of the Marine Services of the Royal Canadian Mounted Police.

Constable Haycock, a member of Marine Services since 1998, has had a lifelong interest in history and genealogy. Taking that interest to another level, Constable Haycock has undertaken to chronicle the history of Marine Services within the Force. Working in collaboration with Lieutenant Commander Bryon Taylor, Canadian Forces Directorate of Maritime Training and Education, Constable Haycock researched the National Archives and has written a book detailing the unique maritime services which the Force has provided to Canada throughout the years. This book will stand as a lasting legacy for future generations to study, learn from and enjoy. Constable Haycock's pride in and commitment to the Marine Services bring credit to himself and are in keeping with the highest traditions of the Royal Canadian Mounted Police.

Gary D. Bass, O.O.M.
Deputy Commissioner – Pacific Region & Commanding Officer, 'E' Division Royal Canadian Mounted Police.

Royal North West Mounted Police officers en route to Yukon Territory, 1905-1906.

Glenbow Archives NA-2703-5

Chapter One

In the Beginning

The history of Canadian marine law enforcement had a beginning that often appears confusing to anyone reviewing the records as to who was responsible for what and where. Some of the Canadian Government offices lasted only a few months, while others remain to this day. As Canada was a very new country and being continually reorganized, the names and responsibilities of some of the early offices were changed frequently. The forerunners of our present day federal offices of the Coast Guard, Department of Fisheries and Oceans, Transport Canada, Canada Customs and Excise, Royal Canadian Navy and Royal Canadian Mounted Police may have had different names, but their primary responsibilities have remained fairly constant.

The first Canadian marine law enforcement agency that actually existed before Confederation was the Ministry of Customs (1841), which in 1921 became Customs and Excise, and in 1927 National Revenue. Another government agency that worked in the marine enforcement was the Department of Marine and Fisheries (1867), which was the forerunner to the Department of Fisheries and Oceans. Over the past 100 years, however, it has had 10 other names. In 1873 the North West Mounted Police was established. It eventually became the Royal Canadian Mounted Police. The Royal Canadian Navy was not formed until 1910 and the Department of Railways and Canals (1879) became the Department of Transport in 1936 along with the Department of Marine, which later became the Canadian Coast Guard (1962). Although marine-related duties were the common thread, their mandates were quite different from one another. Due to limited resources and Canada being so geographically large, some departments utilized the equipment of others to facilitate their needs.

Prior to Confederation in 1867 Britain maintained a fleet of about 20 vessels in Halifax to protect the fisheries of Canada. These were war vessels, which represented maritime law at the time. With the end of the American Civil War, people were tiring of a military presence and looking for a more civil way of settling disputes and protecting their sovereign rights. Therefore the new government of the Dominion of Canada acquired a number of sailing schooners to patrol the fishing grounds and the St Lawrence, as well as to service coastal light stations with equipment and supplies. These ships were titled Canadian Government Ships (CGS) and since they resembled many of the fishing vessels of the day, they patrolled undetected within the fishing fleet and met with considerable success in enforcing fishery laws. They were armed with nine-pounder cannons and a few small arms.

In the Beginning

When a 'series of outrages broke out along the Atlantic coast, consisting of wrecks, piracy, plundering and murder, the government was forced to install a patrol vessel capable of maintaining law and order in Canadian waters. This ship was the sailing vessel *La Canadienne* which patrolled from Labrador to the Bay of Fundy in the late 1870s. It was commanded by Dr Pierre Fortin, who was a medical doctor as well as the captain. He was also the magistrate responsible for the enforcement of maritime laws. This one vessel exercised considerable control over the East Coast and served Canada's interests well.

On the west coast of Canada there was the *Quadra*, the only sea-going government vessel based in Esquimalt, which for years carried a police officer on board. She was commanded by Captain John T. Walbran who was also a magistrate. *Quadra* was the transport vessel for government officials up and down the West Coast until February 1917 when she was beached after a collision with the CPR ship *Charmer*. She was sold in 1917 and operated on the West Coast as a rum runner until the US Coast Guard seized her in 1925.

Along with sailing vessels, the government also used steamers. These vessels provisioned rescue stations, provided training for sailors and served as platforms for other marine police forces. Fisheries operated the Dominion Cruisers, which were armed enforcement vessels that patrolled the Pacific and Atlantic fishing grounds. Many government ships were transferred from one department to another while others were leased or chartered as needed.

In the late 1800s RCMP (NWMP) ships were mainly sailing schooners and yachts, but in 1891 the first steamer, *Constance*, was put into service. Canada's offshore limit was only 12 miles at the time and foreign vessels were notably common in the Gulf of St Lawrence as they travelled and fished in the Gulf or the Grand Banks off Newfoundland. It was imperative that Canada demonstrate an ability to protect its offshore waters. The Fisheries Protection Service accomplished this alongside the Marine Services vessels of the Department of Marine and Fisheries.

The Royal Canadian Navy was established on May 4, 1910. It obtained its first two vessels, the cruiser *Rainbow*, for the West Coast and the cruiser *Niobe* for the East Coast from the Royal Navy. These two ships served in the First World War and were replaced by the destroyers *Patrician* and *Patriot* in 1920. They were subsequently replaced in 1928 by the *Champlain* on the East Coast and the *Vancouver* on the West Coast.

In 1933 the Royal Canadian Navy had a total of four destroyers and two minesweepers, plus one minesweeper in reserve. During the Second World War the RCN grew from 13 ships to 450, one of the largest navies in the world.

From Confederation until 1932 most large sea-going vessels were operated by the Royal Canadian Navy for national defence. They were used by the Customs Department for control of smuggling and the Department of Marine and Fisheries for hydrographic services, lighthouse supply, fishery protection, search and rescue and navigation aids. At the time another agency was rapidly growing and making its mark in the marine environment. The Royal Canadian Mounted Police turned over about 33 vessels along with 209 members to the Royal Canadian Navy and other branches of the Canadian Armed Forces in 1939. This was the culmination of many years marine experience, training and expertise that served to enhance greatly the Canadian contribution to the World War II effort. But where did this force come from and how did it evolve?

Many people are aware that the RCMP was established in 1873 and originally called the North West Mounted Police (NWMP). It had a mere 300 men deployed to the mid-west of Canada to assist in bringing law and order to what was 'Ruperts Land', owned originally by the Hudson's Bay Company. This land was purchased by the Canadian Government in what has been referred to as one of the largest real estate deals in history. In 1871, Canada and the United States agreed to the 49th parallel as the border which divided the two countries and it became the duty of the NWMP to patrol this border as well as the Canadian Territories. In order to perform these patrols it became evident that boats would have to become part of the arsenal of equipment along with horses, wagons, trains, dogs and dog sleds.

From the Office of the Comptroller in Ottawa dated January 4, 1887, there is reference to the building of a ferry to cross 'C' and 'D' Divisions over the Bow River near Calgary in the fall of 1886. Major (Inspector) James Walker had the boat built at the cost of $91.52. The comptroller directed that the boat be taken on charge (as other boats of this type disappeared) and it was subsequently taken on charge by 'E' Division. There was no description of the boat but it was probably a barge, suitable for use as a ferry.

Lake Winnipeg served as a travel route to a distant patrol area in the midwest. In 1890, the sailing vessel *Keewatin* was the first known patrol vessel purchased for the NWMP. It was brought from Selkirk near the mouth of the Red River to Winnipeg where it made patrols over several hundred miles of Lake Winnipeg. Not only did the *Keewatin* become noted as the first patrol vessel of the NWMP but also it became the first vessel to have a collision and first to lose men. Two members, Corporal Harry Morphy and Constable George de Beaujeu, drowned when the *Keewatin* smashed onto some submerged rocks in Lake Winnipeg during a storm in late August 1890. Captain Matthew Watts survived the sinking.

When Inspector Begin, officer in charge of the Lake Winnipeg detachment, heard that the *Keewatin* had sunk he set out to investigate by canoe, the most common mode of travel in the area. He learned that two men were missing and Captain Watts had been taken to Selkirk by the steamer *Aurora*. After an extensive search Inspector Begin could not locate the bodies of Morphy or de Beaujeu (they were recovered months later) so he returned to Selkirk after travelling a distance of some 1,300 miles by canoe.

Commissioner Herchmer interviewed Captain Watts at his bedside in a Winnipeg hospital and heard the tale about how the *Keewatin* had run onto the rocks, rolled on her side and had her centreboard torn off. In his report he stated: "I heard from his own lips the tale of the wreck and his subsequent sufferings. His ability as a sailing master was undoubted, and his efforts to sustain our men after the accident cannot be too highly extolled, while his fortitude during the awful time he remained tied to the wreck almost surpasses belief. I regret to report that after rallying and apparently rapidly approaching recovery, this fine old man had a relapse and succumbed to the results of the frightful exposure and sufferings which he had undergone." Captain Watts was 66.

Gold was discovered in 1886 in the Yukon and by 1893 it became apparent that Canada must send some authority to the north to protect the aboriginal people and satisfy Canadian Sovereignty on its borders with Alaska. On June 1, 1895, Inspector Charles Constantine departed Regina by train to Seattle where he and 19 men boarded the Alaska Commercial Company's vessel *Excelsior* for St Michael, Alaska. From there they travelled up the Yukon River and established the first NWMP post near Fort Cudahy. When more gold was discovered in the Klondike on August 17, 1896, by George Carmack, Skookum Jim, and Tagish Charlie, a gold rush was in the making and a border presence became necessary. The Yukon River was like a highway and in 1899 to patrol this area Superintendent Steele of the NWMP obtained two small steam powered launches called the *Gladys,* which was later converted to gasoline, and the *Jessie*. Soon they were joined by a third vessel, the *Tagish*. In 1902 a larger river steam ship vessel called the *May West*, ideal for the transportation of supplies, equipment and men on the waterway, was purchased at a sheriff's sale for $3,000. She was renamed *Scout* by the NWMP but since there was already a vessel by that name on the registry, the name was changed to *Vidette*.

The *Gladys* was an alco-vapour patrol boat. She arrived in Bennet, B.C. in September 1899. The vessel was 45 feet long with a beam of 10 feet and a loaded draft of three feet. The *Gladys* did not meet the needs of the NWMP as the draft was too much to pass through some of the shallow waters of the Yukon and she was underpowered for the fast current. In 1902 she underwent a number of alterations including a conversion from coal-oil to wood burner. This proved to be efficient as she burned only three-quarters-of-a-ton of wood in a 50-mile trip at a speed of four to five miles an hour on still waters. Despite engineered propellers she lacked sufficient power, so in 1905 she was fitted with a gasoline engine and moved from Whitehorse to Carcross where she patrolled between there and Conrad during the summer. In 1907 she patrolled Lake Tagish and Lake Bennett under S/Sgt O.W. Evans. In 1911 it was determined that the *Gladys* would need $200 in repairs. This was done during the summer of 1912 and she again patrolled the waters in 1913 for the last time under the RNWMP. She was sold to the Pine Creek Power Co. for $780 on August 27, 1913 after 14 years service.

The *Tagish* served until 1907 when she was transferred to the B.C. Government Agent in Atlin. The *Jessie* was taken out of service in 1908 and sold on March 11, 1910.

The *Vidette* was a large river steamer that patrolled between Dawson and Whitehorse. Purchased in 1902, she was the pride of the Yukon. She served for many years but became too expensive for the dwindling force to maintain. In 1908 she was transferred to the Survey Branch of the Department of the Interior. By 1910 the north had settled down, the border was defined between Alaska and Canada, and the RNWMP reduced its manpower in the Yukon to 60 men. The need for vessels was very limited.

At the turn of the century a new and different problem was starting to surface in the Northwest Territories and Arctic. Much of the land was unexplored and it was questionable whether Canada could claim sovereignty to it. There was a major American whaling outpost located on Herschel Island near the Alaskan/Yukon border and the Canadian government was getting complaints about conflicts between the whalers and native inhabitants. Having learned valuable lessons from the Klondike experience, the government planned to use the North West Mounted Police to impose law and order by sending patrols farther north to establish detachments in the Arctic, and farther east to establish detachments in the Northwest Territories and around Hudson Bay.

This sovereignty process was done in three parts. In 1903 a two-man NWMP detachment led by a Sgt Fitzgerald was established on Herschel Island in the western Arctic. The officers arrived on the desolate island in early August. The island was about 12 miles long by two to four miles wide, and was occupied by six Pacific Steam Whaling Co. storehouses and a few huts. The duties of the detachment were to collect customs, enforce Canadian laws and stop the trading of liquor to the Inuit.

They were not too early, for within a couple of weeks the whaling fleet sailed into port. When the vessels *Alexander, Thrasher, Bowhead, Belvedere,*

Baylies, and *Beluga* arrived they were greeted by Sergeant Fitzgerald who politely asked details of the crews and their cargoes. They were advised that the practice of selling liquor to the local natives had to cease, customs and duties had to be paid on all landed goods and Canadian laws would be applied and enforced. Although very surprised, and assuming this would be only a temporary police outpost at best, most captains accepted their authority, although some did challenge it by attempting to smuggle a couple of bottles of liquor ashore. These were promptly seized, and the whalers realized their past illegal activities were over.

The second part of the sovereignty process targeted Hudson Bay with the dispatch of the CGS *Neptune*, a three-masted, 190-foot, 465-ton sealing schooner. With five members and one officer, Inspector J.D. Moodie, the CGS *Neptune,* under Captain Sam Bartlett, sailed in August 1903 from Halifax to Hudson Bay to establish a detachment at Fullerton. CGS *Neptune*, which was built in 1873 and constructed to withstand the pressure of arctic ice, wintered in Chesterfield Inlet in Hudson Bay then continued to Ellesmere Island.

In 1904, now Superintendent, Moodie filed his report and immediately returned to Fullerton when the government sent RNWMP members again to Hudson Bay on the 165-foot barquentine CGS *Arctic,* under the command of Captain Joseph Bernier. This was an old vessel, originally owned by the German government and used as an Antarctic exploration ship called *Gauss* which was renamed when the government purchased her in 1904. The CGS *Arctic* was to serve as a base for patrols to the eastern arctic and to leave plaques throughout, proclaiming Canadian sovereignty over its Arctic waters. This continued for seven years and was instrumental in establishing and supplying RNWMP outposts throughout the Arctic. Many expeditions were sent north to enforce Canadian fishing regulations and lay claim to Melville Island, Baffin Island, Lancaster Sound, Pond Inlet and other areas. These vessels were not owned by the NWMP but were used as transport to get men and supplies into the icy north.

Canada was very complacent about sovereignty in the Arctic Islands but was forced to realize other countries would claim them if they were allowed. A Norwegian Arctic explorer by the name of Otto Sverdrup spent four years from 1898 to 1902 mapping and surveying the Arctic Islands and met with no opposition. He urgently pressed his own Norwegian government to pursue claims but gained no cooperation. In recognition of his exertions and discoveries, Canada awarded Sverdrup a grant of $67,000 in 1903. Canada started to pay attention and when Roald Amundsen, another Norwegian, sailed the North West passage in 1906 on a ship called the *Gjoa*, and Arctic explorers from all over the world began attempting to get to the North Pole, the message was clear, "claim it or lose it". Norwegians, Swedes and Americans were all showing interest in laying claim to these islands in the Arctic.

The third part of securing sovereignty in the north took place many years later, in 1922. The refurbished CGS *Arctic*, again under command of Captain Bernier, headed north and set up detachments on Ellesmere Island, Baffin Island and Devon Island, some areas so remote that even the Inuit had not lived there for hundreds of years. This duty fell upon Inspector C.E. Wilcox, Corporals Jakeman, McInnes, Constables Fairman, Fielder, Anstead, Harry Must, Friel, McGregor and Herbert Lee. On the return of Captain Bernier, the Ottawa Journal reported on October 22, 1922; "Canada's Northern Empire within 850 miles of North Pole, Making our Sovereignty Certain". This statement has been true for over 80 years but is still a challenge for Canada. By 1927 the RNWMP, now the RCMP, had detachments at Port Burwell, Craig Harbour, Pond Inlet, Pangnirtung, Dundas Harbour, Bache Peninsula and Lake Harbour.

In 1904 the NWMP became the Royal North West Mounted Police (RNWMP) and the first vessel built specially for them was constructed in the Government Shipyard at Sorel, Quebec in 1906. It was called the *Rouville*, a single screw patrol steamer of about 130 feet and was a total failure during its test runs. It was going to be a ship solely operated by the RNWMP so they would not have to depend on other government agencies. The vessel was mistakenly built with improper cargo holds, the engines were inefficient and during trials it burned a ton of coal per hour. It was never commissioned by the RNWMP but was turned over to the Department of Marine and Fisheries who used it in the St Lawrence as a buoy tender. The *Rouville* sank in 1931.

After the sinking of the *Keewatin,* on Lake Winnipeg, the next vessel that served on the lake was the *Redwing*. It was a 65-foot motor vessel used from 1904 to 1906 but was deemed unfit for the rough waters of the lake by Inspector Walker and was summarily dispatched to Lake of the Woods. Other vessels like the 122-foot river side-wheeler SS *Northern Light* (renamed *Northland Light* in 1909) and the *Midnight Sun* owned by the Northern Transportation Company, were used by the police for patrols in 1906.

A smaller vessel chartered for use in Hudson Bay on police patrols, was the 47-foot Hudson's Bay Company sailboat called *McTavish*. She was based in Chesterfield Inlet. During the fall of 1909 Superintendent Moodie dispatched Sergeant D. McArthur, Corporal F.W. Reeves, Constable MacMillan, and Constable McDiarmid from Fullerton to Ellis Island on a whale boat. There they were to meet with Inspector E.A. Pelletier and their relief personnel. Pelletier was then to continue on to Churchill on the sailboat *McTavish* while the relief personnel carried on to Fullerton aboard the whale boat.

A few days later the *McTavish* sank during a gale when she became rudderless and was swamped by a huge wave over the bow. After salvaging as many supplies as they could from the sinking sailboat, the members raised a distress signal on the spar. The signal was spotted by some Inuit in a whale boat. They rescued the crew and took them back to Fullerton. In December the members successfully arrived in Churchill, a trip of 450 miles, this time by dog sled.

The *Jeannie* and *Laddie* were two more schooners that were operated by the RNWMP in Hudson Bay. The *Jeannie* was wrecked at Wager Inlet in 1910. The *Laddie* returned to Brigus, Newfoundland in 1911 and served there until 1914 when she succumbed to a grounding. During the summer of 1909 the RNWMP acquired two small launches built for use in Hudson Bay and merely called them *Launch A* and *Launch B*. They are mentioned in the 1909–1914 Commissioner' s Annual Reports along with *Launch C* in 1914.

In Hudson Bay the RNWMP made use of several vessels of the schooner class design. The *Village Belle* was a private vessel which was purchased by the RNWMP in 1914 and set sail for Hudson Bay from Halifax. The RNWMP were to do an investigation into a couple of murders in the Baker Lake and Chesterfield Inlet area led by Inspector W.J. Beyts. It took nearly six years to find the suspects. A member of this search party was a former Royal Navy man, Constable A.B. Kennedy, a good map maker, who spent two years doing surveys of the area and making maps. The *Village Belle* was beached at Port Nelson in 1914 and then had a flywheel of an engine break, severely injuring ex-Cst Chinn, the engineer. Before long it was sold at Port Nelson.

When the First World War broke out in 1914 the government refused to let members of the RNWMP join the military service. However in 1917, the

RNWMP police duties were suspended in Manitoba, Saskatchewan and Alberta and in 1918 members of the force were allowed to volunteer for the war effort. Twelve officers and 726 men were given leave to transfer to the armed forces where they became the 'A' Squadron. Later that same year another six officers and 184 men joined and became 'B' Squadron.

Such was the decimation of the RNWMP that in 1918 only about 303 members remained, down to the level of the March West in 1874. More than half of these men were in the Northwest Territories or the Yukon. It was a demoralizing time for the force as 87 detachments were closed. Realizing the need for a strong federal police force an Order In Council authorized the Force to increase its ranks to 1,200 men and defined its new duties.

In 1919 with the threat of labour strikes and public unrest, the government again ordered the Force to bring up the number of its ranks, this time to 2,500 men. More expansion was soon in the works and on November 10, 1919 the RNWMP Act was amended to create the Royal Canadian Mounted Police. Their authority extended to all of Canada and consisted of four branches, the Criminal Investigation Branch, the Intelligence Branch, the Finance and Supply Branch and the Adjutants Office. It was then that the headquarters were moved from Regina, Saskatchewan to Ottawa, Ontario.

In 1919 the RNWMP had four seagoing motor vessels of its own. They were the *Victory* at Herschel Island, the *Duncan* and *Lady Borden* in Hudson Bay and the *Chakawana* in Prince Rupert on the West Coast. The *Chakawana* was commanded by Inspector A.C. Acland and was based in Prince Rupert from 1919 until 1921. The intent was to provide a vessel that could patrol the west coast of British Columbia in relative safety and facilitate regular visits to logging, mining and fishing communities. The *Chakawana* was acquired from the Imperial Munitions Board in Alert Bay. She was built in 1911 and was 62 feet long, 13 feet wide and fitted with a Wolverine engine. The RNWMP took possession August 1919 in Vancouver but the trip to Prince Rupert was fraught with many engine problems and arrived 12 days later. It was a seaworthy vessel but an engine overhaul was much needed. On August 7, 1921 while tied up to a wharf in Vancouver the *Chakawana* began to sink. Unfit for service, she was eventually sold in October 1921.

In a letter dated February 7, 1923 from Assistant Commissioner Cortlandt Starnes to the Department of Marine and Fisheries, six vessels were confirmed and identified as property of the RCMP. These were the *Fitzgerald*, a 35-foot motor launch located at Fort Norman near present day Tulita on the Mackenzie River in the Northwest Territories; a 30-foot launch *Victory* located at the mouth of the river on Herschel Island; two 30-foot vessels called the *Resolution* and the *Duncan* at Fort Smith on the Slave River; the 34-foot *Lady Borden* on the northwestern shore of Hudson Bay at Chesterfield Inlet; and the 25-foot *Blue Wing* in Halifax, Nova Scotia.

The 1920s brought in an era of border concerns and trafficking in illegal goods. With prohibition in place in the USA, drug and alcohol smuggling became of grave concern to the government. This meant that a large part of the Canadian border with the United States had to be patrolled. The responsibility fell on the greatest controller of lightly armed patrol cruisers–the Department of National Revenue Preventive Service (Canada Customs).

In 1921 the Ministry of Customs became Customs and Excise, which in 1927 became National Revenue. These departments operated numerous vessels in the 1920s, mainly off the East Coast. Some vessels were chartered and others seized and converted for use in the service. In La Havre, Nova Scotia the

RCMP participated in a noted rum seizure on the night of July 3, 1923. Constable F.P. Fahie and Corporal W.A. Caldwell, under the supervision of Detective-Sergeant J. Blakeney, headed to sea in a motor boat to intercept a rum running schooner by the name of *Veda M McKeown*. After giving a known signal to the schooner, Blakeney pulled up beside the vessel, climbed aboard and began to haggle with the captain over the price of the liquor he was selling. A price was agreed to and two 10-gallon kegs of rum were handed over to Fahie and Caldwell. Then the captain demanded payment before any more cargo was off loaded. Blakeney announced he was an officer of the Royal Canadian Mounted Police and told the captain and his eight crew they were under arrest and the cargo was being seized. Silence fell over the group of men as they weighed their options. The crew surrendered without violence, but a lot of grumbling could be heard. The next day the *Veda M McKeown* and her cargo of 2,000 gallons of rum, 200 cases of Scotch whiskey and 35 cases of gin sailed into port under Blakeney's orders.

The 1924 Annual Report – Northern Alberta District – lists several vessels obtained for service in the Northwest Territories. These included power boats by the names of *Ottawa* at Chipewayan, *Calgary* at Fort Smith, *Edmonton* at Simpson, *Macleod* at Norman, *Regina* at Good Hope, the previously mentioned *Resolution* at Resolution, and *Fitzgerald* at Aklavik. These vessels were crucial to security and patrols through the vast expanses of the Canadian north in the summer.

In 1928 the RCMP launched the *St Roch* in Vancouver, B.C. She was a 104-foot schooner specially built for Arctic waters and played a major role in policing the area for the ensuing 25 years. The ship was a floating detachment intended to patrol the Canadian Arctic. Many stories have been written about this historic vessel and the years she spent ice bound while patrolling the Arctic shores. In later years she would be recognized for setting several international Arctic maritime records, which included being the first vessel to conquer the Northwest Passage from west to east from 1940 to 1942.

The *St Roch* was the first ship to find and transit the northerly deep water North West Passage in 1944 when she sailed from Halifax to Vancouver. In doing so she established yet another record for being the first vessel to sail the North West Passage both ways. In 1950 the *St Roch* also became the first ship to circumnavigate North America when she sailed from Vancouver to Halifax through the Panama Canal, then again from the opposite direction in 1954. When she was retired she was placed in a dry dock, which eventually became a covered building and is today the centre piece of the Vancouver Maritime Museum in British Columbia.

The 1929 Commissioner's Annual Report stated that the RCMP had 25 vessels including the *St Roch* in the Force's inventory. In the north, four other small motor vessels used for RCMP patrols were the *Toronto, Lady Byng, Lady Borden* and the *Lady Laurier* (which was the first small vessel to transit Lancaster Sound in the Arctic).

The *Lady Laurier* arrived in Dundas Harbour on Devon Island from Pond Inlet in 1929. She was navigated by Cpl H.A. McBeth and Cst S.H.C. Margetts. This vessel was also operated by Cpl M.M. Timbury and Cst. R.W. Hamilton. The *Lady Borden* was stationed at Cumberland Sound on Baffin Island and operated by Sgt O.G. Petty and Sgt C.G. Moore. The *Lady Byng* was operated by Sgt J.E.F. Wight and Cst P. Dersch at Lake Harbour in the Hudson Strait. The *Toronto* was used at Bernard Harbour, then in 1930 moved about 100 miles south to Coppermine and was renamed *Coppermine*. A sloop called *Halifax* was in service and used by members at Stony Rapids on Lake Athabasca in Northern Saskatchewan. In 1948, the *Lake Harbour* was built for service at Baffin Island, and the *Vancouver* went into service at Rae in the Northwest Territories.

Over the next couple of years other schooners were added to the inventory of the RCMP in the Northwest Territories, Hudson Bay and the Arctic Archipelago. A 38-foot schooner called *Kingston* patrolled the waters of Aklavik to Herschel Island carrying supplies and equipment to the detachments there. The *Lady Willingdon* is mentioned serving in Chesterfield Inlet and the motor launch *Lady Pope* at Dundas Harbour in 1930. The 1931 Commissioner's Annual Report states that northern Alberta had 17 power boats of various sizes on patrol.

When comparing the size of the RCMP vessels to other government agency vessels they were relatively small. The purpose of these vessels was to patrol the lakes and rivers of central and northern Canada and they were quite well suited for that duty. Most of them were operated by RCMP members and although no records of their navigational qualifications could be found, it is clear that most skills were learned on the job or gained from previous experience. This would also explain why when larger vessels were needed by the RCMP they were chartered so that properly trained, certified and experienced crews would be responsible for their navigation and safe operation.

Unlike the larger vessels of the RCMP Marine Section, the smaller vessels were used in isolated detachments, primarily for supply and transport in the summer months. They were operated by one or two men and traversed the local lakes and rivers or Arctic coasts. Details about these vessels are hard to identify as they were usually purchased by local detachments or by Division from previous owners rather than constructed for the RCMP. Official records of these vessels were kept at the local level and most reports to Ottawa with regards to their number and details were vague. The Commissioner's Annual Reports from 1932 to 1945 do not refer to any Divisional boats except to say that a number of smaller motor boats and river craft were being used by detachments in the north and elsewhere.

Changes were to dramatically alter the face and status of the RCMP in 1932. The Force had taken over provincial policing in Saskatchewan in 1928, and four years later took over five more provinces: Nova Scotia and Manitoba on April 1, 1932, New Brunswick on April 30, 1932, Prince Edward Island on May 1, 1932, and Alberta on June 1, 1932.

Along with these additional provincial responsibilities the RCMP took control of the Preventive Service of the Department of National Revenue on April 1, 1932. Soon afterwards, on November 4, 1932, the Marine Section of the RCMP was formally established. This marked the beginning of a large, highly trained and modern federal police force.

The RCMP Marine Section was a separate entity involved primarily with Customs preventive patrols on Canada's coasts and seaways. There were numerous other small vessels that belonged to the Divisions that were used in patrolling the areas of their respective communities.

Vessels of the Customs Preventive Service of the Department of National Revenue

116 ft *Adversus* 1931 - 1939*
116 ft *Alachasse* 1931 - 1939*
85 ft *Baroff* 1927 - 1936 ex-rum runner by the name of *Bo-Peep**
114 ft *Bayhound 2* 1928 - 1936, cruiser formerly known as *Tillicum**
136 ft *Conestoga* 1927 - 1932, later known as *Pathfinder*
165 ft *Fleurdelis* 1929 - 1939*
95 ft *Grib* 1920 - 1926
182 ft *Margaret* 1914 - 1932
85 ft *Patrol Boat No. 4* 1924 - 1934*
This vessel was a rum runner originally called *Stumble Inn*, one of many vessels seized and put back in government service.
165 ft *Preventor* 1929 - 1937*
72 ft *Scatari* 1928 - 1939, ex- rum runner *174**
116 ft *Ulna* 1931 - 1939*
175 ft *Vigilant* 1927 - 1929, ex Great Lakes Fisheries patrol vessel
Patrol Boat No. 1 1920 - 1927, ex-rum runner *Marona*
Patrol Boat No. 2 1920 - 1930, ex-rum runner *Vagrant*
Patrol Boat No. 3 1920 - 1930, ex-rum runner *Edna H*

*Most of these vessels and men would eventually fall under the operation and direction of the RCMP Marine Section in 1932.

Vessels of the Marine and Fisheries Service

Arctic Patrol:
165 ft *Arctic* Barquentine 1904 - 1926

Icebreakers:
207 ft *Stanley* steamer 1888-1935
260 ft *NB McLean* 1930 - 1988
252 ft *Montcalm* steamer 1904 - 1942
212 ft *Saurel* steamer 1929 - 1967
183 ft *Lady Grey* steamer 1906 - 1955
275 ft *Milula* steamer 1923 - 1935

Lighthouse Supply and Buoy Tenders:
180 ft *Aberdeen* steamer 1894 - 1923
100 ft *Brant* (1) steamer 1899 - 1928
160 ft *Druid* steamer 1902 - 1946
104 ft *Scout* steamer 1902 - 1934
210 ft *Lady Laurier* 1902 - 1959
130 ft *Rouville* steamer1906 - 1931
165 ft *Princess* steamer 1906 - 1920

Yukon Archives Accession Number: YA 81-150 #30

115 ft *Newington* trawler 1908 - 1937
212 ft *Estevan* steamer 1912 - 1969
108 ft *Lambton* steamer 1909 - 1922
170 ft *Dollard* steamer 1913 - 1961
104 ft *Argenteuil* steamer 1917 - 1960
241 ft *Aranmore* 1914 - 1939
126 ft *Concretia* steamer 1918 -1935
164 ft *Grenville* 1915 - 1968
149 ft *Laurentian* trawler 1919 - 1946
160 ft *Safeguarder* steamer 1929 - 1967
130 ft *Loos* trawler 1922 - 1937
190 ft *St Heliers* steamer 1930 - 1960
125 ft *Brant* (2) trawler 1928 - 1966
117 ft *Shamrock* steamer 1898 - 1928
123 ft *Bernier* trawler 1930 - 1960

Glenbow Institution NA-3622-25

Fisheries Patrol Vessels:
137 ft *Gulnare* steamer 1902 - 1925, tidal survey ship
162 ft *Malaspina* steamer 1914 - 1939
130 ft *Arleux* trawler 1919 - 1939, East Coast
130 ft *Arras* trawler 1919 - 1939, East Coast
130 ft *Givenchy* trawler 1919 - 1939, West Coast

Hydrographic Survey Ships:
140 ft *Bayfield* (2) tug 1902 - 1935, formerly *Lord Stanley*
140 ft *Lillooet* steamer 1907 - 1939, West Coast
164 ft *Cartier* steamer 1910 - 1939, East Coast, renamed *Charny* in 1941
115 ft *Speedy II* yacht 1912 - 1921, Great Lakes
182 ft *Acadia* (2) steamer 1913 - 1969, East Coast
168 ft *Stadacona* yacht 1920 - 1924, West Coast

Salvage Vessels:
160 ft *Lord Strathcona* tug 1902 - 1947
130 ft *Traverse* steamer 1930 - 1952

Tugs:
100 ft *James Howden* 1903 - 1929
109 ft *Murray Stewart* 1922 - 1939
107 ft *Jalobert* 1923 - 1954

Sounding and Survey Vessels:
130 ft *Bellechasse* steamer 1912 - 1942
147 ft *Detector* steamer 1915 - 1978
128 ft *Berthier* steamer 1916 - 1961
94 ft *Lanoraie II* steamer 1928 - 1956
109 ft *Frontenac* steamer 1930 - 1968

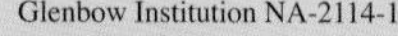

Glenbow Institution NA-2114-17

Divisional Vessels of the NWMP and RCMP prior to 1945

Corporal Joseph Pearson Clemmitt on Royal Canadian Mounted Police patrol, Yukon Territory, 1930s.

Glenbow Archives NA-3622-26

These vessels were purpose-built or purchased locally by the North West Mounted Police, many serving in rivers and lakes of the Yukon and Northwest Territories.

ACTIVE

Sold November 21, 1938

Name: Active
Year Built:
Built By:
In Service: - 1938
Dimensions:
Crew: 1
Code:

Courtesy Pat King

Name: Aklavik (2)
Year Built: 1946
Built By: Alberta Motor Boat Co., Edmonton AB
In Service: 1946 – 1965
Dimensions:
Type: Columbia River fishing boat.
Cost: $4,943.37
Power:
Displacement:
Speed:
Official Number:
Radio Call Sign:
Code: 7413

Left: Courtesy RCMP Historical Collections Unit

Courtesy NWT Archives N-1993-002-0036.

AKLAVIK (2)

The *Aklavik* (2), built in Edmonton in 1946, was used by the RCMP through the 1940s and into the 1950s. She was transferred to the Crown Assets Disposal Corporation (CADC) on April 9, 1965.

Vessel name changes were regular in the world of RCMP marine activities. This often led to a confusion between various craft. *Aklavik I, Herschel* and *Jennings*, all the same boat, are listed elsewhere in this book. This vessel is shown here at the behest of the author, as she was designed and actually under construction and completed probably prior to 1946, for service with the RCMP.

Courtesy Pat King

Above: The Aklavik *(2) at Arctic Red River 1957. Left: RCMP schooner, formerly named* Jennings. *Photo taken in Aklavik spring of 1956. Special officer Otto Binder painting the name. Bill Store, captain, is to Binder's right. Photo by B.W. Brown.*

Courtesy NWT Archives N-1993-002-0010

BAKER LAKE

Name: Baker Lake
Year Built:
Built By:
In Service: – 1943
Dimensions:
Type:
Cost:
Power:
Displacement:
Speed:

BATTLEFORD (1)/PROVIDENCE

Typically, vessel names were carried forward to new vessels in later years, such as the *Battleford II* seen at right.

Courtesy RCMP Historical Collections Unit

Name: Battleford (1)/Providence
Year Built: Alberta Motor Boat Company, Edmonton, Alberta
Built By:
In Service:
Dimensions: 32 x 9
Type: Columbia River fishing boat
Cost:
Power: 25 hp
Displacement:
Speed:
Code: 7217

BLUE WING

The *Blue Wing* was purchased from the Royal Canadian Navy on November 12, 1920 and put into service on the East Coast out of Halifax, Nova Scotia. She was sold December 29, 1938.

Name: Blue Wing
Year Built: 1917
Built By:
In Service: 1920 - 1938
Dimensions: 25 x 7 x 2
Type: Motor
Cost:
Power:
Displacement:
Speed:

Courtesy Vancouver Maritime Museum

Above: An early scene at Tuktoyaktuk, North West Territories. Opposite: Out of the water during the freeze in winter, the Aklavik II, *which was later named* Cambridge Bay, *stands alongside a small commercial vessel on dry land.*

CALGARY

The *Calgary* is a RCMP vessel mentioned in 'Power Boats in the N.W.T. 1924.' In the Annual Report Northern Alberta District. She was stationed at Fort Smith on the Slave River, Northwest Territories, in 1925.

Name: Calgary
Year Built: 1924
Built By: Alberta Motor Boat Company, Edmonton, Alberta.
In Service: 1924 -
Dimensions: 32 x 9
Type: Columbia River fishing boat
Cost:
Power:
Displacement:
Speed:

Courtesy Royal Canadian Signal Corps

CAMBRIDGE BAY

Cambridge Bay, a desolate place for anyone, was a station for early RCMP vessels.

Name: Cambridge Bay
Year Built:
Built By:
In Service: ca. 1939
Dimensions: 32 ft
Type: Motor launch
Cost:
Power: 10 hp
Displacement:
Speed:
Official Number:
Code: 7262

The *Cambridge Bay* was a patrol boat that worked out of the Aklavik, Northwest Territories area. She was the Royal Canadian Signal Corps vessel *Velox* that was transferred to the RCMP in 1939 and renamed *Cambridge Bay*. In 1940 Henry Larsen of the *St Roch*, recorded having towed the *Velox* from Tuktoyaktuk to Coppermine where she went into service as a patrol vessel.

Courtesy Library and Archives Canada e010764892

Below: Aboard the Chakawana. *Right, bottom:* Chakawana *underway.*

Courtesy Don Klancher.

Courtesy RCMP Historical Collections Unit

CHAKAWANA (1)

Name: Chakawana (1)
Year Built: 1910
Built By: D. Martin, Vancouver, B.C.
In Service: 1919 - 1921
Dimensions: 62 x 13.8 x 9
Type: Motor
Cost:
Power: Wolverine gas engine
Displacement: 44.51 GT
Speed:
Official Number: 130441

The *Chakawana* was purchased by the RNWMP on October 22, 1919 from the Imperial Munitions Board and served out of Prince Rupert, B.C. until she was declared surplus on January 15, 1921 and taken to Vancouver.

On August 7, 1921 she almost sank while tied to the wharf. She was sold on October 10, 1921.

Courtesy RCMP Historical Collections Unit

Courtesy Yukon Archives YA 83-22 300

Name: Chakawana (2)
Year Built:
Built By:
In Service: ca. 1928 - 1944
Dimensions: 35 ft
Type: Motor boat, scow type hull
Cost:
Power: 20 hp Kenworth
Displacement:
Speed:
Code: 7234

Left, bottom: Poling a canoe in shallow water on the La Loche River in Saskatchewan.

CHAKAWANA (2)

The *Chakawana* (2) was a transport vessel used in Yukon Territory and was based out of Old Crow. She was built for the Force in 1928. The boat was specially designed for use in the shallow waters of the Porcupine River. The hull was constructed so that the propeller drive shaft could be hauled up and the boat poled or rowed through the shallows. The hull was condemned and destroyed in August 1944 and the engine was transferred to a new hull for Code 7271 *Old Crow*.

Courtesy Glenbow Archives NA-2137-27

Courtesy Vancouver Maritime Museum

COPPERMINE (2)

Name: Coppermine (2)
Year Built: 1944
Built By: Alberta Motor Boat Company, Edmonton, Alberta
In Service: 1944 -
Dimensions: 32 x 9
Type: Columbia River fishing boat
Cost:
Power: 20 hp Kermath engine from the *Ottawa* (7222)
Displacement:
Speed:
RCMP Number:
Code: 7272

The *Coppermine* (2) was purchased in 1944. She was equipped with sail for auxiliary power.

Courtesy NWT Archives N-1990-006:0143

Right and lower right: The Coppermine *in two different configurations.*
Left: A uniformed group at Coppermine.

CRAIG HARBOUR (1)

Name: Craig Harbour (1)
Year Built:
Built By:
In Service:
Dimensions: 21 x 6.5
Type: Trap boat
Cost:
Power: 8 hp
Displacement:
Speed:
Code: 7255

No other information or photograph available.

Courtesy NWT Archives N-1979-003:0181

Courtesy Glenbow Archives NA-1444-2

Courtesy Glenbow Archives NA-1663-50

Left: The NWMP had some very crude vessels in the early days. This was on the 30 Mile River in the Yukon, 1915.

Courtesy Glenbow Archives NA-494-45

Far left: The Sam Steele, *1898, on the Yukon River, which was well patrolled by the NWMP in its heyday during the gold rush.*
Left: Sir Samuel Steele.
Bottom left: RNWMP constables in 1905 at the mouth of the Hart River, Peace River Crossing, Alberta.

DAWSON (1)/CAMERON BAY

Dawson was the Detachment boat at Hay River until transferred to Cameron Bay and renamed *Cameron Bay* circa 1937.

Name: Dawson (1)/Cameron Bay
Year Built:
Built By: Alberta Motor Boat Company, Edmonton, Alberta
In Service:
Dimensions: 32 x 9
Type: Columbia River fishing boat
Cost:
Power: 20 – 25 hp
Displacement:
Speed:
Radio Call Sign:
Code: 7209

DUNCAN (1)

The *Duncan* was a RNWMP motor launch used at and around Fort Smith on Slave Lake. She was purchased from the Department of Railways and Canals in 1919 and first used at Port Nelson in Hudson Bay. Assistant Commissioner Cortlandt Starnes lists her as one of six launches in service in February 1923.

Name: Duncan (1)
Year Built: 1914
Built By:
In Service: ca. 1919 -
Dimensions: 30 ft
Type: Motor
Cost:
Power: 24 hp
Displacement:
Speed:

Yukon Archives YA 9247

Above: RCMP officer delivering mail on the Yukon River, 1924.

Name: Edmonton
Year Built:
Built By: Alberta Motor Boat Company, Edmonton, Alberta
In Service: 1924
Dimensions: 32 x 9
Type: Columbia River fishing boat
Cost:
Power:
Displacement:
Speed:

Name: Fitzgerald
Year Built: 1921
Built By: Northern Boat Building Co. Ltd., Edmonton, Alberta
In Service: 1921 - 1931
Dimensions: 35 x 8.5 x 2.7
Type: Motor boat
Cost:
Power: Single four cylinder gas 30 hp
Displacement: 9.72 GT
Speed:
Official Number: 141355

EDMONTON

The RCMP vessel *Edmonton* was mentioned in the 'Annual Report Northern Alberta District, Power Boats in the N.W.T. 1924' and was stationed in Simpson, Northwest Territories.

Courtesy Glenbow Archives G-1-1712-53

FITZGERALD

The *Fitzgerald* was a RCMP motor launch used at and around Fort Norman in the Northwest Territories. She was purchased in 1921 for service on the Mackenzie River. Assistant Commissioner Cortlandt Starnes lists her as one of six launches in service in February 1923. She was stationed in Aklavik in 1925. The Registry was 'noted' in 1959 as she was presumed to be out of existence.

FRANKLIN/ARCTIC RED RIVER

The *Franklin/Arctic Red River* was a small craft designed for local use. She was an outboard motor propelled whale boat. No further details were available. Photograph opposite page.

Name: Franklin/Arctic Red River
Year Built:
Built By:
In Service:
Dimensions: 22 X 8
Type: Whale Boat
Cost:
Power: 4 hp
Displacement:
Speed:
Code: 7238

Courtesy Don Klancher

Churchill-York Factory, RNWMP patrol, 1910.

Courtesy Glenbow Archives NA-2749-19

GLADYS

Gladys was a 45-foot motor launch that was built for and purchased by the NWMP in 1899 to serve in the Yukon. She was a sister ship of the *Jessie*. She patrolled from Carcross to Conrad, Tagish and Mill Haven. She served until August 27, 1913 when she was sold to the Pine Creek Power Company for $780.

Name: Gladys
Year Built: 1899
Built By: Marine Vapor Engine Co., New Jersey, N.J.
In Service: 1899 - 1913
Dimensions: 45.4 x 10 x 3.9
Type: Steam - screw
Cost:
Power: Alco Vapor steam engine
Displacement: 9.16 GT
Speed:
Official Number: 107722

Top: Crew of the 1933 vessel Herschel *(1) and, above, a photograph of her in the Arctic. Right: The* Arctic Red River *pulled ashore during the freeze in the north.*

Courtesy Library and Archives Canada e010764891

Gull

The *Gull's* home port was Fredicton, New Brunswick where she was used in Preventive Service duties. She was declared surplus on July 16, 1946.

Name: Gull
Year Built:
Built By: Edmonton Alberta
In Service: ca. 1928
Dimensions:
Type: Lobster fishing boat
Cost:
Power: Kermath engine
Displacement:
Speed:
Official Number: Shediac 235
Code: 7405

Courtesy RCMP Historical Collections Unit.

Courtesy Glenbow Archives NA-2617-83

Sergeant K.F. Anderson with Judge Noel and group on a raft on the Peace River, Alberta.

HALIFAX

The *Halifax* was a 'K' Division vessel stationed at Stony Rapids on Lake Athabasca in Northern Saskatchewan just south-east of Great Slave Lake. In 1937 she was transferred to 'G' Division for duty at Simpson.

Name: Halifax
Year Built:
Built By: Alberta Motor Boat Company, Edmonton, Alberta
In Service: ca. 1928
Dimensions: 32 x 9
Type: Columbia River fishing boat
Cost:
Power: 25 HP Karmath engine
Displacement:
Speed:
Official Number:
Code: 7405

Courtesy Vancouver Maritime Museum

Name: Hershel (1)/Aklavik (1)
Year Built: 1930
Built By: George Askew, Vancouver B.C.
In Service: 1938 - 1955
Dimensions: 47 x 12 x 3.5
Type: Auxiliary schooner
Cost: $4,900
Power: 20 hp Frisco engine
Displacement:
Code: 7501

Vancouver Maritime Museum

HERSCHEL (1)/AKLAVIK (1)

The *Herschel* was the detachment boat at Aklavik in the N.W.T. about 1935, according to an interview with ex-Constable Derek Parkes, who was in charge of Coppermine Detachment. He states "It was owned by an Eskimo who died and it was repossessed by the Hudson's Bay Company who in turn sold it to the RCMP at Herschel Island in 1933." She appears to have been called the *Akuvik* prior to that transaction. The record shows the schooner *Akuvik* was purchased from the Hudson's Bay Company March 30, 1933. She was moved to Aklavik and renamed *Herschel* then in 1936 renamed *Aklavik*. She patrolled in the Herschel Island and Aklavik detachment areas. The hull was sheathed in iron bark from keel to above the waterline. She was declared surplus and transferred to War Assets Corporation for disposal in September 1945.

JASPER/MAITLAND

The *Jasper* was a Detachment boat at Aklavik. She was later renamed *Maitland*.

Name: Jasper/Maitland
Year Built:
Built By:
In Service: ca 1938
Dimensions:
Type: Peterhead
Cost:
Power: 9 hp
Displacement:
Speed:
Code: 7403

Courtesy Vancouver Maritime Museum

Courtesy Library and Archives Canada e010788110

Courtesy Glenbow Archives NA-3844-48

Dog team pulling boat over frozen river, Fort Liard area, Northwest Territories.

JEANNE D'ARC

Sir Harry Gignac loaned the *Jeanne D'Arc* to the RCMP at no cost. She was employed out of Windsor, Ontario to patrol the Detroit River to prevent the illegal entry of aliens. Patrols ceased August 1943 because of manpower shortages and the fact that the United States had entered the War. Also, the U.S. Coast Guard was taking a more active interest in patrolling the river.

Name: Jeanne D'Arc
Year Built:
Built By:
In Service: 1940 - 1943
Dimensions: 31 x 9.5
Type:
Cost:
Power:
Displacement:
Speed:
Code: 7263

Opposite page: The Jeannie *was wrecked in a storm at Wager Inlet in the Northwest Territories.*

Name: Jeannie
Year Built:
Built By:
In Service: ca.1910
Dimensions:
Type: Schooner
Cost:
Power:
Displacement:
Speed:
Radio Call Sign:
RCMP Number:
Code:

Courtesy RCMP Historical Collections Unit

JEANNIE

The *Jeannie* was chartered by the RNWMP and wrecked in the same season during a storm at Wager Inlet in the Northwest Territories. Captain Sam Bartlett, a 'life long Navigator' and captain of the Neptune expedition of 1903, had offered his schooner *Jeannie* to police for the season at a fee of $6,000. The Force seized the opportunity to provision the two detachments and send the ship north to Repulse Bay to scout the possibilities of opening a third detachment there. The use of a ship for the whole season also gave the police a chance to make the route between Fullerton and Churchill more secure. Four small prefabricated shelter huts were constructed, to be placed at convenient points on the coast between the two detachments. The huts, containing a stove, lamp, bunks and food, would make the route safer, both by sea and by land. One hut was set up at Eskimo Point, and another at Rankin Inlet. The third, planned for Chesterfield Inlet, could not be set up due to strong winds. The *Jeannie* was totally wrecked in a gale after it reached Wager Inlet, the proposed location of the fourth hut, which was to serve as a way-station to the new post at Repulse Bay.

Courtesy MacBride Museum

JESSIE

The *Jessie* was a 45-foot motor launch that was built for and purchased by the NWMP in 1899 to serve in the Yukon. She was a sister ship of the *Gladys*. The *Jessie* was sold March 11, 1910.

Name: Jessie
Year Built: 1898
Built By: Marine Vapour Engine Co., New Jersey, N.J.
In Service: 1899-1910
Dimensions: 45.4 x 10 x 3.9
Type: Steam - screw
Cost:
Power: Alco Vapor steam engine
Displacement: 9.16 GT
Speed:
Official Number: 107721

Sister to Jessie*, the* Gladys *is seen tied up at Tagish Lake in the photograph left.*

KEEWATIN

The *Keewatin* was a small sailing vessel brought onto Lake Winnipeg from Selkirk near the mouth of the Red River in 1890. She was the first patrol vessel chartered by the North West Mounted Police. The vessel went aground on a sand bar during a storm and two members drowned. The captain survived the wreck but died later in hospital.

Name: Keewatin
Year Built: 1890
Built By:
In Service: 1890
Dimensions:
Type: Sailing
Cost:
Power:
Displacement:
Speed:
Official Number:

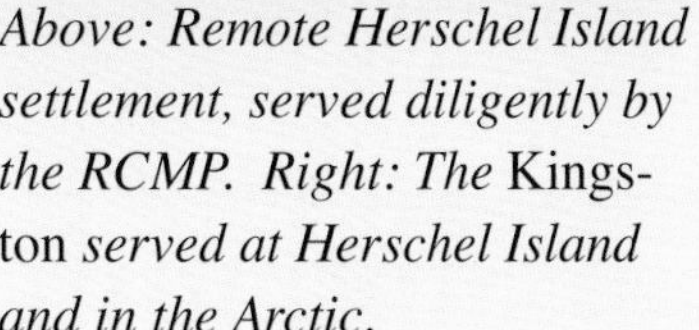

Above: Remote Herschel Island settlement, served diligently by the RCMP. Right: The Kingston *served at Herschel Island and in the Arctic.*

Name: Kingston/Fort Smith
Year Built:
Built By:
In Service: 1930 -
Dimensions: 38 ft
Type: Schooner
Cost:
Power:
Displacement:
Speed:
Official Number:
Code: 7220

KINGSTON/FORT SMITH

The *Kingston* was a single-masted schooner mentioned in the Commissioner's Annual Report for 1930. She was stationed at Aklavik in the Arctic and served between there and Herschel Island. In 1932 the *Kingston* was a shallow draft river boat, according to an interview with ex-Cst Derek Parkes, who was in charge of Coppermine. In April 1933 she was transferred to the Fort Smith Detachment and renamed *Fort Smith*.

Name: Laddie
Year Built:
Built By:
In Service: ca. 1911 - 1914
Dimensions:
Type:
Cost:
Power:
Displacement:
Speed:
Official Number:

LADDIE

Another schooner, that served in the Fullerton area of Hudson Bay in 1911, was the *Laddie*. She served out of Newfoundland until 1914. In the fall of that year she ran aground on a reef en route from the Ottawa Islands to the Belcher Islands.

Courtesy NWT Archives N-1987-033:0030

Courtesy Vancouver Maritime Museum

Courtesy NWT Archives N-1991-041:0070

Top left and opposite: The Lady Borden *at Baker Lake, N.W.T. September 1918.*
Left: Captain Henry Larsen at Albert Chartrand's gravesite in Pasley Bay.
Top right: RCMP graves of Victor Maisonneuve 1899-1926 and William Robert Stephens 1902-1927 on Devon Island.
Above: The Lady Borden *buried in snow in the Arctic, 1924-1927.*

Courtesy RCMP Historical Collections Unit

Name: Lady Borden
Year Built: 1916
Built By: Gidley Boat Co., Penetang, Ontario
In Service: 1916 - 1938
Dimensions: 34 x 8.5
Type:
Cost:
Power:
Displacement:
Speed:

LADY BORDEN

The *Lady Borden* was a motor launch used in and around Chesterfield Inlet on Hudson Bay. Assistant Commissioner Cortlandt Starnes lists her as one of six launches in service in February 1923. In 1924 she was transferred to Pangnirtung Detachment. In 1929 she was located in Baffin Island in the Arctic and was still in service in 1938.

Courtesy RCMP Historical Collections Unit

Name: Lady Byng
Year Built: 1927
Built By: Unknown, Marigomish, N.S.
In Service: 1929 -
Dimensions: 30 x 6.4 x 2.8
Type: Motor
Cost:
Power:
Displacement: 3 GT
Speed:
Official Number: 157012

LADY BYNG

The *Lady Byng* served at one time in and around Devon Island in the Arctic. Commissioner Starnes mentioned the *Lady Byng* in his 1929 Annual Report for Lake Harbour in Hudson Strait where Sgt J.E.F. Wight and Cst P. Dersch covered more than 930 miles patrolling in her.

Name: Lady Foster/Port Harrison
Year Built:
Built By:
In Service: 1935 -
Dimensions: 40 x 11
Type: Fishing boat
Cost:
Power: 9 hp
Displacement:
Speed:
Code: 7230

LADY FOSTER/PORT HARRISON

The *Lady Foster* was the detachment boat at Port Burwell in the Northwest Territories in about 1935. She was moved to Port Harrison Detachment and renamed *Port Harrison*.

Name: Lady Laurier
Year Built:
Built By:
In Service: 1928 -
Dimensions:
Type:
Cost:
Power:
Displacement:
Speed:

LADY LAURIER

The *Lady Laurier* served in and around Devon Island in the Arctic. Commissioner Starnes mentioned her in his 1929 Annual Report on Dundas Harbour on Devon Island. She earned the distinction of being the first small vessel to cross Lancaster Sound. The photograph above shows Devon Island and its spectacular Devon Spires.

Name: Lady Logan
Year Built:
Built By:
In Service: 1935 -
Dimensions: 40 X 11
Type: Peterhead
Cost:
Power: 9 hp
Displacement:
Speed:
Code: 7116

LADY LOGAN

Not much is known about this vessel other than she was a 40-foot Peterhead with a small engine. She was transferred to Port Harrison Detachment from the Department of Mines at Churchill, Manitoba in 1935.

LADY POPE

The *Lady Pope* is mentioned in the Commissioner's Annual Report for 1931. She was stationed at Dundas Harbour in the Arctic.

Name: Lady Pope
Year Built:
Built By:
In Service: 1931 -
Dimensions:
Type:
Cost:
Power:
Displacement:
Speed:
Code: 7232

LADY WILLINGDON/CHESTERFIELD

The *Lady Willingdon* is mentioned in the Commissioner's Annual Report for 1930. She was stationed at Chesterfield Inlet in Hudson Bay.

Name: Lady Willingdon/Chesterfield
Year Built:
Built By:
In Service: 1930 - 1951
Dimensions: 40 x 11
Type: Motor boat
Cost:
Power: 30 - 40 hp
Displacement:
Speed:
Code: 7233

Courtesy Library and Archives Canada e010764888

LAUNCHES A, B and C

All three launches were used in the Yukon Territories for transport and towing purposes. They were mentioned in the Commissioners' Reports from 1909 to 1914. *Launch A* was a 30-foot vessel powered by a 15 hp Buffalo engine and capable of eight knots. *Launch B* was a 17-foot vessel used for towing. There were no further details about *Launch C*.

LETHBRIDGE/HERSCHEL (2)

The *Lethbridge* was the detachment boat at Aklavik, later transferred to Coppermine and renamed *Herschel* ca. 1933. In the summer of 1943 she was damaged beyond repair by drifting onto a rocky ledge during the course of a gale while on patrol in the vicinity of Reid Island. The hull was sold May 1, 1945 and the engine transferred to the new hull of *Coppermine* Code 7222.

Name: Lethbridge/Herschel (2)
Year Built: 1926
Built By: Alberta Motor Co. Ltd., Edmonton, AB
In Service: ca. 1926-1943
Dimensions: 32 X 9
Type: Columbia River fishing boat
Cost: $1,038
Power: 20–25 hp Easthope
Displacement:
Speed:
Code: 7400

An Aurora maritime patrol aircraft flies overhead as part of Operation Lancaster, as sailors, infantry and Canadian Rangers help the RCMP restore a gravesite in Dundas Harbour, Devon Island. The gravesite is for two RCMP members, William Robert Stephens 1902-1927 and Victor Maisonneuve 1899-1926, who died in the 1920s while working in an observation post at this location on the northern coast of Lancaster Sound. Photograph courtesy Pte Darcy Lefebvre, Formation Imaging Services, Canadian Navy, Image Gallery.

Courtesy NWT Archives N-1979-004-0231

MACLEOD (1)

The *Macleod* was a RCMP motor launch used at and around Fort Norman in the Northwest Territories. In the photograph left to right: Isadore Thomas, Cst Williams, Cst Karnac and Inspector A. Eames.

Below: Royal Canadian Mounted Police boat Macleod *after depositing cargo at Liard River, August 1928. A convoy of barges returning to Fort Providence, Northwest Territories, can be seen in the background.*

Courtesy Glenbow Archives NA-3844-10

Name: Macleod (1)
Year Built: 1924
Built By: Unknown, Edmonton, Alberta
In Service: 1924 -
Dimensions: 30 ft
Type: Motor
Cost:
Power:
Displacement:
Speed:

Name: Mallard
Year Built:
Built By:
In Service:
Dimensions:
Type: Lobster fishing boat
Cost:
Power:
Displacement:
Speed:
Official Number: Shediac 232

Name: McTavish
Year Built: 1904
Built By:
In Service: 1909
Dimensions: 47 x 13.5 x 3.5
Type:
Cost:
Power:
Displacement:
Speed:
Official Number:

Modern day Tuktoyaktuk in Nunavut. Few major changes are evident since the early years.

MALLARD

The *Mallard* was a Shediac lobster fishing boat and one of several such vessels used by the RNWMP. Her home port was Fredericton, New Brunswick where she was used for Preventive Service duties. She was declared surplus July 16, 1946.

MCTAVISH

The *McTavish,* not a Shediac boat, was a more substantial vessel at 47 feet in length. For her day, this was a good sized craft in the service of the RNWMP. *McTavish* was chartered from the Hudson's Bay Company for the 1909 summer season. She sank in Hudson Bay September 05, 1909.

Courtesy Don Klancher

Name: Montreal/Reliance (1)
Year Built: 1927
Built By:
In Service: 1927 - 1949
Dimensions: 30 x 9.5
Type: Schooner
Cost:
Power: 20 - 25 hp
Displacement:
Speed:
Code: 7221

Name: Norwells
Year Built: 1939
Built By:
In Service: ca. 1939
Dimensions:
Type:
Cost:
Power:
Displacement:
Speed:

Name: Old Crow
Year Built: 1943
Built By:
In Service: 1943 - 1954
Dimensions: 35 x 7.4
Type: Boat, scow
Cost: $900
Power: 9 hp Kermath gasoline
Displacement:
Speed:
Official Number:
Code: 7271

MONTREAL/RELIANCE (1)

The *Montreal* was an auxiliary sloop that, in July 1927, took Cpl R.A.Williams, Cst S.G. Hooper and Spl Cst P. Burke from Fort Smith, Northwest Territories, to establish the Fort Reliance Detachment on Great Slave Lake. This vessel was renamed *Reliance* and sometimes referred to as *Fort Reliance*. She served for over 20 years on Great Slave Lake until her deteriorating condition rendered her condemned in 1949.

Right: The Norwells. The image below, right is the Chakawana while in service at Old Crow.

Courtesy RCMP Historical Collections Unit

NORWELLS

The *Norwells* was an RCMP vessel built in 1939. This photograph is the only other information available about the craft. Estimated length is 24 feet. She appears to be in use dragging the seabed for some object. In the background are possibly oil storage tanks.

Courtesy Library and Archives Canada e010764889

OLD CROW

Old Crow operated out of the Old Crow Detachment in the Yukon. The hull was purchased in 1943 and was fitted with the engine from *Chakawana* (2). A new engine was purchased in 1946. She was declared surplus June 25, 1954.

Courtesy Library and Archives Canada e010764879

Courtesy Harry Carmen

OTTAWA (1)

Name: Ottawa (1)
Year Built: 1923
Built By:
In Service: 1923 - 1930
Dimensions:
Type: Motor
Cost:
Power:
Displacement:
Speed:

The *Ottawa* was a motor launch that patrolled the areas of Fort Chipewyan on Great Slave Lake in Alberta in the 1920s. She is listed in the Annual Report of Northern Alberta District of 1924. Photograph above.

OTTAWA (2)

Courtesy Vancouver Maritime Museum

Name: Ottawa (2)
Year Built: 1930
Built By: Alberta Motor Boat Co., Edmonton, Alberta
In Service: -1942
Dimensions: 32 x 9
Type: Columbia River fishing boat
Cost: $12,000 (hull only)
Power: 20 hp Kermath
Displacement:
Code: 7222

This vessel *Ottawa* (opposite page) was stationed at Fort Chipewyan. The hull was condemned in October 1942 and destroyed. The photograph in the left column is that of another vessel named *Ottawa*.

Courtesy RCMP Historical Collections Unit

REDWING

The *Redwing* served on Lake Winnipeg and Lake of the Woods from June 1905 to 1906. She was jointly purchased by the RNWMP and the Department of Indian Affairs on May 10, 1905. The RNWMP engaged the crew and operated the boat. The Indian Affairs personnel were carried for no charge and the expenses were shared between the two departments. Inspector W.M. Walke, officer in command for Lake Winnipeg Patrols determined she was too small and underpowered for her duties. The Department of Indian Affairs paid the RNWMP for their share of the vessel and moved her to Lake of the Woods for use by the Indian Agent at Kenora.

Name: Redwing
Year Built: 1904
Built By: William Oserton, Selkirk, Manitoba
In Service: 1905 - 1906
Dimensions: 65 x 10 x 7
Type: Steam - screw
Cost: $2,800
Power: Steam
Displacement: 23.1 GT
Speed:
Official Number: 112303

On patrol in the northern areas aboard the Jennings.

Above: An early days mail delivery–by the RCMP, at Pond Inlet. Photograph Wilfred Doucette, July 1951. Right: In uniform and on duty, an officer aboard a sailing schooner, possibly the St Roch.

Name: Regina (1)
Year Built: 1924
Built By: Alberta Motor Boat Company, Edmonton, Alberta.
In Service: 1924 -
Dimensions: 32 x 9
Type: Columbia River fishing boat
Cost:
Power:
Displacement:
Speed:
Official Number:

Courtesy Vancouver Maritime Museum

REGINA (1)

The *Regina* was a RCMP vessel mentioned in the 'Annual Report Northern Alberta District, Power Boats in the Northwest Territories 1924,' stationed at Good Hope, N.W.T. In 1926 she was transferred to the Arctic Red River area.

Courtesy RCMP Historical Collections Unit

Glenbow Archives NA-3394-56

Above: The RCMP vessel, Resolution *at Yellowknife in the Northwest Territories.*
Below: Two members of the RCMP bringing prisoner Albert Le Beaux to Fort Smith N.W.T., 1921, on his way to the gallows for murdering his wife.

Glenbow Archives NA-781-9

Name: Resolution (1)
Year Built:
Built By:
In Service: 1920 - ca. 1940
Dimensions: 30 x 9.3
Type: Motor/Sail
Cost:
Power: 20 hp Miller gas engine
Displacement:
Speed:
Code: 7600

RESOLUTION (1)

The *Resolution* was a RCMP motor launch used in and around Fort Norman in the Northwest Territories. Assistant Commissioner Cortlandt Starnes lists her as one of six launches in service in February 1923. She was still in service on Great Slave Lake in 1929.

Glenbow Archives NA-3394-55

Name: Resolution (2)
Year Built:
Built By:
In Service: ca 1941
Dimensions:
Type:
Cost:
Power: 20 hp Miller gas engine
Displacement:
Speed:
Official Number:

RESOLUTION (2)

The *Resolution* (2), above, was a much more robust vessel than her predecessor, right and previous page.

ROUVILLE

The *Rouville* was built for the RNWMP to serve in Hudson Bay but was a design failure. She was turned over to the Department of Mines and Fisheries and was put into service as a buoy tender in the St Laurence River. She sank in 1931.

Name: Rouville
Year Built: 1906
Built By: Canadian Govt. Shipyard, Sorel, Que.
In Service: 1906 - 1907
Dimensions: 130 x 26 x 16
Type: Steamer
Cost:
Power: 54 hp
Displacement: 301 GT
Speed:
Official Number: 126528

Photographs courtesy Vancouver Maritime Museum

St Roch in the Arctic

The RCMP schooner *St Roch* was a workhorse of the Arctic. Sergeant Henry Larsen, her skipper, commented that the police force he represented was not one to be feared, but rather respected, and they were, by the public including the people of the north where for many years Larsen and his crew patrolled by boat and overland. The *St Roch* made history in the Northwest Passage, being the first vessel to achieve a number of difficult passages.

Courtesy Vancouver Maritime Museum

The St Roch *spent time icebound on some of her patrols into the Arctic. Her service is well documented in a large collection of writings and photographs.*

BC Archives B_09345

Name: St Roch
Year Built: 1928
Built By: Burrard Dry Dock Company Limited, North Vancouver, B.C.
In Service: 1928 – 1954
Dimensions: 104 x 25 x 12.5
Type: Schooner/ketch
Cost:
Power: 150 hp Union diesel/ 300 hp Union diesel
Displacement: 193.43 GT
Crew: 4
Speed: 8 kts
Official Number: 154809
Radio Call Sign: VGSR

Courtesy RCMP Historical Collections Unit

ST ROCH

The *St Roch* was built in 1928 in Vancouver and sailed north to the Arctic where she served as a floating detachment for 25 years. In 1943-1944 she was re-rigged as a ketch and had a larger engine installed. She was the first vessel to travel the North West Passage in both directions, and first to circumnavigate North America in both directions.

Inset photo: Captain and Mrs W. H. Gillen aboard RCMP St Roch *at Vancouver before sailing on the first voyage June 26, 1928.*

HMCS (later CCGS) LABRADOR was commissioned into the Canadian Navy in July 1954. A state-of-the-art diesel electric icebreaker, LABRADOR was built at Sorel, Quebec for the Royal Canadian Navy.

The ship is similar in design to American Wind Class icebreakers. However, she was modified to include a suite of scientific instruments so she could serve as an exploration vessel rather than a warship like American Coast Guard vessels. On board LABRADOR were a laboratory and a hospital as well as a helicopter pad and rescue boats.

LABRADOR was the first ship to do a continuous circumnavigion of North America when, in 1954, she transited the North West Passage and returned to Halifax through the Panama Canal. She was also heavily involved in the construction of the Distant Early Warning Line, a vast chain of radar stations built in the mid-1950s to detect incoming Soviet bombers.

Opposite: The St Roch, *tied up alongside* HMCS Labrador, *which later, under the same name, went into the service of CCGS. Right:* St Roch *standing at a busy city dock, ready for service. Top:* St Roch *trapped in the ice, the dog team being prepared for an excursion.*
Above: Bathing was a treat during extended patrols. Note the gun for protection against polar bears.

Photographs courtesy Vancouver Maritime Museum

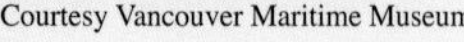

Courtesy Vancouver Maritime Museum

Above: Officers and crew on the RCMP patrol vessel St Roch.

Courtesy RCMP Historical Collections Unit

SHEDIAC 221

The *Shediac 221* was Purchased May 7, 1938. Her home port was Shediac New Brunswick where she served in preventive duties controlled by land force under the direction of Officer Commanding 'J' Division. There were several vessels in the Shediac Class. This one was given the *Shediac* name. She was sold November 15, 1946.

Name: Shediac 221
Year Built:
Built By:
In Service: 1938 - 1946
Dimensions: 38.5 x 9.3 x 3.8
Type: Lobster fishing boat
Cost: $600
Power: Buick 8 cylinder engine
Displacement: 7.8 RT
Speed: 20 kts
Official Number: Shediac 221
Radio Call Sign:
Code: 7406

SNIPE

The *Snipe* was another Shediac type vessel built as a lobster fishing boat. Her home port was Richibucto, New Brunswick where she was used in Preventive Service duties. She was declared surplus July 16, 1946.

Name: Snipe
Year Built:
Built By:
In Service:
Dimensions:
Type: Lobster fishing boat
Cost:
Power:
Displacement:
Speed:
Official Number: Shediac 234

TAGISH (1)

The *Tagish* was a 27-foot motor launch that was built for and purchased by the NWMP in 1899 to serve in the Yukon. She was transferred in 1907 to the British Columbia Government Agent in Atlin.

Name: Tagish (1)
Year Built: 1898
Built By: Marine Vapor Engine Co., New Jersey, N.J.
In Service: 1899 - 1907
Dimensions: 27 x 5.9 x 2.1
Type: Motor steam - screw
Cost:
Power: Alco Vapor steam engine
Displacement: 2 GT
Speed:
Official Number:

Above: Starvation Cove, Nunavut. RCMP patrol vessel Nadon, *on her Voyage of Rediscovery as* St Roch II.

Name: Takulli
Year Built:
Built By:
In Service: ca. 1932
Dimensions:
Type: Motor boat
Cost:
Power:
Displacement:
Speed:
Official Number:

TAKULLI

The *Takulli* was a Yukon Territory transport vessel that served out of the Carcross area in the 1930s.

Courtesy Yukon Archives YA-83-22#6

Courtesy Peter Vassilopoulos

TEAL

Name: Teal
Year Built:
Built By:
In Service:
Dimensions:
Type: Lobster fishing boat
Cost:
Power:
Displacement:
Speed:
Official Number: Shediac 235

The *Teal* was another of the Shediac series of vessels built for the lobster fishing industry on the East Coast. She was used in Preventive Service duties in Chene, New Brunswick. She was declared surplus July 16, 1946.

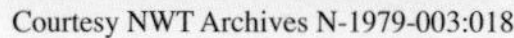

Courtesy NWT Archives N-1979-003:0181

Courtesy NWT Archives N-1990-006:0143

TORONTO/COPPERMINE (1)

Name: Toronto/Coppermine (1)
Year Built:
Built By: Alberta Motor Boat Company, Edmonton, Alberta
In Service: 1929 -1948
Dimensions: 32 x 9
Type: Columbia River fishing boat
Cost:
Power: 20 hp Kermath inboard engine
Displacement:
Speed:
Code: 7404

The *Toronto* is listed in the 1929 Commissioner's Annual Report and served in Bernard Harbour in the N.W.T. She was moved to the Coppermine detachment In 1930 and renamed *Coppermine*.

Photographs above show the Toronto/Coppermine (1).
Opposite: A recent photograph of Carcross in the Yukon, where the Takulli *(page 65) served under the RCMP in the early part of the 20th century.*

Courtesy RCMP Historical Collections Unit

Name: Vancouver/Rae
Year Built:
Built By: Alberta Motor Boat Company, Edmonton, Alberta
In Service: 1931 -
Dimensions: 32 x 9
Type: Columbia River fishing boat
Cost:
Power: 20 - 25 hp
Displacement:
Speed:
Code: 7224

VANCOUVER/RAE

The *Vancouver* was a RCMP vessel referred to in the 1931 RCMP Annual Report. The Report states that this vessel was sent to Rae Detachment at Emile Point in the Northwest Territories. The name was changed accordingly.

Name: Victory
Year Built: 1919
Built By:
In Service: ca. 1919 - ca.1923
Dimensions: 30 ft
Type: Motor boat
Cost:
Power: 15 hp
Displacement:
Speed:
Official Number:

VICTORY

The *Victory* was a motor launch purchased by the RNWMP and used in and around Herschel Island in the Arctic. Assistant Commissioner Cortlandt Starnes lists her as one of six launches in service in February 1923.

Courtesy Vancouver Maritime Museum

Glenbow Archives NA-2114-16

Name: Vidette
Year Built: 1897
Built By: Unknown, St Michaels, Alaska
In Service: 1902 - 1910
Dimensions: 119 x 18 x 3
Type: Steamer
Cost: $3,000
Power: Twin Gillette & Eaton 120 hp
Displacement: 254 GT
Speed:
Official Number: 107869

VIDETTE

The *Vidette*, originally known as *May West,* was purchased by the RNWMP in 1902 for $3,000. Annual Reports state that originally she was to be renamed *Scout* by the NWMP, but when they registered her *Scout* was already taken so they changed the name to *Vidette*. She served on the Yukon River between Dawson City and Whitehorse but became too expensive to maintain, was transferred to the Department of the Interior and replaced by several smaller vessels in 1910. She was wrecked in Lake Lebarge in October 1917.

Courtesy Kenn Haycock

Courtesy Vancouver Maritime Museum

Coming ashore in the high Arctic.

Name: Village Belle
Year Built: 1907
Built By: John Clark, Maitland, Nova Scotia
In Service: 1914 - 1917
Dimensions: 87 x 24.9 x 8.9
Type: Schooner
Cost:
Power:
Displacement: 129.32 GT
Speed:
Official Number: 116556

VILLAGE BELLE

The *Village Belle* was purchased by the RNWMP July 16, 1914 for a police expedition to Hudson Bay led by Inspector W.J. Beyts. She was beached for the winter of 1914 and sold June 22, 1917 at Port Nelson. She was lost off the coast of Newfoundland on October 21, 1920.

VITESSE

The *Vitesse* was a vessel that patrolled out of Prince Edward Island from 1930 to 1933. There is no further information.

Name: Vitesse
Year Built:
Built By:
In Service: 1930 - 1933
Dimensions:
Type:
Cost:
Power:
Displacement:
Speed:
Official Number:

WIDGEON

The *Widgeon* is seen at right. There is no further information.

Name: Widgeon
Year Built:
Built By:
In Service:
Dimensions:
Type:
Cost:
Power:
Displacement:
Speed:
Official Number:

Glenbow Archives NA-2114-17

WINNIPEG/SIMPSON

The photograph is evidence of the existence of this vessel. She was later renamed *Simpson*.

Name: Winnipeg/Simpson
Year Built:
Built By: Unknown, Edmonton, AB
In Service:
Dimensions:
Type:
Cost:
Power:
Displacement:
Speed:
RCMP Number:
Code: 7225

The narrow, current-swept Five Fingers passage, some 200 km north of Whitehorse on the Yukon River, represents tough navigation for vessels of yesterday as well as today.

Courtesy Peter Vassilopoulos

Courtesy RCN P H-761 from DHH, NDHQ

Chapter Two

The RCMP Marine Section

On April 1, 1932 the Royal Canadian Mounted Police formed its first Marine Section when it absorbed all the duties of the Department of National Revenue Preventive Service, along with its seafaring ranks and vessels. This was accomplished through an Order-in-Council P.C. 857 dated April 16, 1932. The new section's primary function was to eliminate the smuggling that was occurring on the St Lawrence, Great Lakes, East and West Coasts and to enforce the Excise Act. Prohibition was in full swing and illegal activity on the borders a major concern. Superintendent M.H. Vernon was appointed Chief Preventive Officer of this new service. According to Superintendent Vernon's report there were 32 vessels and 246 officers and men available for transfer to the Marine Section. Most transferred from the Preventive Service to the RCMP. The new section headquarters were in Moncton, New Brunswick.

Two hundred men and officers took advantage of the transfer into the new Marine Section and 28 of the 32 vessels were accepted by the RCMP. Most of the large vessels were from the Preventive Service but several of the smaller vessels came from other RCMP Divisions: the *Gananoque, Grand Manan* and the *Morrisburg*. Six sea planes from 5 Squadron of the RCAF and their operators were attached to the Marine Section from 1932 until 1936. RCMP members flew in these planes as observers. Air support, radio communications and sea patrols formed an effective network on the border and in its first year of operation this very new section seized 19 boats.

New standards for the men of the Marine Section were set and certification was required in order for them to maintain their ratings. Summer months were too busy for leave so the annual 10 days leave was reserved for the winter months when maintenance of vessels and training allowed more flexible scheduling of time. The rank categories established for the RCMP Marine Section were Officers, Petty Officers and Ratings. Since these men were seamen and had not experienced RCMP training they were precluded from wearing the traditional uniform of the Police.

The uniforms of the RCMP Marine Section 1932 to 1939 were almost identical to those of the Royal Canadian Navy (RCN) and Royal Navy. The officers wore the traditional navy blue peaked cap with a white pique cover that was worn in fine weather. The cap badge was nearly circular with a fouled anchor in the centre surrounded by a wreath of 14 maple leaves under which a scroll was inscribed 'RCMP.' The whole was surmounted by a crown. The officers were issued with a blue Service Dress jacket common to naval services of many nations. It was referred to as a 'reefer' or 'monkey' jacket and was double breasted, dark blue in color, with eight buttons and a turned down collar.

Men in RCMP Marine Section uniform 1934.

On the sleeves of the officers jacket were their gold laced rank insignia which differed from those of the Navy. This jacket was worn with a morning waistcoat, sleeveless blue vest, white shirt and black tie. Blue straight trousers with black shoes completed the officer's uniform.

The following information was supplied by Ms Carmen Harry of the RCMP Historical Collections Unit in Regina, Saskatchewan:

In the Royal Navy and Royal Canadian Navy the badges of rank for officers consisted of rows of gold lace 1-3/4", 9/16" and 1/4" wide on the sleeve cuffs and the epaulets of the great coat. A similar system was adopted for the newly formed Marine Section, which used plain gold stripes, without the circle in the upper stripe used by the Navy, and using instead a gold embroidered crown. In 1932 and 1933 Deck Officers were identified by 3/8" stripes of gold lace on the sleeves surmounted by a crown. The Captain had two stripes with the crown and First and Second Officers one stripe and the crown.

In November 1933 a new rank structure was authorized: Lieutenant, Skipper Lieutenant, Chief Skipper, Skipper, Engineering Lieutenant, Chief Engineer, Warrant Engineer and Cadet, but the badges of rank were not specified. New badges of rank were proposed in 1934, and brought into effect in 1936. According to the Rules and Regulations for that year badges of distinction for officers were to be worn on both sleeves of the jacket and on both epaulets of the overcoat for which Naval braid was used. The full stripes were 9/16" and the half stripe remained 1/4". The lower edge of the top stripe on the jacket was 3 3/4" above the edge of the sleeve, and the stripes were separated by 1/4" and surmounted by a gold embroidered crown with its lower edge 5/8" above the top stripe.

Badges of rank proposed in 1934:

Lieutenant - 2 full stripes, crown

Skipper Lieutenant - 1 full, 1 half stripe, crown

Chief Skipper - 1 full stripe, crown

Chief Engineer - 1 full stripe, crown

Skipper - 1 half stripe, crown

Warrant Engineer - 1 half stripe, crown

Badges of rank used in 1936:

Lieutenant - 2 full stripes, crown

Engineer Lieutenant - 2 full stripes, crown

Skipper Lieutenant - 1 full, 1 half stripe, crown

Chief Skipper - 1 half stripe, crown

Warrant Engineer - 1 half stripe, crown

Cadet - nil

The purple 'lights' to identify Engineer Officers were described as a stripe 1/4" in width, filling the interval between two rows of lace, or placed below a single row of lace. These rank designations were in place until 1939.

RCMP Marine section 1936

Drawings: Courtesy James J. Boulton, ***Uniforms of the Canadian Mounted Police, 1990***

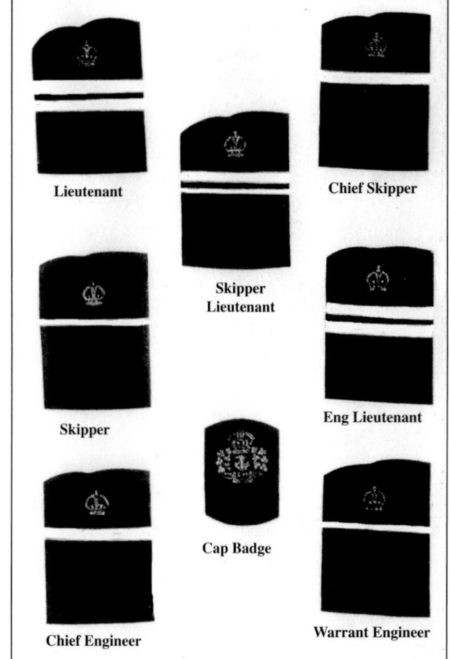

Badges of rank for Officers.

Badges of Ratings.

RCMP Ratings hat.

RCMP Officers hat.

Courtesy Robert F Holtom

Officers and crew of the RCMP vessel Fleurdelis *in 1937*

Courtesy James J. Boulton, ***Uniforms of the Canadian Mounted Police, 1990***

Red embroidered cap badge.

RCMP Marine Section officers cap badge.

The Chiefs and Petty Officers wore uniforms similar to those of the Royal Canadian Navy. Their cap was the same as the officers but the cap badges were quite different. The badges were similar to those worn by the RCN but had the letters RCMP inserted between the crown and the anchor. For Chief Petty Officers the badge was gold embroidered with a silver anchor, and for Petty Officers it was entirely embroidered in red. In 1937 the rules were modified to allow Telegraphists and Leading Telegraphists to wear the red cap badge and Petty Officers and Engine Room Artificers with more than one year service to wear the gold embroidered cap badge.

The Chief Petty Officer's Service Dress jacket was a 'reefer jacket' which was double-breasted with two rows of three buttons, but unlike the Officer's jacket it had no breast pocket. Petty Officers had two buttons placed vertically on the back of the cuff of each sleeve while the Chief Petty Officers had three buttons placed horizontally on each sleeve. Under the jacket they wore a waist-coat. The uniform was completed with a white shirt, black tie, trousers and black shoes. Their rank badges were worn on the upper arm sleeve.

The ratings of the RCMP Marine Section were issued with the 'square rig' uniform common to the Royal Canadian Navy. It consisted of dark blue serge jumper with blue jean collar, dicky, serge bell-bottom trousers and a black silk scarf. The jumper differed from the RCN in that the jacket collars had one wide stripe instead of three thin white stripes. The cap was the standard white or blue Navy Cap worn worldwide by most sailors. It had a tally with 'Marine RCMP Section' on it whereas the RCN tally had the name of the vessel. Since men of the RCMP Marine Section could not wear the same badges as those issued to the RCN, new badges were designed for the whole section. In 1939 there were major changes being planned for the RCMP Marine Section dress that would be a departure from the traditional Navy uniform. War broke out before these changes could be implemented and the men were absorbed by the RCN and no longer considered RCMP members.

Until 1934 members of the RCMP Marine Section had not been considered regular members but rather Special Constables of the RCMP. After they had served several months under the direction of the Royal Canadian Mounted Police in Preventive Service duties they became regular members. The RCMP had control of the Marine Section but it was not officially recognized by Parliament as a constituent of the RCMP until the amendment of the Police Act in 1934. Two hundred and seven officers and men then became uniformed members of the force.

The vessels of the RCMP Marine Section were called 'cruisers'. There were four types, known as Class 'A', 'B', 'C', and 'D'. The Class 'A' cruisers required 14 or more men and were used for patrolling up to 200 miles off-shore. These vessels ranged from 120 to 180 feet long and were equipped to stay at sea for long periods of time. They travelled from Newfoundland, St Pierre and Miquelon and on to Canadian waters. (Newfoundland had not yet joined confederation and St Pierre and Miquelon are French Islands). Coastal search and rescue and detection of rum runners were their main mandates.

The Class 'B' cruisers required six to 14 men, were only 75 to 80 feet long and were constructed of wood. They had speed rather than size and were assigned to the coastal 12-mile limit patrols. Their mandate was the same as that of 'A' class cruisers, but they were restricted closer to shore as they had limited abilities to stay at sea.

The Class 'C' cruisers required four men or less, were about 40 to 50 feet long, and did inshore work. They functioned mainly at night, the crew watching the bays and harbours for activity. They had no wireless radios so operated out of a local base or detachment and were limited to a small area. Each vessel had only one watch so they could not operate on a continuous basis.

The Class 'D' cruisers, also known as the 'Mosquito Fleet', required three men or less and were not equipped with suitable living accommodations so crews lived on shore. They were limited to patrolling sheltered waters and harbours. The variety in size and patrol areas of these vessels suited the RCMP and its purpose well. The Royal Canadian Navy worked entirely under one command, with one goal: to fight an enemy of the nation. This was unlike the RCMP vessels that worked independently in all weather and in all sea conditions to enforce Canadian laws in Canadian waters.

'A' Class cruisers could no more patrol a small inner harbour or shallow bay than small 'D' Class cruisers could go miles offshore for several days in foul weather. This diversity allowed for very effective and widespread patrols. The two government departments, the RCMP and the Navy, worked very closely and together afforded a very strong coastal defence.

The vessels transferred from the Preventive Service as Class 'A' cruisers were the *Fleurdelis, Adversus, Ulna, Preventor, Bay Hound, Baroff, Alachasse* and the *Patrol Boat No. IV.* Class 'B' cruisers were the *Scatarie, Chaleur and Madawaska*. These made up the eleven ocean going vessels of the new Marine Section. For operation expense considerations two other vessels, the *Margaret* and the *Conestoga* were not commissioned but sold.

There were 20 other smaller vessels of the Class 'C' and 'D' type. The Class 'C' vessels were the *Vigil, Ellsworth* and *Fernand Rinfret*. Class 'D' type were the motor boats and outboard motor boats called *Beebe, Behave, Guardian, Margaret's Launch 'H', No. 10, Stalwart, Tenacity, Bristle, Neguac, O-27,*

Patrol Boat S, Grand Manan, G, Despatcher, Imperator, Gananoque, and the *Morrisburg*. The motor boats *Fort Frances* and the *O-28* were determined to be unfit for patrol work and hence disposed of.

In October 1932 RCMP Commissioner J.H. MacBrien proposed to the Department of National Defence that the Marine Section become a unit of the Royal Canadian Naval Volunteer Reserve, citing that similar training, organization and operational functions would benefit both services. However, due to conflicts in financial responsibilities and policy differences it was believed this would create a problem and was rejected by the Minister.

A new proposal was submitted that would benefit both organizations, especially in times of emergency. The RCMP Marine Section personnel would take RCNR training in the winter months in order to be familiar with military protocol, weapon operations and communication systems. This idea was accepted and for the next seven years the RCMP sent approximately 21 men of the ranks each year to the Canadian Naval Reserve training centre in Halifax, Nova Scotia for four months of winter training. This proved to be an exceptional move for when Canada went to war in 1939 these men were fully trained and ready for deployment.

With most of the larger vessels running out of Her Majesty's Canadian (HMC) Dockyard in Halifax and winter training also being conducted there, the HQ of Marine Section was transferred from Moncton, N.B. to Halifax, N.S. in 1933. Their duties were twofold: one was to provide law enforcement and the second search and rescue support. One report states that the Marine Section conducted about 70 to 80 rescues each year. Most of the time law enforcement involved enforcing the Customs Act and dealing primarily with smuggling.

Smuggling of liquor was very popular and lucrative in the 1930s. It cost the Canadian Government millions in revenue. The seizure of contraband and vessels was an effective deterrent to this activity and in fact in the seven years of the Marine Section it was almost entirely eliminated. This involved the cooperation of three partners. First were the RCAF aircraft which would save hours of sea patrols by simply flying over the coast of the eastern shores and spotting suspicious vessels. They in turn radioed the larger patrol vessels with details of the given location. The larger ships would 'dog' the suspect vessels until they attempted to unload cargo to smaller vessels to be taken ashore. This was relayed to the smaller patrol vessels which chased down the suspect craft, or to the local detachments who attempted to locate a destination on shore.

R.A.S. MacNeil, a skipper of one of these vessels, wrote a description of rum running in those days and how the Marine Section intervened. Because he had experienced this it is best to use his own words:

A sea-going motor vessel, of about 200 tons gross tonnage, capable of a speed approximating 15 knots, and with a hold capacity of some 4,500 five-gallon kegs of rum, proceeds to a West Indian or South American port, loads and returns to a point off the Canadian coast. Here the cargo is transferred to similar but smaller vessels, which take up strategic positions off the coastline. Acting on instructions received by wireless transmission (W/T), these vessels in turn are contacted by small, high-speed launches which, when conditions are favourable, attempt to run their cargoes of some 300 kegs past the police blockade and thence ashore in some remote cove. If successful, the rum is loaded into trucks, or cached until a more convenient time for transportation.

—That was the side of the picture for the rum runner.

Above: Rum runner boat Liberty *with seized rum barrels stacked on the dock. Right, top to bottom: Rum cache seized by the RCMP Marine Section in 1936; rum runner boat* Liberty; the *RCMP vessel* Acadian *with a load of seized rum barrels on her decks, 1936.*

Photographs courtesy Roy Holtom

The police activity is as follows:

> *Immediately a rum runner arrives off the coast, an intensive effort is made to locate the vessel and commence surveillance. This effort usually lasts for a period of 24 hours, in the course of which aircraft and patrol craft cover the waters adjacent to the coast, and extending seaward for about 150 or 200 miles. Upon the location of the rum craft, she is picketed by one of the larger cruisers, the duty of which is to maintain continuous contact and observation. The object of establishing this contact, of course, is to provide Headquarters on shore with all information of the transfer of cargo, and the arrival and departure of contact boats. From this information the necessary action is taken with regards to the disposition of the remaining cruisers and patrol boats.*

MacNeil goes on to describe the evasive manoeuvres the suspects executed, including using smoke screens at night while zig zagging, using quick and unpredictable course changes. The Marine Section vessels responded by running at 'Full Speed' into the smoke with all search lights blazing. This had many risks but the threat of a large vessel bearing down on a target made the suspects reassess their manoeuvres in future trips. He continued:

Irrespective of whether or not the mother-ship is picketed by a police cruiser, the shore boat eventually makes contact and loads preparatory to making a dash shorewards. Upon receipt of a W/T (wireless transmission) signal from shore, the contact boat casts off and proceeds at full speed towards her destination, without burning the regulation navigating lights. The picketing ship refrains from giving chase because of the lack of high speed and the inability to navigate in shoal waters, and transmits the necessary information in connection with the boat's speed, course, weather conditions, etc. Then the hunt is on.

Sometimes these boats succeed in running the gauntlet, sometimes they are seized in Canadian waters, and sometimes they are chased or driven off shore by the inner patrol. It is a game of 'Blind Man's Bluff' played in inky darkness, when the slightest error of judgment on either side could easily turn the tables. All that is seen from the police vessel, if anything, is the phosphorescent, translucent feather of wake astern of the rum boat. In a few seconds the searchlights must flare on, and a warning shot must be laid across her bows before the rum runner sheers off in an attempt to escape under cover of a smokescreen. After warning shots have been fired, aim is directed at the boat itself, but the gunners in a small ship are under a severe handicap from the unpredictable motion of their own vessel and that of the target. Such a situation usually results in a seizure, but occasionally boats escape from this type of predicament. In recent years there was an incident in which a contact boat returned to St Pierre with one rudder and propeller knocked off by machine-gun fire—a fair indication of the reception she had received from a police cruiser off Sydney Harbour.

The radio was a new, wonderful and exciting tool for the RCMP patrolling the coasts of Canada. There were 15 vessels equipped with radios which were believed to have been Marconi LTT4s. The four letter Radio Call letters used by some Marine Section vessels consisted of the first three letters CGP—Canadian Government Police. This assignment acronym also provided the rum runners with useful information. Any ship monitoring the radio would hear the call sign, recognize it as a police vessel and then use the direction finder to tell immediately where the police were. If two or more rum runners were listening they could triangulate and even get an exact location for the police vessel.

RCMP vessels that carried radios, and their call signs:

CGPB – *Baroff*
CGPD – *Acadian*
CGPJ – *Bayhound*
CGPL – *Fleurdelis*
CGPQ – *Interceptor*
CGPS – *Chaleur*
CGPV – *Ulna*
CGPX – *Adversus*
CGPZ – *Detector*
CGSR – *French*
CGPC – *Laurier*
CGPF – *Macdonald*
CGPK – *Preventor*
CGPN – *Patrol Boat No. IV*
CGPR – *Madawaska*
CGPT – *Scatarie*
CGPW – *Alachasse*
CGPY – *Captor*
CGSJ – *Arresteur*
VGSR – *St Roch*

In the early 1930s smuggling was a very profitable venture. Due to the size of the Canadian coast it was not difficult for craft to slide in under the cover of darkness, dispose of contraband and then head out to sea without fear of getting caught. In fact, it was so easy that offenders along the St Lawrence waterway became careless and over-confident in their operations. Unknown to them, for months the Mounted Police had been compiling information on the players, cargo, warehouses and vessels. When satisfied that their investigations were complete they went into action and soon 60 men, including the ring leaders and seven vessels, were seized in the lower St Lawrence River. This brought a new respect to the Mounted Police and their enforcement techniques, and terminated contraband smuggling for several months.

An interesting event took place off Cape Breton on the East Coast in December 1933. A schooner called *Kromhout* skippered by Ross Mason was preparing to off load her cargo of 5,000 gallons of liquor when the RCMP *Patrol Cruiser No. IV* came into view. Mason refused to stop and headed out to sea. Thirty miles off shore the *Kromhout* surrendered to the police boat after a daring chase, and the RCMP took over command of the offending vessel. Crewed now by First Officer Mackenzie and three other RCMP members, the *Kromhout* was taken in tow. However, under cover of darkness the smugglers regained control from the RCMP, cut the tow line, and escaped to the open sea. The RCMP made a general radio broadcast that the vessel was fleeing Canadian justice and dispatched orders for her immediate seizure.

The *Kromhout* headed for the French island of St Pierre where the authorities seized her and arrested Mason. He was taken into custody and transported to Halifax where he was found guilty of theft of the vessel *Kromhout* from legal seizure, theft of her cargo from legal seizure, and obstruction of the RCMP in performance of their duty. This was a warning to the criminal element that an effective police presence was now in operation.

Although firearms are now an everyday part of Canadian law enforcement officers' equipment, they were, as a rule, used minimally in this time period. On some occasions, however, they were necessary. One night in May 1933 skipper J.C. Kelly of the patrol boat *Acadian* surprised the rum runner *Lucky Peggy* and two other rum running vessels exchanging cargo. The *Lucky Peggy* immediately tried to escape and the *Acadian* opened fire on her. This brought her to a stop and on inspection it was found that a William Tanner had been killed by a bullet that had ricocheted off a rum keg. The RCMP skipper was charged with manslaughter but a Grand Jury found 'no bill' and concluded that the shooting was justified.

Aside from smuggling, other law enforcement duties included Excise, Fisheries Protection, Shipping Acts and provincial marine statutes. From March to January the men worked 10 days at sea with one day to replenish supplies. During the very few days they were not at sea, the crews participated in local regattas, transportation of various people to remote places and assisting in beach searches. Commissioner MacBrien wrote that prior to March 31, 1934 the service had investigated 6,000 cases under the Customs and Excise Acts.

A marine advisor made plans for replacement vessels that would meet the needs of the RCMP after a survey of the fleet indicated that due to their age the cost of maintenance and operation would be excessive. Over the next seven years several vessels were added to the fleet and others were retired. In 1936 the RCMP had 23 cruisers and patrol boats, which was down from the 1932 inventory, but still an overly large fleet. Prohibition ended in 1936 so the need for border patrols and vessels was diminished.

Marine Section

The obsolete 'A' Class Police cruisers *Preventor* and *Bayhound* were replaced by the *Macdonald* and the *Laurier*. These new cruisers were sister ships, launched at Quebec City on August 20, 1936, and were specially built and designed for the Marine Section. A seized rum runner speed boat was added to the fleet and commissioned as the *Beaver*. Two more new speed boats were being constructed for the Marine Section that would join the existing vessels *Islander, Alarm* and *Alert,* which were also added before 1936.

From 1932 to 1936 the RCMP Marine Section used aircraft of the Royal Canadian Air Force (RCAF) to spot smugglers. Under the command of Squadron leader F.C. Higgins, this RCAF section was part of 5 Squadron which was equipped with Vickers Vancouver 'Flying Boats' and Fairchild 71 float planes and worked out of Rimouski, Gaspé, Shediac and Dartmouth in the summer months. When the RCAF could no longer fulfill its duties with the police force the RCMP initiated its own Air Services on April 1, 1937 with the purchase of four DeHaviland DH-90 Dragonfly aircraft. They were identified as CF-MPA, CF-MPB, CF-MPC, and CF-MPD. Eight qualified pilots were drawn from RCMP ranks under the direction of S/Sgt T.R. Michelson. The new service was based in New Brunswick and carried on where the RCAF left off.

The 1938 Quarterly refers to the Marine Section Vessels and lists their classes and numbers. There were seven 'A' Class, eight 'B' Class, nine 'C' Class and nine 'D' Class vessels for a total of 33 vessels. In 1939 the RCMP had negotiated with three marine construction companies to build four brand new 'D-2' type fast patrol boats. These 48-foot vessels were in the construction phase when Canada declared war on Germany, so the Royal Canadian Navy took over the final delivery of the RCMP vessels *D-14, D-15, D-16* and *D-17*. Although never officially classed as police vessels, they were designed and constructed for the RCMP.

In September 1939 Canada elected to participate in the Second World War in Europe and 155 of a total of 209 officers and men in the Marine Section were transferred with their ships to the Navy. Twenty-six men transferred to the RCAF and became the core of the Marine Section of the Air Sea Rescue and one man joined the army. The remaining 27 were discharged mainly due to age or physical impairments. Some of them later joined various other forces. Ironically, many of the rum runner skippers also joined in the effort of the Second World War along with their law enforcement counterparts, to be united in this common cause. The sea skills both groups had acquired during prohibition came to a very good purpose during the war, a purpose that no doubt saved their own and many other lives. Due to wear and tear most of the vessels never returned to active service with the RCMP after the war ended in 1945.

In 1939 the RCMP Marine Section had come to the end of an era. The world was changing and Canada moved its focus from prohibition, contraband and rum running to the protection of its harbours and waterways from intrusion by Nazi Germany and later Imperial Japan. This was where the men of the RCMP Marine Section were to meet their next challenge. Not until April 1947 would the RCMP again see the likes of a marine service that it had enjoyed for the past seven years.

Class A and B Vessels Transferred to the New RCMP Marine Section in 1932

In 1932, the Marine Section was formed with the RCMP takeover of Department of National Revenue Preventive Services' duties and vessels. With 35 ships (11 seagoing craft), its primary duty was to curtail smuggling in the Gulf of St Lawrence and on the east and west coasts of Canada.

In Ontario the Marine Division of the RCMP entered '0' Division waters in 1946, stationing police boats at Sarnia and Windsor. Later other vessels saw service at Hamilton and Niagara Falls. Police Boat Shaunavon *arrived in Toronto during June, 1948 where she saw service until 1956. In May of that year this vessel was replaced by the PB* Shaunavon II.

In 1972, Shaunavon II *was decommissioned and replaced by Patrol Vessel* Manyberries. *At present Marine Services operate Patrol Vessels in Sarnia Windsor, and Toronto, and play a vital support role to land operations, by enforcing the Small Vessels Regulations, Customs and other Acts.*

Courtesy RCMP Historical Collections Unit

These vessels came from the Preventive Services.

Watercolour sketch courtesy Canadian naval artist John M. Horton, depicting Canadian Naval vessels in the 1940s.

Courtesy James J. Boulton, *Uniforms of the Canadian Mounted Police, 1990*

Name: Adversus (1)
Year Built: 1931
Built By: Ditchburn Boats Ltd, Gravenhurst, Ontario
In Service: 1932 – 1939
Dimensions: 112.3 x 19 x 11
Type: Class 'A' cruiser
Cost:
Power: Twin screw diesel, 750 hp
Displacement: 155 GT
Crew: 12
Speed: 12 kts
Armament: One .303 machine gun
Official Number: 157002
Radio Call Sign: CGPX
Code: 7000

Courtesy Vancouver Maritime Museum

ADVERSUS (1)

The *Adversus* was built for the Preventive Service and then transferred to the RCMP in 1932. She was sent to North Sydney, Nova Scotia, but in 1933, she was reassigned to the Pacific, becoming the first RCMP vessel to transit the Panama Canal. On August 7, 1937 she returned to the East Coast and in 1939 was transferred to the Royal Canadian Navy and became HMCS Adversus. On December 20, 1941 she was lost at sea when caught in a blizzard and ran aground on McNutts Island near Shelburne, N.S. The *Adversus* was sister ship to the *Alachasse*.

Courtesy RCN

Name: Alachasse
Year Built: 1931
Built By: Les Chantiers Manseau, Sorel, Quebec
In Service: 1932 – 1939
Dimensions: 116.4 x 19 x 11.3
Type: Class 'A' cruiser
Cost:
Power: Twin screw diesel, 750 hp
Displacement: 157 GT
Crew: 14
Speed: 12 kts
Armament: One .303 machine gun
Official Number: 157001
Radio Call Sign: CGPW
Code: 7001

The Alachasse *was based in Shediac, New Brunswick before being transferred to the RCN as HMCS* ALACHASSE.

ALACHASSE

The *Alachasse* was built for the Preventive Service and transferred to the RCMP in 1932. A sister ship to the *Adversus,* she was based in Shediac, New Brunswick. In 1939 the *Alachasse* was transferred to the Canadian Navy and became HMCS ALACHASSE with pennant number Z18. She was declared surplus and turned over to CADC on January 3, 1946 and sold to Marine Industries Limited and then scrapped in 1957.

Courtesy RCMP Historical Collections Unit

The Baroff *was a former rum runner that was seized and put into service of the RCMP. She patrolled out of Gaspé, Quebec.*

Name: Baroff
Year Built: 1918
Built By: College Point Boat Corporation, College Point, N.Y.
In Service: 1932 – 1936
Dimensions: 87.8 x 14.6 x 8
Type: Class 'A' cruiser
Cost:
Power: Single Fairbanks-Morse 60 hp semi diesel
Displacement: 76 GT
Crew: 15
Speed: 18 kts
Armament: One 3 pounder
Official Number: 150546
Radio Call Sign: CGPB

Courtesy Robert F. Holtom

BAROFF

The *Baroff*, was a former American submarine chaser that became a rum runner. Formerly known as the *Bo-Peep,* she was seized by the Preventive Service in 1927 and turned into a government vessel. She was transferred to the RCMP in 1932 and patrolled out of Gaspé until taken out of service in 1936. *Baroff* was sold June 27, 1938 and was operated by Marine Industries of Montreal, Quebec until finally dismantled in 1945. *Baroff* was a sister ship to *Patrol Boat IV*.

Courtesy Vancouver Maritime Museum

Courtesy RCMP Historical Collections Unit

BAYHOUND

The *Bayhound* was formerly a private yacht named *Tillicum* owned by Sir Charles Gordon. She was purchased by the Preventive Service in 1928 where she served until 1932 when she was transferred to the RCMP. She went out of service in 1936 and was replaced by the *Laurier*. She was refitted as a 'depot' vessel and used as living quarters in Halifax for crews in training. The *Bayhound* was sold to Pictou Foundry and Machine Co. Ltd in Pictou, Nova Scotia. Later she was sold to her original owner and finally reported out of existence in 1945.

Name: Bayhound
Year Built: 1910
Built By: William Gardner, New York
In Service: 1932 – 1936
Dimensions: 114 x 17.2 x 6
Type: Class 'A' cruiser
Cost:
Power: Single screw diesel, 400 hp
Displacement: 135 GT
Crew: 15
Speed: 15 kts
Armament: Small arms
Official Number: 152367
Radio Call Sign CGPJ

Name: Chaleur
Year Built: 1930
Built By: Ditchburn Boats Ltd, Gravenhurst, Ontario
In Service: 1932 – 1939
Dimensions: 73.3 x 13.7 x 8.1
Type: Class 'B' cruiser
Cost:
Power: 2 – 300 hp Sterling gasoline engines
Displacement: 60.16 GT
Crew:
Speed: 13 kts
Armament: Machine gun Colt automatic 303
Official Number: 156505
Radio Call Sign: CGPS

Courtesy of RCMP Historical Collections Unit

CHALEUR

The *Chaleur* is a common name among Navy vessels but this one was a somewhat smaller vessel than most and very similar to the *Madawaska*. The RCMP received this ship from the Preventive Service in 1932 and used her until she was turned over to the Royal Canadian Navy in 1939. She was based out of Charlottetown, Prince Edward Island from 1932 to 1935. In 1939 she became HMCS CHALEUR, an examination vessel with pennant number Z20 from 1939 to 1945. The vessel was declared surplus and turned over to CADC on August 8, 1945. She was sold August 23, 1946 and finally dismantled in 1947.

Name: Conestoga
Year Built: 1896
Built By: Racine Boats Mfg. Co., Racine, Wisconsin
In Service: Not put in Service
Dimensions: 136 x 18.3 x 10
Type: Class 'A' cruiser
Cost:
Power: Four-cylinder triple expansion
Displacement: 167.6 GT
Speed: 13 mph
Crew: 19
Armament: Ross and Winchester rifles
Official Number: 138220

CONESTOGA

Conestoga was a steel oil-fired Customs vessel on the Great Lakes, transferred to the RCMP in June 1932 but not taken into the Marine Section. She was transferred to CADC, sold to the Georgian Bay Tourist Company of Midland, Ontario and re-named *Pathfinder*.

Courtesy Robert F Holtom

Name: Fleurdelis
Year Built: 1929
Built By: Canadian Vickers Ltd, Montreal, Quebec
In Service: 1932 – 1939
Dimensions: 164.8 x 21.1 x 11.7
Type: Class 'A' cruiser
Cost:
Power: 3 – Winton triple screw diesel engines 1,800 hp each
Displacement: 316 GT
Crew: 23
Speed: 12-18 kts
Armament: One .303 machine gun
Official Number: 156502
Radio Call Sign: CGPL
Code: 7005

Crew of the Fleurdelis.

FLEURDELIS

The *Fleurdelis* was a Preventive Service vessel that was transferred to the RCMP in 1932 and based out of Halifax, Nova Scotia checking rum running. She was transferred to the Royal Canadian Navy as an examination vessel in 1939 and renamed HMCS FLEUR DE LIS, pennant number Z31 and later J16.

She was declared surplus and turned over to CADC on January 3, 1946 and sold on April 15 that year to Marine Industries Ltd, who operated her until 1952 when she was scrapped. *Fleurdelis* was a sistership to *Preventor* (1).

Name: Madawaska
Year Built: 1930
Built By: Ditchburn Boats Ltd, Gravenhurst, Ontario
In Service: 1932 – 1939
Dimensions: 73.3 x 13.7 x 8.1
Type: Class 'B' cruiser
Cost:
Power: 2 – 300 hp Sterling engines
Displacement: 60.16 GT
Crew: 6
Speed:
Armament: Machine Gun Colt Auto .303
Official Number: 156507
Radio Call Sign: CGPR
Code: 7103

Courtesy RCMP Historical Collections Unit

MADAWASKA

The *Madawaska* was a Preventive Service vessel that was transferred to the RCMP in 1932 and was based out of Rivière du Loup, Quebec. In 1939 the ship was transferred to the Royal Canadian Navy and served as HMCS MADAWASKA with pennant number Z21. She was declared surplus and turned over to CADC on December 21, 1945 and sold for breaking up May 28, 1946.

Photograph from RCMP Quarterly

The Baroff *shown left, was a sister ship to the* Patrol Boat No. IV.

Name: Patrol Boat No. IV
Year Built: 1917
Built By: Unknown, Brooklyn, New York
In Service: 1932 – 1935
Dimensions: 87.8 x 14.6 x 8
Type: Class 'A' cruiser
Cost:
Power: Triple screw gasoline, 660 hp, (re-powered in 1928 with two Fairbanks Morse 180 hp diesel engines)
Displacement: 76 GT
Crew: 13
Speed: 18 kts (15 kts after re-engined)
Armament: One 3 pounder
Official Number: 152653
Radio Call Sign: CGPN

PATROL BOAT NO. IV

Patrol Boat No. IV was a former American submarine chaser turned into a rum runner called *Stumble Inn* (1). This vessel was a main participant in running contraband in the Great Lakes with her sister ship *Stumble Inn* (2) from Canada to a hotel called Stumble Inn on Grand Island just opposite the city of Buffalo on the Niagara River. During a raid by the American Coast Guard the *Stumble Inn* (2) was seized but *Stumble Inn* (1) escaped back to Canadian waters and dumped her cargo in the Niagara River. Having failed to report to Customs, she was seized and then forfeited to the Crown in 1924. She was abandoned on the shore near Bridgeburg, Ontario until taken over by the Preventive Service and turned into a government vessel in 1929. With much difficulty the patrol boat was taken by a crew to North Sydney, Nova Scotia. The engines were in such disrepair that they were removed and new diesel engines installed. She was now renamed *Patrol Boat No. IV* of the Preventive Service. In 1932 she was turned over to the RCMP where she served out of North Sydney, N.S. She was sold in 1935 to Manseau Shipyards then in 1938 to Marine Industries who resold her in 1941 for $1.00 to the RCN and she was renamed HMCS Montreal and in 1943 renamed HMCS Donnacona II.

Courtesy James J. Boulton, *Uniforms of the Canadian Mounted Police, 1990*

Couartesy RCMP Museum, Regina

Name: Preventor (1)
Year Built: 1929
Built By: Canadian Vickers, Montreal, Quebec
In Service: 1932 – 1937
Dimensions: 164.8 x 21.1 x 11.7
Type: Class 'A' cruiser
Cost:
Power: 3 - Winton diesel engines 1,800 hp (600 hp each)
Displacement: 316 GT
Crew: 23
Speed: 12 kts
Armament: One .303 machine gun
Official Number: 156504
Radio Call Sign: CGPK

PREVENTOR (1)

The *Preventor* (1) was a Protective Service vessel built in 1929 and turned over to the RCMP in 1932. The ship was transferred to the RCN in 1937 and sold to Marine Industries in 1938. She was broken up in 1953. She was a sister ship to the *Fleurdelis*.

In 2009 the newest vessel with the name *Preventor* was commissioned in Halifax. She is seen at right on the day of her RCMP acceptance after a major refit since being acquired from the Canadian Coast Guard. Details on page 280.

Courtesy RCMP Historical Collections Unit

Courtesy Robert F Holtom

Name: Scatarie
Year Built: 1926
Built By: Ditchburn Boats Ltd., Gravenhurst, Ontario
In Service: 1932 – 1939
Dimensions: 71.7 x 13.7 x 6
Type: Class 'B' cruiser
Cost:
Power: Two 120 hp diesel engines
Displacement: 41 GT
Crew: 9
Radio Call Sign: CGPT
Speed: 35 kts (possibly exaggerated)
Armament: small arms
Official Number: 151156
Code: 7171

SCATARIE

The *Scatarie* was a seized rum runner known as *One Seventy Four* that was used to transfer contraband from the schooner *I'm Alone* to American shores. It was the *Baroff* that seized the rum runner in 1928 at Chaleur. She was sent to Cheticamp, Nova Scotia as a Preventive Service vessel. In 1932 she was transferred to the RCMP and served until 1939 when she was again transferred to the Royal Canadian Navy as HMCS Scatarie, pennant number Z22. She was declared surplus and turned over to CADC on January 3, 1946.

Courtesy RCMP Historical Collections Unit

Above: The Ulna*, courtesy Robert F. Holtom. Right: The* Ulna *in her prime. Following page: The* Ulna *with an accompanying float plane, on patrol, from an early period newspaper clipping.*

Name: Ulna
Year Built: 1909
Built By: Day Summers & Co. Ltd., Southampton, England
In Service: 1932 – 1939
Dimensions: 125.7 x 18.5 x 10.2
Type: Class 'A' cruiser
Cost:
Power: Single screw steam triple expansion 41 hp
Displacement: 167 GT
Crew: 17
Radio Call Sign: CGPV
Speed: 13 kts
Armament: One 3 pounder
Official Number: 124518

Courtesy RCMP Historical Collections Unit

ULNA

The former yacht *Ulna*, chartered in 1931, and subsequently purchased by the RCMP in 1932, was based out of Gaspé, Quebec. She was built by Day Summers & Co. Ltd and purchased from Margaree Steamship Co. Ltd of Sydney, Nova Scotia. In 1939, she was sold to Canso Steamship Company of Sydney and was chartered by the RCN where she became HMCS Ulna. Used as examination vessel until 1940, she was returned to her owner and served as a coastal freighter.

Courtesy of Don Klancher

Class 'C' and 'D' Vessels Transferred to the New RCMP Marine Section in 1932

Courtesy of RCN Photo S-38 DHH, NDHQ

These were former Preventive Service vessels that were turned over to the RCMP.

Courtesy RCMP Historical Collections Unit

BEEBE

The *Beebe* was a Canada Customs vessel that was turned over to the RCMP in 1932. She served on the East Coast out of Jedore, Nova Scotia. In Archive files 'RG 24, Vol 5676 – Work done for Police Dept by the RCN,' it was reported that work was completed on this vessel in 1929. She is listed as 38 feet long. The RCMP annual report for 1936 states she was taken out of service. She was dismantled in 1938.

Name: Beebe
Year Built: 1927
Built By: Ditchburn Boats Ltd., Gravenhurst, Ontario
In Service: 1932 – 1936
Dimensions: 38 x 8 x 4.2
Type: Class 'D' cruiser
Cost:
Power: 290 hp Sterling Dolphin gasoline engine
Displacement: 8.62 GT
Crew: 2
Speed: 30 mph
Official Number: 154587

The vessel shown at right, identified as Vigil II, *possibly* Vigil *(1), was similar to the* Beebe *and* Behave. *No photographs of these two craft were located.*

Name: Behave
Year Built: 1927
Built By: Ditchburn Boats Ltd., Gravenhurst, Ontario
In Service: 1932 – 1936
Dimensions: 38 x 8 x 4.2
Type: Class 'D' cruiser
Cost:
Power: 290 hp Sterling Dolphin gasoline engine
Displacement: 8.62 GT
Crew: 2
Speed: 30 mph
Official Number: 154588

Name: Bristle
Year Built: 1928
Built By: Ditchburn Boats Ltd., Gravenhurst, Ontario
In Service: 1932 – 1936
Dimensions: 38 x 8 x 4.2
Type: Class 'D' cruiser
Cost:
Power: 290 hp Sterling Dolphin gasoline engine
Displacement: 9 GT
Crew: 2
Speed: 30 mph
Official Number: 154801
Code: 7208

Courtesy RCMP Historical Collections Unit

BEHAVE

The *Behave* was a Canada Customs vessel, listed at 38 feet long, that was turned over to the RCMP in 1932. She served on the East Coast out of Ingrahamport, Nova Scotia. In Archive files 'RG 24, Vol 5676 – Work done for Police Dept by the RCN,' work was completed on this vessel in 1929. She was sold March 27, 1936 and was in operation until broken up in 1946.

BRISTLE

The *Bristle* was a Canada Customs vessel that was turned over to the RCMP in 1932. She served on the East Coast out of Saint John, New Brunswick. The RCMP annual report for 1936 states she was taken out of service and sold September 19, 1936. The Registry was noted February 9, 1959: 'Vessel presumed out of existence.'

Courtesy Peter Caron

DESPATCHER

The *Despatcher* was a Canada Customs vessel in Vancouver, British Columbia, launched on April 12, 1928. Under the command of Captain Malcolm Finlay MacDonald, she patrolled the west coast of BC for rum runners. She was turned over to the RCMP Marine Section in 1932 along with her skipper who became a member of the RCMP. This vessel was sold on November 17, 1933 and subsequently renamed *Spring*. Many years later she was rebuilt and on her 80th birthday, April 12, 2008, she was rechristened *Despatcher* by her new owner.

Name: Despatcher
Year Built: 1928
Built By: S.R. Wallace, North Vancouver, B.C.
In Service: 1932 – 1933
Dimensions: 49 x 10.5 x 4.9
Type: Class 'D' cruiser
Cost: $17,400
Power: Twin 290 hp Stirling Dolphin gasoline engines
Displacement: 20.56 GT
Crew: 4
Armament: Model 1949, Colt Automatic gun .303
Speed: 30 kts
RCMP Number: 154590
Code: 7104

Name: Ellsworth
Year Built: 1928
Built By: O.A. Ham, Mahone Bay, N.S.
In Service: 1932 – 1939
Dimensions: 52.5 x 12.8 x 8.5
Type: Class 'C' cruiser
Cost:
Power: Fairbanks-Morse diesel engine
Displacement: 27.28 GT
Crew: 4
Speed: 10 kts
RCMP Number: 155054
Code: 7102

Courtesy Robert F Holtom

ELLSWORTH

The *Ellsworth* was originally a Canada Customs vessel and was turned over to the RCMP in 1932. She worked out of the Barrington Passage area of Nova Scotia. In 1939 she was turned over to the RCN and became HMCS ELLSWORTH from 1939 to 1942 when she was renamed HMC HC 43. She was declared surplus and turned over to CADC on October 20, 1945 and was sold January 14, 1946.

Courtesy RCN Photo HS-0050-82 from DHH, NDHQ

Name: Fernand Rinfret
Year Built: 1928
Built By: O.A. Ham, Mahone Bay, N.S.
In Service: 1932 – 1939
Dimensions: 34.4 x 9.4 x 4.6
Type: Class 'C' cruiser
Cost:
Power: Sterling 150 hp horizontal crude oil engine
Displacement: 10.65 GT
Crew: 3
Speed: 12 kts
Official Number: 155056
Code: 7213

FERNAND RINFRET

The *Fernand Rinfret* was a Canada Customs vessel that was turned over to the RCMP in 1932. She worked out of Quebec. In 1939 she was turned over to the RCN and became HMCS Fernand Rinfret from 1939 to 1942 when she was renamed HMC HC 46. She was declared surplus and turned over to CADC on July 23, 1945.

Name: G (Launch G)
Year Built:
Built By:
In Service: 1932
Dimensions:
Type: Class 'D' cruiser
Cost:
Power:
Displacement:
Speed:
Official Number:

G

The *G* (also known as *Launch G*) was a Canada Customs vessel. She was turned over to the RCMP in 1932. She worked out of Gaspé, Quebec. This vessel is not mentioned in any RCMP Marine Section annual reports after 1932.

Name: Gananoque
Year Built: 1931
Built By: Greavette Boats Ltd, Gravenhurst, Ontario
In Service: 1932
Dimensions: 18.5 ft
Type: Class 'D' cruiser motor launch
Cost:
Power:
Displacement:
Speed: 33 mph
Crew: 1
Official Number:

GANANOQUE

The *Gananoque* was a motor launch transferred from the Customs Service in 1932. She patrolled the islands in the vicinity of Gananoque, Ontario and east and west of that point.

Courtesy Library and Archives Canada e010764875

Name: Grand Manan
Year Built: 1930
Built By: Peerless Motor & Machine Works Ltd, St John, New Brunswick
In Service: 1932
Dimensions: 21 ft LOA
Type: Class 'D' cruiser
Cost:
Power: Outboard
Displacement:
Speed:
Official Number:

GRAND MANAN

The *Grand Manan* was a motor patrol boat transferred from the Customs Service in 1932. She worked out of Grand Manan, New Brunswick. The photograph shows Corporal Mallory aboard the vessel in 1936.

Courtesy RCN Photo S-38 DHH, NDHQ

GUARDIAN

The *Guardian* was a Canada Customs vessel that was turned over to the RCMP in 1932. She worked out of Halifax, Nova Scotia. In 1939 she was turned over to the RCN and became HMCS Guardian from 1939 to 1942 when she was renamed HMC HC 47. She was scrapped in 1945.

Name: Guardian
Year Built: 1929
Built By: O.A. Ham, Mahone Bay, Nova Scotia
In Service: 1932 - 1939
Dimensions: 34.8 x 8 x 4
Type: Class 'D' cruiser
Cost:
Power: Sterling gasoline engine
Displacement: 7.64 GT
Crew: 3
Speed: 12 kts
Official Number: 156501
Code: 7202

Name: Imperator
Year Built: 1927
Built By: Hoffar-Beeching Shipyards, Vancouver, British Columbia
In Service: 1932 - 1939
Dimensions: 35.1 x 8.6 x 4.8
Type: Class 'D' cruiser
Cost: $7,650
Power: 180 hp Hall-Scott gasoline engine
Displacement: 10 GT
Crew: 4
Speed: 26 kts
Official Number: 154589
Radio Call Sign: CGJN
Code: 7105

Courtesy RCMP Historical Collections Unit

IMPERATOR

The *Imperator* was a Canada Customs vessel, turned over to the RCMP in 1932. She worked out of Vancouver, British Columbia and the Sunshine Coast up to Powell River, B.C. In 1939 she was turned over to the RCN and became the HC 18 until 1945. She was declared surplus and turned over to CADC on August 30, 1945. The vessel was sold January 4, 1946 and the Registry was noted in 1977 because the existence of the vessel could not be verified.

Name: Margaret's Launch H
Year Built: 1914
Built By: U.K.
In Service: 1932
Dimensions: 182.4 x 32.3 x 12.1
Type: Class 'D' cruiser
Cost:
Power: 2,000 hp
Displacement:
Speed: 15 kts
Official Number:
Armament: Ross and Winchester rifles

MARGARET'S LAUNCH H

The *Margaret's Launch H* was a twin-screw, steel oil-fired Canada Customs vessel that was turned over to the RCMP in 1932. She worked out of Halifax, Nova Scotia. This vessel is not mentioned in any RCMP Marine Section Annual reports after 1932, when she was put up for sale.

Courtesy NWT Archives

The photograph at left shows Frank Dunn and a RCMP boat on the Yukon River at Dawson City. It is small but convenient for the local conditions.

MORRISBURG

The *Morrisburg* was a motor boat transferred from the Canadian Customs Service in 1933. She worked out of Morrisburg, Ontario.

Name: Morrisburg
Year Built: 1930
Built By: Flatterly Co. Ltd, Morrisburg, Ontario
In Service: 1932
Dimensions:
Type: Class 'D' cruiser
Power:
Displacement:
Crew:
Speed:
Official Number: 130415

NEGUAC

The *Neguac* was a Canada Customs vessel that was turned over to the RCMP in 1932. She worked out of Shippigan, New Brunswick. This vessel is not mentioned in any RCMP Marine Section Annual Reports after 1932 except for the annual report of 1936 which states she was taken out of service that year.

Name: Neguac
Year Built: 1926
Built By:
In Service: 1932 - 1936
Dimensions: 45 x 9.6 x 4
Type: Class 'D' cruiser
Power: 100 hp Kermath
Displacement:
Crew: 3
Speed:
Official Number:
Code: 7209

O-27

The *O-27,* formerly the *Alice G*, was a Canada Customs vessel, and was turned over to the RCMP in 1932. She worked out of New Brunswick and was sold June 18, 1934.

Name: O-27
Year Built:
Built By:
In Service: 1932 - 1934
Dimensions: 35 x 8 x 3.5
Type: Class 'D' cruiser
Power:
Displacement:
Crew: 3
Official Number:
Code: 7210

Right: Tranquil waters at Little Bras d'Or, Nova Scotia, where numerous RCMP patrol boats have been in operation. The vessels shown here are not RCMP.

Name: Patrol Boat No. 10
Year Built: 1906
Built By: B.J. Walters, Halifax, N.S.
In Service: 1932 - 1936
Dimensions: 39 x 9 x 4.8
Type: Class 'D' cruiser
Cost:
Power:
Displacement: 12.74 GT
Crew: 3
Speed:
Official Number: 12212
Code:

PATROL BOAT No. 10

The *Patrol Boat No. 10* was a Canada Customs vessel turned over to the RCMP in 1932. She worked out of Big Bras d'Or, Nova Scotia. She was sold December 4, 1935.

Name: S
Year Built:
Built By:
In Service: 1932
Dimensions::
Type: Class 'D' cruiser
Cost:
Power: Buffalo gasoline engine
Displacement:
Speed:
Official Number: 122129

S

The *S* was a Canada Customs vessel that was turned over to the RCMP in 1932. She worked out of Shediac, New Brunswick. This vessel is not mentioned in any RCMP Marine Section Annual reports after 1932.

Courtesy RCMP Historical Collections Unit

STALWART

The *Stalwart* was a Canada Customs vessel that was turned over to the RCMP in 1932 and served on the East Coast out of Little Bras d'Or, Nova Scotia. She was sold May 14, 1940 and was finally destroyed in the ice in December 1945 off Cape Breton Island. She was a sister ship to the *Tenacity*.

Unwanted

Some vessels acquired by the RCMP never made it into service. Such was the *O-28* (formerly *Swordfish*) a Customs vessel that was turned over to the RCMP in 1932 at Dalhousie, New Brunswick. The vessel was almost 20 years old and it was considered not worthwhile to spend money on the extensive repairs required. She was determined to be of the vessel type required for Chaleur Bay, but was not fast enough and the deckhouse was too high. She was never commissioned and was turned over to CADC on receipt and sold.

Name: Stalwart
Year Built: 1928
Built By: Woodard McCrea Boats, Inc., North Hatley, Quebec
In Service: 1932 - 1940
Dimensions: 31 x 7.6 x 3.8
Type: Class 'D' cruiser
Cost:
Power: 150 hp Sterling Petrel motor
Displacement: 4.81 GT
Crew:
Speed: 25 kts
Official Number: 154806

Name: Tenacity
Year Built: 1928
Built By: Woodard McCrea Boats Inc., North Hatley, Quebec
In Service: 1932 - 1939
Dimensions: 32 x 7.6 x 4.3
Type: Class 'D' cruiser
Cost:
Power: 150 hp Sterling Petrel motor
Displacement: 4.76 GT
Crew: 3
Speed: 25 kts
Official Number: 154805
Armament:
Radio Call Sign:
RCMP Number:
Code:

Courtesy RCMP Historical Collections Unit

TENACITY

The *Tenacity* was a Canada Customs boat that was turned over to the RCMP in 1932 as a Class 'D' vessel. She served on the East Coast out of North Sydney, Nova Scotia until 1939 when she was sold. This vessel is not mentioned in any RCMP Marine Section Annual Reports after 1932. However in National Archive Files RG 24 Vol 5676, and File 910701 Vol 1 and Vol 2 the *Tenacity* is mentioned in June 1938 and November 1938 as work having been done for the Police Department, and in the Summary of Police Patrol Boats.

The above photograph is Vigil II. *See* Vigil II *on page 145.*

Name: Vigil
Year Built: 1928
Built By: Ditchburn Boats. Ltd., Gravenhurst, Ontario
In Service: 1932 - 1935
Dimensions: 38 x 8 x 3.7
Type: Class 'D' cruiser
Power: 290 hp Sterling Dolphin
Displacement: 9 GT
Speed: 30 mph
Official Number: 154802

VIGIL

The *Vigil* was a Canada Customs vessel that was turned over to the RCMP in 1932. She worked out of Riverport, Nova Scotia and in 1934 was listed as working out of New Brunswick. She was sold December 4, 1935. The *Vigil* has similar dimensions to her sister ships *Beebe, Bristle* and *Behave.*

A Selection of Vessels Built in British Columbia for Police Services

Courtesy BC Archives F-03481

Not much detail is available about these vessels. They were built and used on the West Coast in the early years by the British Columbia Police Service before being transferred into other services.

Courtesy BC Archives F-03478

Courtesy BC Archives E-04181

PML 16, *above, and the vessel at right, were among those built and used in British Columbia by local police services. The* PML 16 *was one of six put into RCMP Service.*

In August, 1950 the RCMP took over the duties of the B.C. Provincial Police and their motor launches stationed along the Pacific Coast. The fleet consisted of about 12 vessels, mostly 40 to 70 feet in length and identified by PML numbers.

RCMP-2
MP-80

Courtesy BC Archives F-03474

Courtesy BC Archives E-04177

Courtesy BC Archives E-04185

Courtesy BC Archives G-03713

The vessels on these pages were purpose-built in British Columbia.
Opposite: The Tahsis, *(MP 80) locally-built for area waters, is seen plying the inlets of the west coast of Vancouver Island, out of the town for which she was named. Right: ML 15 high and dry on an unchartered rock near Port Essington, B.C.*

Vessels added to RCMP Marine Section 1933-1939

Courtesy of RCN photo S51 from DHH, NDHQ

Some vessels were built specifically for the RCMP. Some were seized from rum running and other illegal activities and transferred to the RCMP.

Courtesy Vancouver Maritime Museum

Above: Royal Canadian Mounted Police officer William S. Carter, Cambridge Bay, Nunavut 1932.

Name: Acadian (1)
Year Built: 1934
Built By: W.C. MacKay & Sons Ltd., Shelburne, Nova Scotia
In Service: 1934 - 1939
Dimensions: 46.5 x 12.3 x 6.1
Type: Class 'B' cruiser
Cost:
Power: 1-160 hp Gleniffer diesel
Displacement: 22 GT
Speed: 11 kts
Crew: 5
Official Number: 158158
Radio Call Sign: CGPD
RCMP Number:
Code: 7110

Courtesy of RCMP Historical Collections Unit

ACADIAN (1)

The *Acadian* was a wood-hulled vessel built for the RCMP. She worked on the East Coast. The boat was turned over to the RCN in 1939 and became HMCS Invader pennant P13 and Z09, and later renamed HMC HC50. She was declared surplus August 28, 1945.

Courtesy RCN photo H-736 from DHH, NDHQ

Courtesy Vancouver Maritime Museum

Name: Advance (1)
Year Built: 1934
Built By: Canadian Vickers Ltd., Montreal, Quebec
In Service: 1935 - 1939
Dimensions: 24.6 x 6.8 x 3.6
Type: Class 'D' cruiser
Cost:
Power: 100 hp Buchanan gasoline engine
Displacement: 3.6 GT
Speed: 25 mph
Crew: 3
Official Number: 158840
Radio Call Sign:
Code: 7247

ADVANCE (1)

The *Advance* was purchased by the RCMP in 1935 and served in eastern Canada out of Ste Anne des Monts, Quebec until 1939. She was turned over to the Royal Canadian Navy in 1939 and renamed HMC HC27. She was declared surplus on July 10, 1945.

Courtesy RCMP Historical Collections Unit

Courtesy Glenbow Archives NA-2137-27

Left: RCMP crew poling a canoe in shallow water on La Loche River, Saskatchewan, 1909.

Name: Alarm
Year Built: 1930
Built By: Alfred Stubbart, Souris, P.E.I.
In Service: 1936 - 1939
Dimensions: 34 x 6.5 x 3.5
Type: Class 'D' cruiser
Cost:
Power: 25 IMP Nash gasoline engine
Displacement: 5 GT
Speed: 10 kts
Crew: 1
Official Number: 158833
Radio Call Sign:
Code: 7253

ALARM

The *Alarm* was a seized vessel that was turned over to the RCMP Marine Section in 1936 and was stationed in Charlottetown, Prince Edward Island. She was turned over to the RCN in 1939 but was found to be unfit for service and was not put into operation by the RCN. On April 19, 1940 she was transferred to the Department of Transport.

Name: Alert (1)
Year Built: 1933
Built By: Ditchburn Boats Ltd., Gravenhurst, Ontario
In Service: 1936 - 1939
Dimensions: 24 X 5.6 X 3.2
Type: Class 'D' cruiser
Cost:
Power: 120 hp Buchanan gasoline engine
Displacement: 3 GT
Speed: 30 mph
Crew: 1
Official Number: 158156
Radio Call Sign:

ALERT (1)

The *Alert* (1) was a RCMP vessel that replaced the *Chaleur* in 1936 and was stationed in Charlottetown, Prince Edward Island. She was sold on May 28, 1939.

Photographs courtesy Bryon Taylor

Name: Arresteur
Year Built: 1937
Built By: Ditchburn Boats, Gravenhurst, Ontario
In Service: 1937 - 1939
Dimensions: 67 x 13.7 x 5.4
Type: Class 'B' cruiser
Cost:
Power: 2-300 hp Auto Engine Works gasoline engines
Displacement: 40.66 GT
Speed: 26 kts
Crew: 2
Official Number: 170172
Radio Call Sign: CGSJ
Code: 7118

ARRESTEUR

The *Arresteur* was built for the RCMP in 1937 and patrolled the East Coast out of Dartmouth, Nova Scotia. She was turned over to the RCAF in 1939 and became RCAF M 305 Arresteur, pennant number B114, from 1939 to 1945. When she was returned to the RCMP at the end of the war, they turned her over to CADC on September 6, 1946. In 1947 she was renamed *Linda Belle* and in the same year she was wrecked and considered a total loss.

Courtesy RCMP Historical Collections Unit

ARROW

The *Arrow* was a seized vessel (*Tracy Smith*), turned over to the RCMP in 1936 to work out of Nova Scotia. She was turned over to the RCN in 1939 and renamed HMCS Arrow, a harbour defence craft from 1939 to 1942, then renamed HMC HC29. She was condemned and disposed of in March 1943.

The Beaver (1), *opposite page, was previously called the* Hard Times. *See page 134. Photograph courtesy of the Royal Canadian Navy. Below: A remote RCMP outpost at Aklavik in the Northwest Territories.*

Courtesy Vancouver Maritime Museum

Name: Arrow
Year Built: 1933
Built By: Charles Boudreau, Wedgeport, Nova Scotia
In Service: 1936 - 1939
Dimensions: 40.8 x 11 x 5.4
Type: Class 'D' cruiser
Cost:
Power: 25 IMP Acadia gasoline engine
Displacement: 14 GT
Speed: 12 kts
Crew: 1
Official Number: 158831
Radio Call Sign:
RCMP Number:
Code: 7114

Courtesy RCN photo H-759 from DHH, NDHQ

BURMA

The *Burma* was a very small craft, turned over to the RCN in 1939. The RCN named her HMCS Burma from 1939 to 1942 then she was renamed HMC HC36.

Name: Burma
Year Built:
Built By: Unknown, Detroit, Michigan
In Service: 1939
Dimensions: 16 x 5.5 x 2.4
Type: Class 'D' cruiser
Cost:
Power:
Displacement:
Speed:
Official Number:
Radio Call Sign:
RCMP Number:
Code:

Name: Captor (1)
Year Built: 1935
Built By: Shelburne Shipbuilders Ltd., Shelburne, Nova Scotia
In Service: 1935 - 1939
Dimensions: 59.2 x 13 x 7
Type: Class 'B' cruiser
Cost:
Power: Diesel engine
Displacement: 33.7 GT
Speed: 11kts
Official Number: 158159
Radio Call Sign: CGPY
Code: 7112

Courtesy RCN photo H-443 from DHH, NDHQ

CAPTOR (1)

The *Captor* (1) was built for the RCMP Marine Section in 1936. She was turned over to the RCN in 1939 and became HMCS Captor from 1939 to 1942 then renamed HMC HC37. She was declared surplus and turned over to CADC on August 14, 1945. She was still registered in 2010.

Courtesy RCN photo S-76 from DHH, NDHQ

D-1

The *D-1* was a seized vessel originally called *86* and was purchased by the RCMP in 1938 for service in and around Prince Edward Island. In 1939 she was renamed HDPC 11 when she was turned over to the RCN, who operated her in harbour defence duties until 1945. On September 18 that year she was declared surplus and turned over to CADC.

The vessel D-1 *looking forlorn, tied to a wharf and listing to port with another craft rafted alongside.*

Name: D-1
Year Built: 1933
Built By: Capt. Alfred Trenholm, Cape Tormentine, New Brunswick
In Service: 1938 - 1939
Dimensions: 38.8 x 7.3 x 3.5
Type: Class "D" (Lobster fishing boat)
Cost:
Power: Gasoline engine
Displacement: 7 GT
Speed: 16 kts
Crew: 3
Official Number: 158806
Radio Call Sign:
Code: 7407

Name: D-2
Year Built: 1931
Built By: C.M. Nickerson, Clarke's Harbour, Nova Scotia
In Service: 1938 - 1939
Dimensions: 43.3 x 13 x 5.4
Type: Class 'D' cruiser
Cost:
Power: Gasoline engine
Displacement: 16 GT
Speed: 18.5 kts
Crew: 3
Official Number: 157056
Radio Call Sign:
Code: 7256

Courtesy RCN photo S51 from DHH, NDHQ

D-2

The *D-2* was a seized vessel originally called *Ted* and was turned over to the RCMP in 1938 for service in and around Prince Edward Island. She was transferred to the RCN in 1939 and renamed HDPC 12 and used in harbour defence duties until 1945. This vessel proved so ideal for the RCMP that they had four new models built specially for the service. She was turned over to CADC on November 27, 1945 and was sold for breaking up on February 6, 1948.

Name: D-10
Year Built: 1936
Built By: Spurgeon Hickox, Bonshaw, Prince Edward island
In Service: 1938 - 1939
Dimensions: 38.4 x 8 x 3.4
Type: Class 'D' cruiser
Cost:
Power: 120 hp Buchanan gasoline engine
Displacement: 7 GT
Speed: 20 mph
Crew: 3
Official Number: 158807
Radio Call Sign:
Code: 7257

D-10

The *D-10* was a seized vessel (*Sea Witch*) that was purchased by the RCMP in 1938 and used for inshore work at Prince Edward Island. She was transferred to the RCN in 1939. They named her HDPC 13 and used her in harbour defence duties until 1942 when she was renamed HC180. She was turned over to CADC on August 4, 1945.

Courtesy RCN. Photo H-597 from DHH, NDHQ

Name: D-14
Year Built: 1939
Built By: John Etherington Shipbuilding Co. Ltd., Shelburne, Nova Scotia
In Service: Not taken into service
Dimensions: 48.6 x 13 x 6.7
Type: Class 'D' cruiser
Cost: $17,318
Power: Twin Sterling 6 cylinder gas engines 225 hp
Displacement: 12 GT
Speed: 18 kts
Crew: 3
Official Number:
Radio Call Sign:

D-14

The *D-14* was a high speed patrol boat built for the RCMP but was turned over to the RCN in 1939 during construction. The RCN named her HDPC 14. The vessels *D-15, D-16* and *D-17* were sister ships.

The vessel D-15, *opposite, like her sister ships, was a good seagoing craft whose fine bow entry and narrow beam gave a fairly comfortable ride in rough water.*

Name: D-15
Year Built: 1939
Built By: John Etherington Shipbuilding Co. Ltd., Shelburne, Nova Scotia
In Service: Not taken into service
Dimensions: 48.6 ft
Type: Class 'D' cruiser
Cost: $17,318
Power: Twin Sterling 6 cylinder gas engines 225 hp
Displacement: 12 GT
Speed: 18 kts
Crew: 3
Official Number:
Radio Call Sign:

D-15

The *D-15* was another high speed patrol boat built for the RCMP. She was turned over to the RCN in 1939 while under construction. The RCN named her HDPC 15. She capsized in heavy seas in the main channel of the entrance to Saint John Harbour April 14, 1943 and was lost. Photograph opposite page.

Courtesy RCN Photo H-761 from DHH, NDHQ

Courtesy RCN. Photo HS-0050-82 from DHH, NDHQ.

Name: D-16
Year Built: 1939
Built By: John LeBlanc, Weymouth, N.S.
In Service: Not taken into service
Dimensions: 48.6 ft
Type: Class 'D' cruiser
Cost: $18,158
Power: Twin Sterling 6 cylinder gas engines 225 hp
Displacement: 12 GT
Speed: 18 kts
Crew: 3
Official Number: 176593
Radio Call Sign: CGDM
Code: 7260

D-16

D-16 was a high speed patrol boat built for the RCMP but was turned over to the RCN in 1939 during construction. The RCN named her HDPC 16.

The vessel D-17*, opposite, had a low sheerline and lots of deck space. Her wheelhouse was small but below decks was quite extensive.*

Name: D-17
Year Built: 1939
Built By: Stanley Mason, Tancook, N.S.
In Service: Not taken into service
Dimensions: 48.6 ft
Type: Class 'D' cruiser
Cost: $18,158
Power: Twin Sterling 6 cylinder gas engines 225 hp
Displacement: 12 GT
Speed: 18 kts
Crew: 3
Official Number:
Radio Call Sign: CGDN
Code: 7261

D-17

The *D-17* was a high speed patrol boat built for the RCMP but, like the *D-14, D-15* and *D-16*, was turned over to the RCN in 1939 during construction. The RCN named her HDPC 17.

Courtesy RCN. Photo H-756 from DHH, NDHQ.

Courtesy Spud Roscoe

DETECTOR (1)

The *Detector* was built for the RCMP in 1937 and patrolled the East Coast out of Dartmouth, Nova Scotia. She was turned over to the RCAF in 1939 and became RCAF M.306 Dectector, pennant number B115 from 1939 to 1945. When she was returned to the RCMP at the end of the war she was turned over to CADC on September 6, 1946 and sold. She was renamed *Noruna*. In 1950 she was renamed *Lady Beth II,* and again in 1970 renamed *Surveyor*.

Name: Detector (1)
Year Built: 1937
Built By: Ditchburn Boats, Gravenhurst, Ontario
In Service: 1937 - 1939
Dimensions: 67 x 13.7 x 5.4
Type: Class 'B' cruiser
Cost:
Power: 2 – 300 hp Auto Engine Works gasoline engines
Displacement: 40.66 GT
Speed: 26
Crew: 5
Official Number: 170171
Radio Call Sign: CGPZ
Code: 7117

A later vessel named French *was the former HMCS* Transcona. *She was transferred to the RCMP after WWII in 1945 and served on the east coast of Canada until 1960.* *See page 172.*

Name: French (1)
Year Built: 1938
Built By: Davie Shipbuilding & Repairing Co. Ltd., Lauzon, Quebec
In Service: 1938 - 1939
Dimensions: 138.1 x 22.1 x 10.8
Type: Class 'A' cruiser
Cost:
Power: 2-Glenniffer 420 hp diesel engines
Displacement: 226 GT
Speed: 12 kts
Crew: 18
Official Number: 170177
Radio Call Sign: CGSR
RCMP Number: MP 84
Code: 200-84

Courtesy Don Klancher

FRENCH (1)/MACKENZIE

The *French* was the last vessel built for the RCMP Marine Section. The following year she was turned over to the Royal Canadian Navy and became HMCS French. She had pennant number S01 and Z23 during the war and was used as an Escort vessel and later an Examination Vessel. For her actions as an Escort Vessel she was awarded the Battle Honour 'GULF OF ST LAWRENCE 1942'. She was returned to the RCMP in 1946 and renamed RCMPS *MacKenzie* but was never re-commissioned as an RCMP vessel. She was turned over to CADC on September 3, 1946 and sold February 4, 1947 and her name was changed to *Le Francais*. She was severely damaged in a hurricane off Cape May, New Jersey in August 1953 and abandoned to the Underwriters.

GREAVETTE

The *Greavette* was a patrol boat based in Montreal, Quebec. She went into service in 1936 for one year.

Name: Greavette
Year Built:
Built By:
In Service: 1936-1937
Dimensions:
Type:
Cost:
Power:
Displacement:
Speed:
Official Number:
Radio Call Sign:
Code:

Courtesy RCN

HARD TIMES/BEAVER (1)

The *Hard Times* was a high speed former rum runner that was seized and turned over to the RCMP Marine Section in 1935. She was renamed *Beaver* in 1936. The vessel was turned over to the RCN in 1939 and became HMCS Caster, pennant number S10, from 1939 to 1942. In 1942 she was renamed HMC HC38. In June 1944 she was condemned and disposed of.

Name: Hard Times/Beaver (1)
Year Built: 1902
Built By: Charles Boudreau, Wedgeport, Nova Scotia.
In Service: 1935 - 1939
Dimensions: 36.9 x 12.2 x 4.6
Type: Motor launch
Cost:
Power: 40 hp diesel
Displacement: 19 GT
Speed: 11 kts
Crew: 3
Official Number: 158832
Radio Call Sign:
Code: 7252

Right: The harbour at Esquimalt. It is a prominent naval base adjacent to the city of Victoria, B.C. It was one of the places Helac II *stopped at for repairs. No photographic record was found of the* Helac II. *The vessel pictured above was the* Ellsworth, *a vessel of the same era.*

Name: Helac II
Year Built: 1928
Built By: Vancouver Dry Dock & Salvage Co. Ltd., Vancouver, B.C.
In Service: 1932
Dimensions: 53.6 x 16.3 x 7.3
Type: Tug
Cost: $6,798
Power: Diesel
Displacement: 44.29 GT
Speed:
Official Number: 154930

HELAC II

Skipper Joe Olsen Reg #10372 wrote the story of the *Helac II* in the book 'The Way it Was–50 Years of RCMP Memories' 1990 by RCMP Veterans. *Helac II* was a 53-foot diesel tug boat owned by Pacific Salvage of Vancouver. The RCMP were looking for a replacement vessel for the *Despatcher* which was tied up and being taken out of service. They decided to charter this vessel, a month at a time, to see if it was suitable for RCMP service in the late fall of 1932. The first trip took 10 hours to go from Vancouver to Esquimalt due to clutch problems and fuel issues. They then made the vessel suitable for their purposes. It was to be an unmarked, covert vessel, to patrol Juan de Fuca Strait looking for rum runners. Their second trip was to Port Angeles in Washington to confer with the US Coast Guard in Puget Sound. On the trip home they discovered the vessel was leaking badly. It was pumped out but the source of the leak could not be found. Their next patrols took them up the coast towards Bamfield but again they ran into problems with the clutch and were ordered to Port Alberni for repairs. En route the vessel took on a vibration caused by the propeller which had lost a blade. Repairs were made over several days in dry dock in Port Alberni and they decided to head back to Vancouver on December 22, for Christmas. Again, en route, the vessel took on water from an unknown source and had to be pumped continually. During the night they struck a log but suffered no apparent hull damage. While crossing the Strait of Georgia to Vancouver they had engine problems again and arrived in Vancouver on December 24. They tied the vessel to the dock and went home only to get a call on Christmas Day that the vessel was sinking. She was taken to dry dock. The charter ended. Pacific Salvage sued the Force for damages apparently caused by the log strike. Several years later it was discovered that this vessel had a habit of sinking for no apparent reason, but possibly due to the construction of the hull which consisted of a mix of wood and steel.

Courtesy RCMP Historical Collections Unit

INTERCEPTOR (1)

The *Interceptor* was built as part of the replacement programs for older, worn vessels received from the Preventive Service and worked out of Matane, Quebec. She was the first vessel built of a new material called Birmabright, an aluminum alloy, making it light and fast. Mrs H. Guthrie, wife of the Minister of Justice, christened her May 13, 1934. In 1939 she was turned over to the RCN becoming HMCS INTERCEPTOR with pennant number Z15 and Q15 based at Matane, Quebec. She was declared surplus and turned over to CADC on October 3, 1945. On July 23, 1946 she was sold to the Aluminum Company of Canada Ltd. In 1949 the Registry was transferred to Georgetown, British Guiana.

Name: Interceptor (1)
Year Built: 1934
Built By: Les Chantiers Manseau, Sorel, Quebec
In Service: 1934 - 1939
Dimensions: 65.5 x 12 x 8.0
Type: Class 'B' cruiser
Cost:
Power: Twin Gleniffer diesel engines of 320 hp each
Displacement: 38 GT
Speed: 12 – 16 kts
Crew: 9
Official Number: 158157
Radio Call Sign: CGPQ
Code: 7107

Name: Islander
Year Built: 1933
Built By: Alfred Stubbart, Souris, P.E.I.
In Service: 1933 - 1939
Dimensions: 45.2 x 8.3 x 4.5
Type: Class 'C' cruiser
Cost:
Power: Twin Chrysler Majestic Marine 8-cylinder Type 'C' engines
Displacement: 14 GT
Speed: 15 mph
Crew: 1
Official Number: 154889
Code: 7246

Courtesy RCN. Photo S-55 from DHH, NDHQ

ISLANDER

In October 1933, the seized vessel *Fripon* was purchased from the Department of National Revenue and renamed RCMP *Islander*. She was transferred to the RCN in 1939 and became HMCS Islander and in 1943 renamed HMC HC51. She was declared surplus and turned over to CADC on October 3, 1945.

Courtesy Vancouver Maritime Museum

Name: Laurier
Year Built: 1936
Built By: Morton Engineering & Drydock Ltd, Quebec City, Quebec
In Service: 1936 - 1939
Dimensions: 113 x 21 x 10.3
Type: Class 'A' cruiser
Cost:
Power: Twin screw diesel
Displacement: 201 GT
Speed: 12 kts
Crew: 16
Armament: One 12 pounder, Hotchkiss gun and one .303 machine gun
Official Number: 158985
Radio Call Sign: CGFL
RCMP Number: MP82
Code: 7011

LAURIER

The *Laurier* was one of the first 'A' class cruisers built for the RCMP Marine Section. She was the sister ship to the *Macdonald*. In 1939 she was transferred to the Royal Canadian Navy in Sydney and Mulgrave, Nova Scotia and became HMCS Laurier, pennant number Z34 and S09. In 1945 she was returned to the RCMP, but not put into commission. She was sold in 1946 and became a Fisheries Patrol Vessel on the west coast of Canada and named CGS *Laurier*. In 1984 the Department of Fisheries sold the *Laurier* and in 2008 she was still listed in the List of Ships on Register in Canada as *Laurier II*. She was a sister ship of the *Macdonald*.

Name: Lincoln II
Year Built: 1917
Built By: United States Government, Jacksonville, Florida
In Service: 1933
Dimensions: 102 x 15 x 8.5
Type: Class 'B' cruiser
Cost:
Power: 180 HP Fairbanks-Morse crude oil engine
Displacement: 77 GT
Speed: 7 kts
Official Number: 156807

LINCOLN II

The *Lincoln II* was chartered by the RCMP from May 15, 1933 to November 15, 1933. On October 12, 1933 the *Lincoln II* assisted the SS *Dollard* with the rescue of the *Edna F Parsons,* a vessel in distress.

Courtesy Robert F Holtom

Name: Louisburg
Year Built: 1926
Built By: Daniel Plant, Lunenburg N.S.
In Service: 1935 – 1939
Dimensions: 41.4 x 10.5 x 5.1
Type: Class 'C' cruiser
Cost:
Power: Twin gasoline engines
Displacement: 13.66 GT
Speed: 9 kts
Crew: 2
Official Number: 155022
Radio Call Sign:

LOUISBURG

The *Louisburg* was a seized vessel taken over by the RCMP Marine Section in 1935. She was sold commercially July 28, 1939 and was purchased by the RCN August 05, 1941.

Fred Doucet and Roy Holtom stand on the deck of the Louisburg *in the photo right.*

Courtesy Vancouver Maritime Museum

Name: Macdonald
Year Built: 1936
Built By: Morton Engineering & Drydock Ltd, Quebec City, Quebec
In Service: 1936 - 1939
Dimensions: 113 x 21 x 10.3
Type: Class 'A' cruiser
Cost:
Power: Twin screw diesel
Displacement: 201 GT
Speed: 12 kts
Crew: 15
Armament: One 12 pounder, one .303 machine gun
Official Number: 158986
Radio Call Sign: CGPF
RCMP Number: MP83
Code: 7012

MACDONALD

The *Macdonald* was built the same as her sister ship *Laurier*. Constructed for the RCMP in 1936, she was sent to the West Coast until transferred to the RCN in 1939. Known as HMCS MACDONALD with pennant number Z07 and P07 she was stationed in Halifax, Nova Scotia. In 1945 she was returned to the RCMP but was not put in commission. The ship was transferred to the Department of Fisheries on the West Coast and renamed CGS *Howay* with call sign CGCZ. In 1982 the Department of Fisheries sold the *Howay* and in 2010 she was still registered in Canada, as *Jenny Marcel*.

Watercolour sketch by John M. Horton showing wartime naval vessels HMCS Sackville *and* HMCS Saskatchewan *heading through The Narrows out of St John's Harbour in Newfoundland. They were part of a convoy on the noted Atlantic run. Note the similar hull lines to those of* Macdonald (opposite), *an obvious architectural influence of the times. Many of the RCMP marine members were transferred to the Canadian Navy.*

MISS WINDSOR

The *Miss Windsor* was a RCMP vessel purchased in 1936 to work at 'C' Division in Montreal, Quebec and was stationed on Lake Champlain.

Name: Miss Windsor
Year Built:
Built By:
In Service: 1936 - 1938
Dimensions:
Type:
Cost:
Power:
Displacement:
Speed:
Official Number:
Radio Call Sign:

Courstesy RCMP Historical Collections Unit

NEW BRUNSWICKER

The *New Brunswicker* was originally called the *K Don* and was purchased by the RCMP July 17, 1934 and renamed. She served on the East Coast until 1939 when she was turned over to the Royal Canadian Navy and renamed HC88. The ship was declared surplus and turned over to CADC on March 9, 1945. In 1947 she was sold and in 1949 her registry was closed after she sank.

Name: New Brunswicker
Year Built: 1931
Built By: Jerome Michaud, Buctouche, New Brunswick
In Service: 1934 - 1939
Dimensions: 41 x 10.7 x 5.6
Type: Class 'C' cruiser
Cost:
Power: 1-100 hp Kermath gasoline engine and 1-75 hp Redwing gasoline engine
Displacement: 21 GT
Speed: 12 kts
Crew: 3
Official Number: 154606
Radio Call Sign:
Code: 7248

Courtesy James J. Boulton, *Uniforms of the Canadian Mounted Police, 1990*

The vessel to the right was a patrol boat in Newfoundland. She had the typical lines of early days.

Name: Nokomis/Alacrity
Year Built: 1927
Built By: J.B. Outhouse, Tiverton, N.S.
In Service: 1935
Dimensions: 37.3 x 9.4 x 3.6
Type: Class 'D' cruiser
Cost:
Power: 150 hp Kermath gasoline engine
Displacement: 9 GT
Speed:
Crew: 3
Official Number: 158834
Radio Call Sign:
Code: 7235

NOKOMIS/ALACRITY

The *Nokomis* was purchased by the RCMP in 1935 after she had been chartered for a couple of years to patrol out of New Brunswick. She was renamed *Alacrity* in 1936 and sold March 2, 1939. Photograph of *Nokomis*, right, shows her rakish lines.

Courtesy RCMP Historical Collections Unit

Courtesy RCN Photo S83 from DHH, NDHQ

PROTECTOR/No. 78

The *No.78* was a seized vessel taken over by the RCMP Marine Section in 1935 and renamed *Protector*. She worked out of New Brunswick. The vessel was turned over to the RCN in 1939 and renamed HMCS PROTECTOR from 1939 to 1942 then renamed HMC HC63. The *Protector* was declared surplus and turned over to CADC on August 30, 1945.

Name: Protector/No. 78
Year Built: 1932
Built By: Unknown, Salmon River, N.S.
In Service: 1935 - 1939
Dimensions: 39.9 x 10.5 x 2.6
Type: Class 'D' cruiser
Cost:
Power: 140 hp Thornycroft gasoline engine
Displacement: 15 GT
Speed: 9 kts
Crew: 2
Official Number: 158835
Radio Call Sign:
Code: 7251

Right: Vigil II *on patrol. The lower photograph while identfied as* Vigil II *is more likely that of the* Vigil (1). *See also page 101.*

Name: Vigil II
Year Built: 1935
Built By: Joseph Deveau, Salmon River, Nova Scotia
In Service: 1936 - 1939
Dimensions: 41.3 x 13.4 x 5.7
Type: Class 'D' cruiser
Cost:
Power: 100 hp diesel engine
Displacement: 20 GT
Speed: 10 kts
Crew: 3
Official Number: 158836
Radio Call Sign:
Code: 7254

Courtesy Vancouver Maritime Museum

VIGIL II

The *Vigil II* was built for the RCMP Marine Section in 1935, to replace the *Vigil*. She was turned over to the RCN in 1939 and became HMCS VIGIL II from 1939 to 1942 then HC104. She was sold in 1945, re-named *Fala* in 1947 and then *Blue River III* in 1950. She was eventually destroyed by fire in 1951.

Courtesy RCMP Historical Collections Unit

An oil painting of Halifax Harbour during WW II by Canadian naval war artist John M. Horton, showing vessels marshalling for the large trans-Atlantic convoys in the safety of Bedford Basin. Note the diversity of naval ships and merchant ships within the harbour defences. Courtesy Naval Museum of Canada.

Chapter Three

The War Years

On September 10, 1939 Canada declared war on Nazi Germany and was set to enter a six-year battle on land, at sea and in the air. Thanks to the foresight of Commissioner MacBrien in 1932 who proposed that RCMP Marine Section personnel undertake military training every winter, they were prepared to become a part of the war effort immediately. The ships were refitted for their new tasks and transferred to the Royal Canadian Navy and RCMP personnel were allowed to volunteer for naval service. The 30 vessels and 155 men were a huge asset to the Canadian Navy and would play a major role in protecting Canadian coastlines and harbours. The RCMP Marine Section ceased to exist during the war years.

The Royal Canadian Navy had only 13 ships at the start of the war but at the end they had over 500 vessels of various sizes. The 13 vessels operated by the RCN in 1939 were six destroyers, HMCS SAGUENAY, HMCS SKEENA, HMCS FRASER, HMCS ST LAURENT, HMCS RESTIGOUCHE and HMCS OTTAWA, four minesweepers: HMCS COMOX, HMCS FUNDY, HMCS GASPE and HMCS NOOTKA, and three training vessels: HMCS SKIDEGATE, HMCS VENTURE (a sailing schooner), and HMCS ARMENTIERES (a trawler).

The loss of the RCMP Marine Section did not mean there were no marine vessels left in the service of the RCMP. Officers carried on with their duties patrolling lakes, shorelines and the north in vessels such as the *St Roch* and the *Aklavik* in the Arctic, the *Resolution* and the *Reliance* on Great Slave Lake, and the *Baker Lake* in Hudson Bay. Some of the remaining Class 'D' vessels of the RCMP Marine Section continued to patrol on the coasts and Great Lakes. These men and vessels were deployed to participate in early anti-submarine patrols on both coasts. Eventually this expanded into trans-Atlantic escort convoy duties. The battle at sea turned out to be a battle against an unseen force by way of the Nazi U-boat. Supplies, equipment, troops, munitions, fuel and food had to get to England, and the ocean was the only highway. The U-boats concentrated all their resources to hinder this process, many times with alarming success. In the early part of the war the action was confined to the western approaches to England, but after France fell to Germany the action spread westward towards North America. The examination of vessels leaving and entering the Nova Scotia ports of Sydney and Halifax became crucial, and anti-submarine warfare a part of everyday life.

During a 1940 conference held to discuss the growth and expansion of the naval forces a question arose about where to obtain the seamen for the requisitioned ships. One senior representative is reported to have said "Seamen? I have no seamen except the Mounties and the rummies they used to chase".

Another story that expressed the speed of the 'drafting' of crews recounts:

"A petty officer in HMCS Stadacona was greeted at the Petty Officers' mess by the president who said 'Just come in, eh? You had better join the mess. It will cost a dollar to join and 25 cents a month.'

The new P.O. replied 'Okay, guess I will.'

'What are you, RCNR?' 'Yes, why?'

'Well,' said the president, 'Perhaps you had better not join, you can be a temporary member at a quarter a month. You don't happen to be ex-Marine Section, do you?'

'Yes, I am. So what?' The president smiled. 'That settles it. Don't bother joining. You won't be here long enough.'"

Courtesy Vancouver Maritime Museum

Four hours later the P.O. was drafted to sea. It appears that the Marine Section personnel were not only needed anywhere and everywhere but were respected to a large degree by their naval counterparts.

The larger vessels of the RCMP Marine Section lost their peacetime appearance as they were equipped with heavier armament, guns, depth-charge gear and Anti-Submarine Detection Investigation (ASDIC) apparatus. For a while they escorted merchant vessels out to the 'Western Rendezvous' location for the overseas voyage. These duties continued until newer vessels were constructed and properly equipped to take over the escort tasks. They then returned to their local patrolling and investigation duties outside the harbours and beyond coastal patrol areas.

While many of the RCMP Marine Section officers saw lots of wartime action, there were others who filled in the huge task of administrative duties on shore. Their continuous efforts played a major role in the success of these vessels and men as they supplied, repaired and fulfilled all other aspects of maintaining a fighting force at sea. Concurrent with this was the never-ending training of new crews for the numerous vessels that were under construction. Many of the engineers and officers from the RCMP Marine Section shared their skills with the newly recruited personnel who eventually formed a new ship's company. The ever-expanding navy was beginning to take shape and the RCMP Marine Section was playing an important role.

The RCMP Marine personnel who joined the war effort played no small role in the operation, deployment, maintenance and provisioning of Canadian war assets. Although most vessels and manpower went to the Canadian Navy there were a few resources that went to the Royal Canadian Air Force, including two RCMP vessels that went to the Air Sea Rescue unit of the RCAF. They were the two high-speed launches *Arresteur* and *Detector*. These vessels were instrumental in delivering badly-needed supplies to outposts, rescuing people from downed aircraft, and coming to the aid of numerous coastal communities for the duration of the war.

In the year 2000 a story, which was kept secret for over 50 years, surfaced regarding a RCMP Marine vessel. The schooner *St Roch* had patrolled the Arctic for over 10 years when the war broke out. The skipper, Sergeant Henry Larsen, knew the Arctic waters very well. In October 1939, Larsen was approached and asked if he and his crew could traverse the North West Passage from Vancouver, B.C. to the Atlantic.

This was a lifelong dream of Larsen and he felt very confident that it could be accomplished. His task was to proceed to Greenland where a cryolite mine was located. Cryolite was an important ingredient in the manufacturing of aluminium, and important to the manufacturing of aircraft for the war effort. The *St Roch* was to patrol the coast of Greenland, ferry in supplies and support an occupying force in the effort to legally secure the mines for the allies, a top secret mission that failed to materialize.

Officially the voyage through the Arctic was to exercise Canadian Sovereignty by patrolling through the North West Passage to Halifax. The ship and crew departed in June 1940, but due to the worst winters conditions in over 50 years the *St Roch* became ice bound for two years and never reached the north Atlantic coast until September 1942. The top secret mission was long past, but Sergeant Larsen had succeeded in commanding the first vessel ever to pass through the North West Passage from west to east. His 'official' mission was accomplished and a dream had come true for Larsen.

Right: A watercolour sketch of war at sea by John M. Horton, Canadian naval artist. Courtesy John M. Horton. Opposite page: The St Roch *locked in winter ice, 1942.*

Courtesy Roy Holtom

An article written by A/Cpl W.E.F. Bell in the July 1946 RCMP Quarterly magazine listed in detail the duties taken on by the RCMP Marine Section and warrants mention here to demonstrate the huge contribution these men made to the Canadian war effort. The following is his list of Commissions Won, and Retiring Rank of ex-RCMP Marine Section members:

NAVAL SERVICE:
Commanders, RCNR - 2
Commanders (E), RCNR - 2
Lieutenant Commanders RCNR - 10
Lieutenant Commanders (SB) RCNVR - 1
Lieutenants RCNR - 27
Lieutenants RCNVR - 1

Lieutenants (E) RCNR - 8
Mates RCNR - 2
Chief Skippers RCNR - 5
Commissioned Engineers RCNR - 3
Gunner (T) RCNR - 1
Warrant Engineers RCNR - 4
Warrant Shipwrights RCNR - 1
Total = 67

CANADIAN ARMY:
Major (acting Lieutenant Colonel) - 1
Lieutenant (Eng.) RCASC - 1
Total = 2

AIR FORCE:
Wing Commander, RCAF - 1
Flight Lieutenants, RCAF - 4
Flying Officers, RCAF - 4
Total = 9

Total number commissioned in all services = 78

Ships with RCMP Marine Section Engineers

HMCS Acadia
HMCS Adversus * **
HMCS Alachasse *
HMCS Beaver
HMCS Brockville
HMCS Captor *
HMCS Caribou
HMCS Chaleur *
HMCS Charney
HMCS Digby
HMCS Esquimalt **
HMCS Fleur De Lis *
HMCS French*
HMCS Husky
HMCS Interceptor
HMCS Lachine
HMCS Laurier *
HMCS Lynx
HMCS Macdonald
HMCS Melville
HMCS Noranda
HMCS Otter **
HMCS Puncher
HMCS Sans Peur
HMCS Skeena
HMCS Transcona
HMCS Trois Rivieres
HMCS Vision

RCASC *General Schmiddlin*

Ships commanded by RCMP Marine Section Officers

HMCS Acadia
HMCS Acadian *
HMCS Adversus * **
HMCS Alachasse *
HMCS Algoma
HMCS Armentieres
HMCS Bantie
HMCS Barrie
HMCS Blairmore
HMCS Bras d'Or **
HMCS Burlington
HMCS Captor*
HMCS Chaleur *
HMCS Charlottetown **
HMCS Columbia
HMCS Comox
HMCS Courtney
HMCS Cowichan
HMCS Dauphin
HMCS Dawson
HMCS Drummondville
HMCS Dundalk
HMCS Dundurn
HMCS Eastore
HMCS Fleur de Lis *
HMCS French *
HMCS Gananoque
HMCS Glenbrook
HMCS Goderich
HMCS Helena
HMCS Interceptor *
HMCS Jolliette
HMCS Kam
HMCS Kipawo
HMCS Laurier *
HMCS Lisgar
HMCS Macdonald *
HMCS Macsin
HMCS Madawaska *
HMCS Matapedia
HMCS Marie Therese
HMCS Nootka
HMCS North Shore
HMCS North Wind
HMCS Ottawa
HMCS Portage
HMCS Pugwash
HMCS Restigouche
HMCS St Catharines
HMCS Saskatoon
HMCS Scatarie *
HMCS Seretha
HMCS Shediac
HMCS Sorel
HMCS Transcona
HMCS Valinda
HMCS Venosta
HMCS Venture
HMCS Wallaceburg
HMCS Waskesiu
RCAF M.305 *Arresteur* *
RCAF M.208 *Nootka*
RCAF M.306 *Detector* *
RCAF M.200 *Elaine W.*

* denotes RCMP Marine Section Ship
** denotes lost at sea

Decorations awarded RCMP Marine Section personnel

Officer of the Order of the British Empire (Operational)

- A/Cmdr R.J. Herman, O.B.E., RCNR
- Lt Cmdr R.A.S. MacNeil, O.B.E., RCNR
- Lt Cmdr R.R. Kenny, O.B.E., RCNR

Officer of the Order of the British Empire (Non-operational)

- Cmdr (E) C.M. O'Leary, O.B.E., RCNR

Distinguished Service Cross

- Lt Cmdr J.P. Fraser, D.S.C., RCNR

British Empire Medal

- Chief Skipper N.C.C. Roberts, B.E.M., RCNR
- Chief SBS. R.P. Arseneault, B.E.M., RCNR

Mention in Despatches

- Cmdr R. McD. Barkhouse, RCNR
- Lt Cmdr K.W.N. Hall, RCNR
- Lt H.D.G. Bould, RCNR
- Lt. (E) R.A. Conarad, RCNR
- CPO R.J. Cook, RCNR
- Chief Motor Mechanic 1st Cl D.E. Gillis, RCNR
- P.O M.P. Furlong, RCNR

Commendation

- Lt. F.E. Smith, RCNR
- Lt. W.E.F. Bell, RCNR

Foreign Decorations:

French Croix De Guerre

- Lt. Cmdr K.W.N. Hall, RCNR

Norwegian Krigsmedaljen

- Lt Cmdr R.A.S. MacNeil, O.B.E., RCNR
- Lt Cmdr J.W. Bonner, RCNR - killed in action
- Lt P.R.F. Milthorpe, RCNR - killed in action
- FO A.H. LeMaistre, RAF - shot down
- Ch. Motor Mech D.E.Gillis - died of exposure while rescuing others
- Ldg Tel A.W. Armstrong, RCN - lost in HMCS MARGAREE
- 2nd Officer J. Cassidy, M/N - lost when SS *Pink Star* sank
- 2nd Eng A. Allard, M/N - lost when ship sank
- Sgt S Kenny, RCAF - lost in Ferry Command
- Flt Sgt Heeney, RCAF - lost in 10th bomber squadron
- Mr Kennedy - lost as civilian member of Ferry Command
- St PO C. Palmer - died
- Ck Stwrd W.F. Roberts - died
- Lt F.E. Smith, RCNR - died
- Ch Tel H.N. Walker - killed on duty
- Ex-Oiler W.J. Curtis, RCAF - killed in flying accident

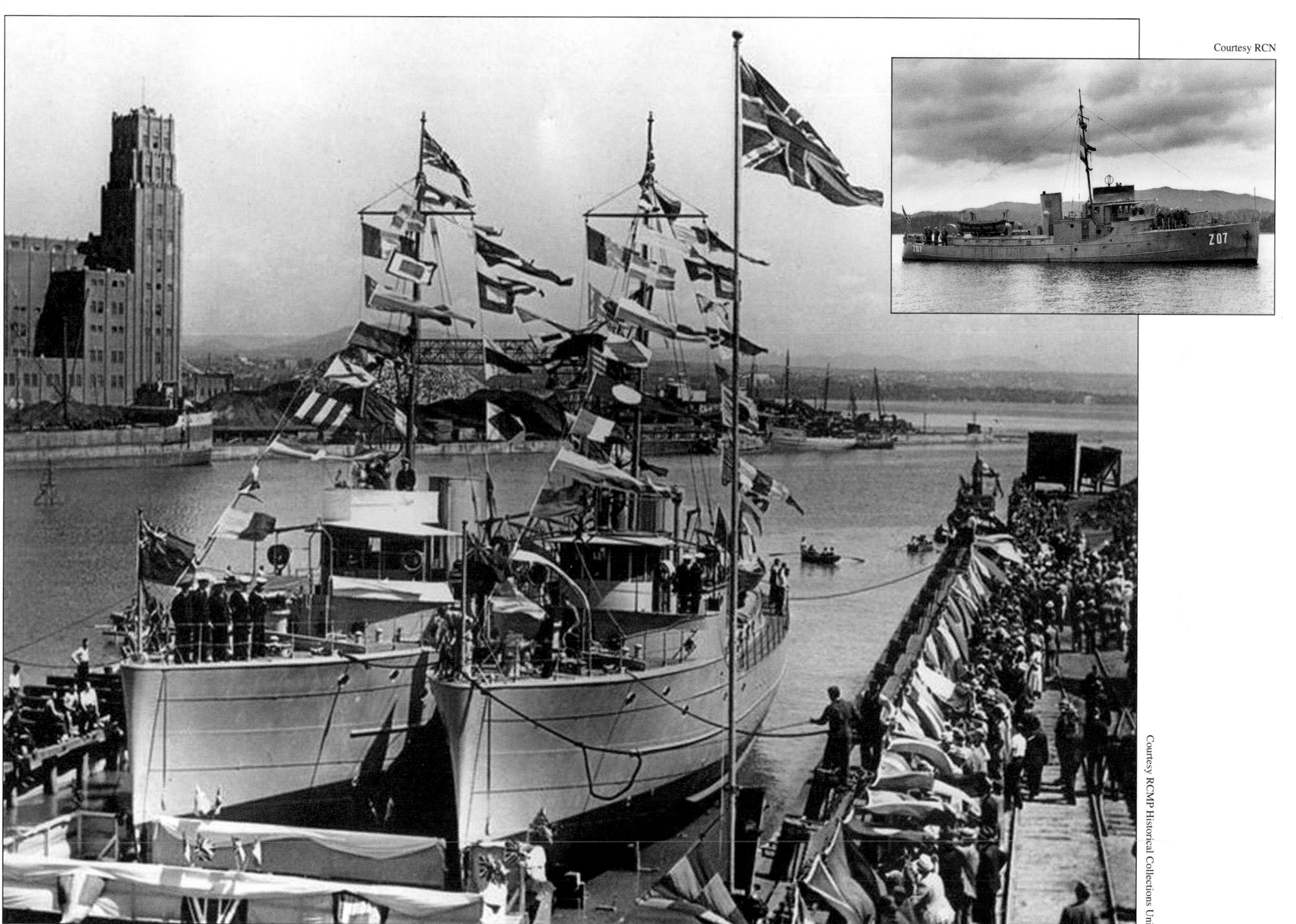

Courtesy RCN

Courtesy RCMP Historical Collections Unit

The Macdonald *and the* Laurier *on the day of their launching in Quebec. Above, right: The* Macdonald *with her Navy pennant Z07 added.*

Richardson-built PB Dauphin *MP 45 on patrol. Richardson was a noted builder of fine wooden pleasure cruisers. The yard was in Meaford, Ontario and saw its heyday in the 1960s.*

Courtesy RCMP Historical Collections Unit

Chapter Four

The RCMP Marine Division

As the war drew to a close, the effort to return to pre-war civilian life began and the huge task of re-organizing former institutions like the RCMP Marine Section started to take place. Much of the original equipment was lost, too old, or otherwise unsuitable. Many of the former RCMP Marine members had retired or moved on to other careers, cutting the number of returning members to about half.

The task of organizing the post-war Marine Division fell on the shoulders of Commissioner Wood who in 1945 arranged with the War Assets Corporation to acquire replacement vessels for the new RCMP Marine Section. A survey of the former RCMP Marine Section vessels showed that they were substantially worn out after six years of war duty and were not useful for the peacetime duties assigned them. The former RCMP *Detector*, *Arresteur* and the *French* (now called *Mackenzie*) were returned to the RCMP but were deemed unsuitable and turned over to the Crown Assets Distribution Centre (CADC) in September 1946.

The Marine Section was re-instated in 1945 and 1946 with a fleet of patrol vessels formerly used by the Royal Canadian Navy. Of the 54 Bangor class minesweepers constructed for the war effort, eight 162-foot, 600-gross-ton, diesel-powered, twin-screw vessels were turned over to the RCMP Marine Service. These became known as 'Commissioner' class. Each vessel carried a crew of 35 men. The class 'B' vessels came from the former 112-foot, 79-gross-ton Fairmile submarine chasers known in the RCMP as 'Fort' class. These were also diesel powered and had twin screws. Four of the 88 vessels built for the war were turned over to the RCMP. They carried a crew of 14 men. Of 30 Harbour Defence Craft (HDC) built for the Royal Canadian Navy during the war, 13 went to the RCMP in 1945. These 48-foot HDC, 18-gross-ton vessels were named after historic detachments and became known as 'Detachment' class vessels. All of these vessels carried three to four men and required some alterations and modifications to bring them up to date for their new duties in a civilian marine force.

In a memorandum to OC 'H' Division Halifax, dated September 6, 1945, Commissioner S.T. Wood explains the code and pennant numbers of RCMP ships. Prior to beginning operations these pennant numbers were to be placed in the appropriate position on the bow of each vessel. The code numbers reflected the pennant number. For example the *Colonel White was* Code No. 20010 and had pennant MP-10. All vessels turned over to the RCMP Marine

Section received code and pennant numbers even if they were immediately sold, disposed of, or returned to the RCN.

With manpower, budget and equipment issues, some of these vessels never came into full use by the RCMP, and were transferred back to the RCN or sold for other purposes. The Commissioner class vessels *Herchmer, Starnes, Perry, Macleod, MacBrien, Irvine* and the *French* were renamed after former commissioners. Only the *Colonel White* was not named for a former RCMP commissioner, but rather in honour of Lt Col Frederick White, C.M.G. In 1878 White was appointed comptroller of the North West Mounted Police and served in that position for 45 years. Out of eight Commissioner class vessels received, the RCMP kept only four. The *Herchmer, Starnes, Colonel White* and *Perry* were returned to the War Assets Deptartment. The *Herchmer* was sold and renamed *Gulf Mariner* while the *Starnes* was converted to a tugboat and assumed its former RCN name LACHINE. The *Colonel White* and the *Perry* were returned to the RCN. The former became HMCS GRANDBY again, and the *Perry* became HMCS DIGBY.

The class 'B' vessels were former RCN motor launches called *ML 112, ML 114, ML 117* and *ML 119*. These four Fairmile, Fort Class vessels became the *Fort Walsh, Fort Selkirk, Fort Steele* and *Fort Pitt*, but only the *Fort Pitt* and *Fort Walsh* were retained and the other two were returned to CADC.

The Detachment class vessels were former Harbour Defence Patrol Craft. The 13 vessels turned over to the RCMP were originally Patrol Boats named *Brule, Little Bow, Carnduff, Chilcoot, Cutknife, Fitzgerald, Grenfell, Aklavik, Moosomin, Shaunavon, Slideout, Tagish* and *Yellowknife*. In a letter from the RCMP Commissioner to Deputy Minister Naval Service dated August 29, 1946, it was discovered that three names on these vessels were already in use. To remedy this they changed the names of the *Yellowknife* to *Willow Bunch*, *Fitzgerald* to *Big Bend* and the *Aklavik* to *Standoff*. Of the 25 vessels turned over to the RCMP at the end of the war, only 19 were retained for service.

Vessels were generally floating detachments and worked as part of a team with the detachments where they were based. Vessels based on command to the Land Division were under the operational control and discipline of the Commanding Officer of the Division or Officer Commanding the Sub-Division. Vessels not based on command to any Land Division were under the operational control of the Commanding Officer Marine Division/Marine Sub-Division. All other functions such as promotions, postings, transfers, annual leave, refits, repairs, acquisitions and training fell under the control of the Marine Division in Ottawa.

The new fleet needed to be maintained and a works yard was needed for this so the wartime agreement between the RCMP and the Canadian Navy was renewed. Repairs, inspections, vessel surveys and training were to be conducted by the Navy. In return the RCMP agreed to make available to the Navy all of its marine resources in the event of another war. This agreement suited the RCMP greatly as it lowered their costs by reducing the technical manpower required ashore to train the men and equip the vessels.

All vessels of the RCMP Marine Section were manned by experienced captains who held certificates of competency issued by the Department of Transport. The captain of each vessel had the authority to decline an assigned task if in his view the operation would endanger the lives of his crew, or his vessel.

Returning crews formed the basis of the Marine Section and were called on to share their knowledge and train new recruits. Most of these returning members had been out of touch with law enforcement duties for six years and had to attend refresher courses at 'N' Division and 'Depot' Division.

For the men of the RCMP Marine Section there was another major change.

Courtesy RCMP Historical Collections Unit

Little Bow, *one of the 13 Detachment class vessels turned over to the RCMP from Harbour Defence Patrol.*

Uniforms: Courtesy James J. Boulton, *Uniforms of the Canadian Mounted Police, 1990*

Marine Division 'Sea Dress' uniform.

Marine Division beret.

On September 12, 1945, Commissioner Wood approved the issue of a regular brown serge uniform when members went ashore. At sea they wore a black beret with dark blue battle-dress called 'Sea Dress', which was actually the 'Battle Dress' from Canadian military surplus that had been worn by the RCN since 1942. This Sea Dress was not to be worn ashore. The beret had an unbacked metal cap badge and the blouse had the embroidered letters 'RCMP' on each shoulder. The beret was never approved for officers, but rather Special Constables and Constables only, until it was abolished on July 18, 1963. A winter cap, which was a ski cap in nature, was approved for use by the Marine Section in foul weather. It was a blue peaked hat with fold-down ear and brow protectors.

The Special and Regular Constables of the RCMP Marine Section wore different kit depending on where they were deployed. Constables employed on shore were issued scarlet serge jacket, breeches, overalls with stripes, long boots and riding crop, while those assigned sea duties were not. In 1948 when the RCMP Marine Section became the RCMP Marine Division, scarlet serge uniforms were issued to all members provided they had completed the standard police training.

In 1953 the blue Sea Dress was replaced by a brown serge uniform called 'Brown Service Dress' for Inland Water Transport and West Coast personnel. It was worn with the beret when aboard a vessel, and with a forage cap when on shore. The East Coast did not get approval for this uniform until late 1957 when inventory of the blue Sea Dress was depleted. This was a happy departure from the military type uniforms and served to make Marine members appear as part of the regular force.

There were four classifications assigned to Marine members and each had its own badge. The Deck Department wore a fouled anchor badge, the

Engineering Department wore a three-bladed propeller, the Communications Department wore wings with a lightning bolt, and the Victualling Department wore a letter 'V'. These badges were placed on the right sleeve and were yellow on a dark blue background. A new breast badge was also worn on the serge of Marine members. It was gold on blue for scarlet serge and gold on red for the blue jacket worn by the Staff Sergeants. These badges were worn from 1948 to 1970 by RCMP Marine Division members.

Marine Officers wore the same uniform as members in the land force and Marine Staff Sergeants wore the blue serge jackets and blue overalls, the same as the Staff Sergeants of the land force. The Victualling Department of the Commissioner and Detachment Class ships wore white jackets, white trousers, white aprons and white cook's caps.

After the RCMP Marine Division was terminated in 1970, members of the RCMP Marine Service continued to wear a Marine badge above their left breast pocket on their duty jackets and scarlet serge until the 1990s.

Another welcome change was that pay and allowances were standardized with all other members of the Force. New recruits became police officers first, then attended an additional three-month-long marine specialty course at Rockcliffe, Ontario. This course gave them a working knowledge of the laws applicable to marine and customs areas and allowed them to learn the lay of the 'water' which would be critical in their new border patrol role. NCOs in charge of the smaller vessels were also given a two week course at Ottawa Headquarters regarding legal questions and tactful diplomacy when dealing with cross border issues.

On April 1, 1947 the RCMP turned the Marine Section into the new RCMP Marine Division. Headquarters for the 195 returning members, 24 new members and some 19 vessels was in Halifax. This new Division was to last for 23

1948 King's Marine Division breast badge.

1953 Queen's Marine Division breast badge.

1970 – 1990s RCMP Marine Service badge.

Courtesy Don Klancher

Crew of the RCMP MacBrien. *Front l-r: Ernie Boulet, H. Deslauriers, Joe Cooper, Insp Cassive, Ralph Conrad, Bennie Roach, Roy Sharp.*
2nd row: Frank Myress, L Clattenburg, Lee Stewart, Unknown, K. Perry, Dom Day, George Zack, Joe Desrosiers, Maurice Duffy.
3rd row: Frank Connelly, Red McNeil, Unknown, Unknown–cook, Pete Breard, Canuel–cook, Al Long, John Bozac, Stew McLean.
4th row: John Stevens, Lawren Bourser, Herb Roberts, Lavoie, F. Charlton, M. Jennex, J.B. McKinnon, Art Doney, Ernie Parsons.

years. The main responsibilities of this division were the enforcement of the Customs and Excise Act, Canada Shipping Act, Immigration Act, Indian Act, Migratory Birds Act, Fisheries Protection Act, Illegal Commercial Guiding Regulations, border patrols in the Great Lakes and St Lawrence, and Search and Rescue operations.

Many of the 48-foot Detachment class boats were distributed at strategic positions along the St Lawrence and Great Lakes to enhance border patrols. This reinforced Canadian policing links with the U.S. Coast Guard as both countries shared information on cross-border activities. In 1947 two new motor boats appeared in the Great Lakes in the form of the MP 90 *Kenora* (1) and the MP 91 *Fort Frances* (2). In 1949, Newfoundland joined the Canadian confederation and, as the result of an agreement between that province and the Government of Canada, the RCMP assumed all duties of the Newfoundland Ranger Force, in addition to selected jurisdictions formerly policed by the Newfoundland Constabulary. Two police vessels, the *Point May* and the *Shulamite*, acquired by the RCMP, were never commissioned but turned over to CADC for disposal.

In August, 1950 the RCMP took over the duties of the B.C. Provincial Police and with this came their Police Motor Launches which were stationed all along the Pacific Coast. This fleet consisted of approximately 12 vessels, most of which were 40 to 70 feet long and were identified by PML numbers. Six vessels were taken over by the RCMP and their names modified to RCMP with

ML numbering. The RCMP Commissioner's Report for 1950 indicates that only the ML *6* (MP 73), ML *9* (MP 74), ML *10*, ML *15* (MP 76), ML *16* (MP 77) and ML *17* (MP 78) were put into RCMP service.

Now that the RCMP had assumed contract policing for two coastal provinces it was time for the force to assess the organization. It needed to reflect the coast to coast operations and increased responsibility for the Great Lakes and the St Lawrence.

In 1954 when the Marine Headquarters was transferred to Ottawa, Halifax became a Sub-Division which dealt with repairs and stores. The Marine Division was set up much the same as the Land Divisions. Three Sub-Divisions were administered through the Commanding Officer at Headquarters in Ottawa. These were located in Halifax, Nova Scotia (East Coast), in Bagotville, Quebec (Great Lakes) and in Esquimalt, British Columbia (West Coast).

Part of the reconstruction and rebuilding of the RCMP Marine Division included a list of newer, faster and better equipped replacement vessels that were needed to modernize the Force. Most of the vessels that made up the RCMP Marine Division had a life expectancy of 10 years so a replacement schedule had to be established for the repossessed and former Navy vessels. From 1952 to 1962 a replacement program was initiated, although the first vessel was not launched until 1954. The plan called for the 165-foot minesweepers to be replaced by similar sized twin-screw vessels. The 112-foot Fairmile replacements had not yet been determined, but 60-foot inshore single-screw coastal boats and a Great Lakes 49-foot high-speed patrol boat were planned to replace the 48-foot harbour defence patrol craft.

In September 1954 the first vessel constructed for the RCMP on the West Coast was the 35-foot wooden-hulled *AML 1*. She was launched in Victoria, B.C. by McKay-Cormack Ltd and was stationed at Zeballos in Esperanza Inlet on Vancouver Island. Another vessel constructed on the West Coast was the 30-foot motorboat MP 60 *Fort St James* constructed by Star Shipyards (Mercer's) Ltd in New Westminster, B.C. In 1962 she was transferred to Marine Division where she served until January 1968.

In the fall of 1954 the RCMP Marine Division's first replacement vessel was launched. She was the 49-foot MP 81 *Chilcoot II* in Toronto, Ontario.

This was followed in the summer of 1955 with three other new vessels. On June 24 the 48-foot MP 84 *Burin* was launched in Nova Scotia, on July 6 the 49-foot MP 82 *Cutknife II* was launched in Toronto, Ontario and on August 8, 1955 the 60-foot MP 83 *Interceptor* was launched in Shelburne, Nova Scotia.

In the mid 1950s the Bird Class patrol vessels were being built for the Royal Canadian Navy. Eight of them were originally ordered but this was soon reduced to four. The third vessel built was turned over to the RCMP in 1957 for use on the East Coast. That vessel was the 92-foot MP 32 *Blue Heron,* which reportedly carried about 21 men. The RCMP liked it so much they built another called the MP 31 *Victoria*. The RCMP soon had two more constructed specially for them to their own design specifications. These were the MP 17 *Wood* and the MP 34 *Fort Steele* (2). Other vessels were added to the fleet to replace some of the aging vessels.

Marine Operations in Ottawa managed all the marine resources of the Land and Marine Division and controlled the purchasing, supplying and repairing of their vessels. All Marine Division vessels were given a 'MP' number. Vessels without a number were Land Division or Detachment boats.

In the Commissioner's Report for 1961, it was stated that there were 32 vessels in the RCMP Marine Division, one vessel in 'A' Division (Ont.), nine vessels in 'B' Division (Nfld.), two vessels in 'D' Division (Man.), one vessel in 'E' Division (B.C.), 27 vessels in 'G' Division (N.W.T.) and one vessel in

Sgt Gilles Gagne on the bridge of the PB Moosomin II *MP 96.*

Bottom, this page and opposite: Photographs of interior of unknown vessel, but details are similar to that of PB Captor *MP 50.*

Courtesy Don Klancher

'K' Division (Alta.) for a total of 73 vessels operating with 232 officers in the RCMP. This may have been the apex of the RCMP Marine assets. The 1969 Commissioner's Report states that the RCMP Marine Division had 48 vessels, the largest number listed in the RCMP Annual Reports up to 1973.

By the end of 1962 the 22 vessels taken from the Canadian Navy, the three RCMP vessels built in 1947, and seven vessels seconded from B.C. and Newfoundland had been taken out of service. The replacement program provided 33 new Marine Division and 16 new Land Division vessels. A report submitted in 1964 indicated that there were 35 vessels operated by 232 officers and men in the Marine Division, with 14 vessels on the West Coast, 13 in the Great Lakes and St Lawrence, and eight on the Atlantic Coast.

Costs for the Marine Service were very high and its budget was huge compared to that of other RCMP departments. One report stated that one ship in the marine section cost more money than all of the patrol cars the force owned. This, plus the fact that in 1962 the Canadian Coast Guard was formed as part of the Department of Transport, would inevitably influence the future of the RCMP Marine Division.

One of the major roles of the RCMP Marine Division was search and rescue and now the new Coast Guard would eventually fulfil that role. In the meantime construction of new replacement vessels continued. In 1967 there was a short burst of construction as seven vessels were built to enhance the security for Expo 67 to be held off Montreal, Quebec on Île Sainte-Hélène, in the St Lawrence River. These were named the *Slideout, Moose Jaw, Battleford, Lac La Ronge, Dauphine*, *Brule* and *Athabasca.*

On April 1, 1970 the RCMP Marine Division was reorganized into the RCMP Marine Services. This consisted of 249 members and 41 vessels including one Commissioner class, two Fort class and 38 patrol craft ranging from

30 to 75 feet (9 East Coast, 16 Great Lakes and 16 West Coast). The RCMP Marine Division was terminated and all personnel, officers and patrol vessels now reported directly to the Land Division Commanding Officers. During the ensuing year the fleet was further reduced to 31 vessels. The Marine Services however inherited the responsibility for all water transport including the 310 outboard motor boats and skiffs operated by Land Division personnel.

The last of the large vessels, the *Wood* on the East Coast, was sold to the Department of Transport (Canada Coast Guard) in 1970. The 180-foot vessel had its name changed to *Daring* and served for many more years. She was later sold privately, but in September 1987 the vessel was arrested and seized in Puerto Barrios, Guatemala for taking on 2,375 kg of cocaine from Columbia. It was a sad end to a prized Canadian government vessel.

The 92-foot *Victoria* on the West Coast was turned over to CADC for disposal. After 1970 most vessels were in the 40- to 75-foot range.

The RCMP Marine Division became 'M' Directorate – Marine Services, and was controlled by a director at Headquarters in Ottawa. This Directorate acted as an advisory for overall operations, maintenance and procurement of patrol vessels. The Marine Services administrative branches were established in Halifax, Montreal, Toronto, Winnipeg and Victoria to advise Commanding Officers on training and personnel. A Marine Services officer was assigned to each Division as needed. In 1974 the responsibility of the Marine Services Directorate was transferred to the new Transport Management Branch, Services and Supply Directorate, and in 1994 the Transport Management Branch was incorporated as Fleet Program Administration, Material & Services Management Branch. In 2003 Fleet Program Administration, Material & Services Management Branch was incorporated into the new Assets & Procurement Branch, Corporate Management & Comptrollership.

Canadian Prime Minister Pierre Elliott Trudeau on lookout aboard the Valleyfield II, *1976.*

Courtesy Gilles Gagne

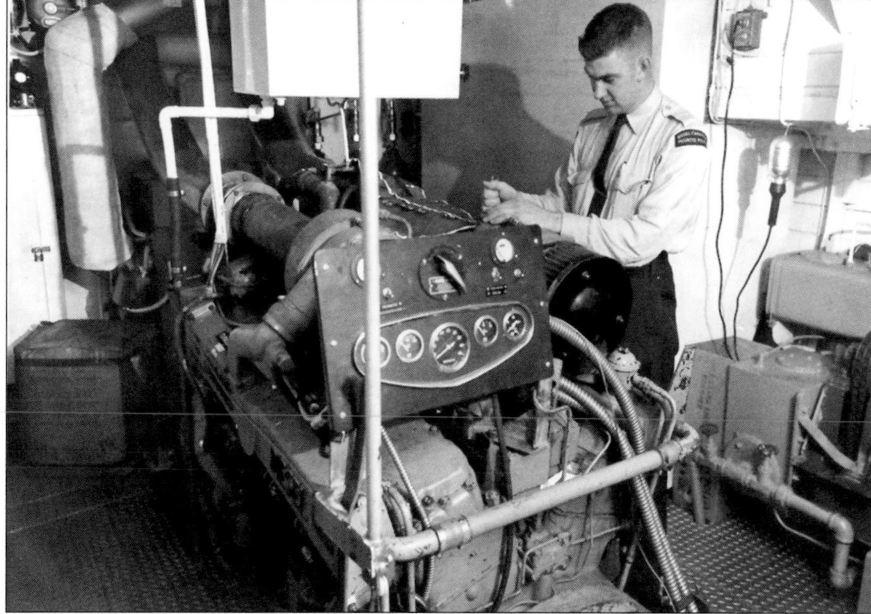

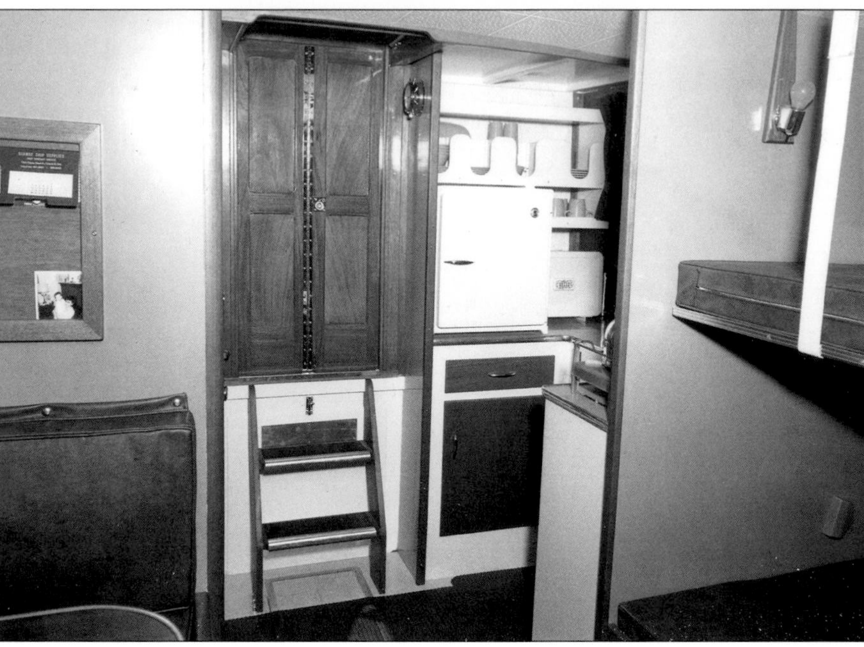

Based on window details, position of helm, galley and stateroom it is believed that these are photographs of the inside of the PB Dauphin *MP 45 or similar vessel such as the* Moosamin, *above.*

Courtesy RCMP Historical Collections Unit

Ships transferred to new RCMP Marine Section from the Royal Canadian Navy in 1945/46

Courtesy RCN

Courtesy RCMP Historical Collections Unit

World War II was over. As vessels deployed during the war became redundant, there was a surplus available for other uses and many of these went into service with the RCMP.

Photographs courtesy the RCMP Historical Collections Unit

Name: Big Bend
Year Built: 1944
Built By: Walter Pinaud's Yacht Yard, Baddick, Nova Scotia
In Service: 1946 - 1955
Dimensions: 48 x 13.6 x 5.3
Type: Harbour Defence Patrol Craft Detachment Class
Cost:
Power: Twin 225 hp Kermath Seawolf engines
Displacement: 18 GT
Speed: 12 kts
Official Number:
Radio Call Sign: CGPS
RCMP Number: MP 65
Code: 200-65

BIG BEND

Harbour defence patrol craft HPC-27 was transferred to the RCMP from the RCN on January 14, 1946 and renamed RCMP PB *Fitzgerald* but when it was discovered there was another vessel of the same name they changed it to RCMP PB *Big Bend*. She served on the East Coast out of Halifax, Nova Scotia until December 14, 1955 when she was turned over to CADC.

BRULE (1)

Harbour defence patrol craft HPC-20 was turned over to the RCMP on January 30, 1946 and renamed RCMP PB *Brule* (1). She served out of North Sydney, Nova Scotia until March 26, 1959 when she was turned over to CADC.

Name: Brule (1)
Year Built: 1943
Built By: Silver Agencies, Dartmouth, N.S.
In Service: 1946 - 1959
Dimensions: 48 x 13.6 x 5.3
Type: Harbour Defence Patrol Craft Detachment Class
Cost:
Power: Twin 225 hp Kermath Seawolf engines
Displacement: 18 GT
Speed: 12 kts
Official Number:
Radio Call Sign: CGPC
RCMP Number: MP 61
Code: 200-61

Name: Carnduff
Year Built: 1944
Built By: Palmer & Williams, Summerside, Prince Edward Island
In Service: 1946 - 1959
Dimensions: 48 x 13.6 x 5.3
Type: Harbour Defence Patrol Craft Detachment Class
Cost:
Power: Twin 225 hp Kermath Seawolf engines
Displacement: 18 GT
Speed: 12 kts
Official Number:
Radio Call Sign: CGPD
RCMP Number: MP 62
Code: 200-62

Library and Archives Canada e0107649900

CARNDUFF

Harbour defence patrol craft HPC-25 was transferred to the RCMP from the RCN on January 14, 1946 and renamed RCMP PB *Carnduff*. She served on the Great Lakes, usually out of Kingston, Ontario until February 16, 1959 when she was turned over to CADC. Photograph above.

Name: Chilcoot (1)
Year Built: 1944
Built By: Walter Pinaud's Yacht Yard, Baddick, Nova Scotia
In Service: 1946 - 1955
Dimensions: 48 x 13.6 x 5.3
Type: Harbour Defence Patrol Craft Detachment Class
Cost:
Power: 2-225 HP Kermath Seawolf engines
Displacement: 18 GT
Speed: 12 kts
Official Number:
Radio Call Sign: CGPF
RCMP Number: MP 63

CHILCOOT (1)

Harbour defence patrol craft HPC-29 was turned over to the RCMP on January 30, 1946 and renamed RCMP PB *Chilcoot*. She served on the Great Lakes out of Sault Ste. Marie, Ontario, until February 3, 1955 when she was turned over to CADC. Photograph right.

Library and Archives Canada e010764893

Courtesy RCN

Name: Colonel White
Year Built: 1942
Built By: Davie Shipbuilding and Repairing Co. Ltd., Lauzon, Quebec
In Service: Not taken into service.
Dimensions: 162 x 28 x 8.3
Type: Harbour Defence Patrol Craft Detachment Class
Cost:
Power: Diesel
Displacement: 592GT
Speed: 16 kts
Armament: 1-12 pdr, 2-20 mm
Official Number:
Radio Call Sign:
RCMP Number: MP 10
Code: 200-10

COLONEL WHITE

HMCS GRANDBY was a Bangor class minesweeper that was transferred to the RCMP from the RCN on August 3, 1945 and renamed RCMP *Colonel White*. She was never commissioned by the RCMP but was turned over to War Assets on August 12, 1946. She was recommissioned on May 23, 1953 as HMCS GRANDBY again by the RCN and used as a diving tender until she was paid off on December 15, 1966.

Name: Cutknife (1)
Year Built: 1943
Built By: Silver's Agencies, Dartmouth, Nova Scotia
In Service: 1946 - 1957
Dimensions: 48 x 13.6 x 5.3
Type: Detachment class
Cost:
Power: 2-225 HP Kermath Seawolf engines
Displacement: 18 GT
Speed: 12 kts
Official Number:
Radio Call Sign: CGPG
RCMP Number: MP 64
Code: 200-64

CUTKNIFE (1)

Harbour defence patrol craft HPC-19 was transferred to the RCMP from the RCN on January 30, 1946 and renamed RCMP PB *Cutknife*. She served on the Great Lakes out of Sarnia, Ontario until February 19, 1957 when she was turned over to CADC.

Name: Fort Pitt
Year Built: 1943
Built By: Minnet-Shields Ltd., Bracebridge, Ontario
In Service: 1945 - 1957
Dimensions: 112 x 17 x 4.8
Type: Fort class
Cost: $50,000
Power: 10 cyl, OHV Vivian diesel
Displacement: 79 GT
Speed: 13 kts
Crew: 17
Armament: 303 rifle, Very pistol
Official Number: 193893
Radio Call Sign: CGMM
RCMP Number: MP 30
Code: 200-30

FORT PITT

HMC ML-119 was a wood-constructed vessel that was transferred to the RCMP from the RCN on August 3, 1945 and renamed RCMP PB *Fort Pitt.* She was commissioned by the RCMP in June 1948 and went into service off the coast of Newfoundland out of Grand Banks until June 1957 when she was turned over to CADC and sold. She was later renamed *Sondra II.*

Courtesy Don Klancher

Name: Fort Selkirk
Year Built: 1943
Built By: Greavette Boats Ltd, Gravenhurst, Ontario
In Service: Not taken into service.
Dimensions: 112 x 17 x 4.8
Type: Fairmile
Cost:
Power: Twin 700 hp Sterling diesels
Displacement: 79 GT
Speed: 22 kts
Crew: 16
Armament: 3-20 mm
Official Number: 192332
Radio Call Sign: CGMR
RCMP Number: MP 31
Code: 200-31

FORT SELKIRK

HMC ML-114 motor launch was transferred to the RCMP from the RCN on August 3, 1945 and renamed RCMP PB *Fort Selkirk.* She was never commissioned by the RCMP although this photograph shows her with the Force's pennant number MP 31. She was turned over to War Assets on January 22, 1947 and sold to H.P. Leask and Roy Pyke of Halifax, Nova Scotia. She was renamed *Amy Mae* and hauled lobsters in the Bay of Fundy.

MP33

Name: Fort Steele (1)
Year Built: 1943
Built By: Grew Boats Ltd., Penetanguishene, Ontario
In Service: Not taken into service.
Dimensions: 112 x 17 x 4.8
Type: Fairmile
Cost:
Power: Twin 550 hp 10 cyl Vivian diesel engines
Displacement: 79 GT
Speed: 22 kts
Crew: 16
Armament: 3-20 mm
Official Number:
Radio Call Sign: CGMQ
RCMP Number: MP 32
Code: 200-32

Oppposite: Fort Walsh on patrol.

Name: Fort Walsh
Year Built: 1943
Built By: J.J. Taylor and Sons, Toronto, Ontario
In Service: 1945 - 1958
Dimensions: 112 x 17 x 4.8
Type: Fort class
Cost:
Power: Twin 560 hp Vivian diesels
Displacement: 79 GT
Speed: 22 kts
Armament: 3-20 mm
Official Number:
Radio Call Sign: CGMR
RCMP Number: MP 33
Code: 200-33

FORT STEELE (1)

HMC ML-117 was transferred to the RCMP from the RCN on August 3, 1945 and renamed RCMP PB *Fort Steele*. She was never commissioned by the RCMP and was turned over to War Assets on January 22, 1947.

Courtesy RCMP Historical Collections Unit

FORT WALSH

HMC ML-112 was transferred to the RCMP from the RCN on August 3, 1945 and renamed RCMP PB *Fort Walsh.* She was commissioned by the RCMP in 1946 and served on the East Coast and Gulf of St Lawrence out of Rimouski, Quebec until October 1958 when she went aground on Scatarie Island off Nova Scotia during a hurricane. There she remained.

"The waves beat the boat against the rocks, she was taking on water, and the crew quickly formed a human chain and waded through the cold water to shore. Freezing cold, wet, hungry and feeling ill and emotionally drained, they carefully made their way in the dark toward the lighthouse. In due time the light keeper and his wife saw the struggling men and rushed to help. They were fed and made warm. Each very grateful to be alive, and it was a close call they would never forget." *—Bonnie Lowe*

Courtesy RCN

Library and Archives Canada e010764883

Abov: Crew aboard the HMCS French. *The photo at lower left, identified as aboard the* French, *is apparently of a different vessel with the same name.*

Name: French (2)
Year Built: 1941
Built By: Marine Industries Ltd, Sorel, Quebec
In Service: 1945 - 1960
Dimensions: 162 x 28 x 8.3
Type: Commissioner class
Cost:
Power: 2 shafts, 1,000 hp each Dominion Sultzer
Displacement: 592 GT
Speed: 16 kts
Armament: 1-12 pdr, 2-20 mm
Official Number:
Radio Call Sign: CGMB
RCMP Number: MP 11
Code: 200-11

Library and Archives Canada e010764882

FRENCH (2)

HMCS Transcona was transferred to the RCMP from the RCN on November 10, 1945 and renamed RCMP *French*. She served in the Marine Services on the East Coast out of Halifax, Nova Scotia until October 1960 when she was turned over to CADC and sold for scrap in 1961 at La Have, Nova Scotia. This was the second vessel called *French* for the RCMP as there was another one of the same name at the outset of World War II (page 133).

Courtesy RCMP Historical Collections Unit

Name: Grenfell
Year Built: 1945
Built By: Walter Pinaud's Yacht Yard, Baddick, Nova Scotia
In Service: 1946 - 1959
Dimensions: 48 x 13.6 x 5.3
Type: Harbour Defence Patrol Craft
Cost:
Power: Twin 225 hp Kermath Seawolf engines
Displacement: 18 GT
Speed: 12 kts
Official Number:
Radio Call Sign: CGPK
RCMP Number: MP 66
Code: 200-66

GRENFELL

Harbour defence patrol craft HPC-33 was transferred to the RCMP from the RCN on January 14, 1946 and renamed RCMP PB *Grenfell*. She served in Eastern Canada out of Bagotville, Quebec until May 4, 1959 when she was turned over to CADC.

Courtesy RCN

HERCHMER

HMCS Truro was a Bangor class minesweeper that was transferred to the RCMP from the RCN on August 3, 1945 and renamed RCMP *Herchmer*. She was never commissioned by the RCMP but was turned over to War Assets on August 6, 1946 and sold. She was renamed *Gulf Mariner*. The ship was abandoned ashore on the Fraser River in British Columbia and broken up in 1964.

Name: Herchmer
Year Built: 1942
Built By: Davie Shipbuilding and Repairing Co. Ltd., Lauzon, Quebec
In Service: Not taken into service
Dimensions: 162 x 28 x 8.3
Type: Commissioner class
Cost:
Power: Diesel
Displacement: 592 GT
Speed: 16 kts
Armament: 1-12 pdr, 2-20 mm
Official Number: 177616
Radio Call Sign:
RCMP Number: MP 12
Code: 200-12

Name: Irvine
Year Built: 1941
Built By: Davie Shipbuilding and Repairing Co. Ltd., Lauzon, Quebec
In Service: 1945 - 1962
Dimensions: 162 x 28 x 8.3
Type: Commissioner class
Cost:
Power: Twin 1,000 hp Dominion Sultzer diesel engines
Displacement: 592 GT
Speed: 16 kts
Armament: 1-12 pdr, 2-20 mm
Official Number: 330084
Radio Call Sign: CGMF
RCMP Number: MP 13
Code: 200-13

Courtesy RCMP Historical Collections Unit

IRVINE

HMCS Noranda was transferred to the RCMP from the RCN on August 28, 1945 and renamed RCMP *Irvine*. She served in the Marine Services on the East Coast in Halifax until 1962 when she was sold and renamed *Miriana* after her conversion to a yacht. She sank in Montego Bay, Jamaica in 1971.

Courtesy RCMP Historical Collections Unit

Name: Little Bow
Year Built: 1945
Built By: Victoria Motor Boat & Repair Works Ltd., Victoria, British Columbia
In Service: 1946 - 1958
Dimensions: 48 x 13.6 x 5.3
Type: Harbour Defence Patrol Craft
Cost:
Power: Twin 225 hp Kermath Seawolf diesel engines
Displacement: 18 GT
Speed: 12 kts
Official Number:
Radio Call Sign: CGPL
RCMP Number: MP 67
Code: 200-67

LITTLE BOW

Harbour defence patrol craft HPC-31 was transferred to the RCMP from the RCN on January 14, 1946 and renamed RCMP PB *Little* Bow. She served on the West Coast out of Vancouver, British Columbia until March 29, 1958 when she was turned over to CADC.

Library and Archives Canada e010764897

Library and Archives Canada e010764899

Library and Archives Canada e010764898

Left, bottom: RCMP crew activities aboard the HMCS MacBrien.

Name: MacBrien
Year Built: 1941
Built By: Marine Industries Ltd, Sorel, Quebec.
In Service: 1945 - 1959
Dimensions: 162 x 28 x 8.3
Type: Commissioner class
Cost:
Power: Dominion Sultzer diesel engines 2 shafts, 1,000 hp each
Displacement: 592 GT
Speed: 16 kts
Armament: 1-12 pdr, 2-20 mm
Official Number:
Radio Call Sign: CGMG
RCMP Number: MP 14
Code: 200-14

Courtesy Don Klancher

MACBRIEN

HMCS Trois Rivieres was transferred to the RCMP from the RCN on August 3, 1945 and renamed RCMP *MacBrien*. She served in the Marine Services on the East Coast until 1959 when she was transferred to the RCN on permanent loan for conversion to a Naval Research Vessel. She was not converted but declared surplus June 13, 1959, was turned over to CADC and sold for scrap in 1960.

Name: Macleod (2)
Year Built: 1941
Built By: Marine Industries Ltd, Sorel, Quebec
In Service: 1945 - 1950
Dimensions: 162 x 28 x 8.3
Type: Commissioner class
Cost:
Power: Diesel - 2 shafts, 2,000 hp
Displacement: 592 GT
Speed: 16 kts
Armament: 1-12 pdr, 2-20 mm
Official Number:
Radio Call Sign: CGMJ
RCMP Number: MP 15
Code: 200-15

Courtesy RCN

MACLEOD (2)

The HMCS Brockville was transferred to the RCMP from the RCN on August 28, 1945 and renamed RCMP *Macleod*. She served in the Marine Services on the East Coast until July 1, 1950 when she was returned to the RCN and re-commissioned on April 5, 1951 as HMCS Brockville then later transferred to the West Coast where she served until paid off on October 31, 1958. In 1961 she was broken up.

Name: Moosomin
Year Built: 1943
Built By: Walter Pinaud's Yacht Yard, Baddick, Nova Scotia
In Service: 1946 - 1958
Dimensions: 48 x 13.6 x 5.3
Type: Harbour Defence Patrol Craft Detachment Class
Cost: $200,000
Power: Twin 225 hp Kermath Seawolf engines
Displacement: 18 GT
Speed: 12 kts
Official Number:
Radio Call Sign: CGPM
RCMP Number: MP 68
Code: 200-68

MOOSOMIN

Harbour defence patrol craft HPC-32 was transferred to the RCMP from the RCN on March 29, 1946 and renamed RCMP PB *Moosomin*. She served on the St Lawrence River out of Montreal, Quebec until September 19, 1958 when she was turned over to CADC.

Name: Perry
Year Built: 1942
Built By: Davie Shipbuilding and Repairing Co. Ltd., Lauzon, Quebec
Built By:
In Service: Not taken into service
Dimensions: 162 x 28 x 8.3
Type: Commissioner class
Cost:
Power: Diesel
Displacement: 592 GT
Speed: 16 kts
Armament: 1-12 pdr, 2-20 mm
Official Number:
Radio Call Sign:
RCMP Number: MP 16
Code: 200-16

PERRY

HMCS Digby was a Bangor class minesweeper that was transferred to the RCMP from the RCN on August 3, 1945 and renamed RCMP *Perry*. She was never commissioned by the RCMP but was turned over to War Assets on August 16, 1946. She was in Sorel, Quebec until the RCN took her over in 1951, refitted her for training and recommissioned her on April 29, 1953 as HMCS Digby again until she was paid off on November 14, 1956 and scrapped.

Courtesy RCN

SHAUNAVON

Harbour defence patrol craft HPC-26 was transferred to the RCMP from the RCN on January 14, 1946 and renamed RCMP PB *Shaunavon*. She served on the Great Lakes out of Toronto, Ontario until December 14, 1955 when she was turned over to CADC.

Name: Shaunavon
Year Built: 1943
Built By: Walter Pinaud's Yacht Yard, Baddick, Nova Scotia
In Service: 1946 - 1955
Dimensions: 48 x 13.6 x 5.3
Type: Harbour Defence Patrol Craft
Detachment Class
Cost:
Power: Twin 225 hp Kermath Seawolf engines
Displacement: 18 GT
Speed: 12 kts
Official Number:
Radio Call Sign: CGPM
RCMP Number: MP 69
Code: 200-69

Courtesy RCMP Historical Collections Unit

Opposite: The Slideout *was a former Defence Patrol Vessel.*

SLIDEOUT (1)

Harbour defence patrol craft HPC-30 was transferred to the RCMP from the RCN on January 14, 1946 and renamed RCMP PB *Slideout*. She served on the East Coast out of Halifax, Nova Scotia until July 28, 1960 when she was turned over to CADC.

Name: Slideout (1)
Year Built: 1945
Built By: Walter Pinaud's Yacht Yard, Baddick, Nova Scotia
In Service: 1946 - 1960
Dimensions: 48 x 13.6 x 5.3
Type: Harbour Defence Patrol Craft
Cost:
Power: Twin 225 hp Kermath Seawolf engines
Displacement: 18 GT
Speed: 12 kts
Official Number:
Radio Call Sign: CGPP
RCMP Number: MP 70
Code: 200-70

MP 70

Courtesy John Kerster

STANDOFF (1)

Harbour Defence Patrol Craft HPC-28 was turned over to the RCMP and commissioned on August 31, 1946 as RCMP PB *Aklavik*. When it was discovered there was another vessel of the same name they changed it to RCMP PB *Standoff*. She served on the West Coast out of Vancouver and Victoria until 1951.
She eventually became a tugboat on the Fraser River.

Below: Constable R. H. Davies ties up Standoff at a West Coast dock. The vessel served in Vancouver and Victoria in the late 1940s.

Courtesy John Kerster

Name: Standoff (1)
Year Built: 1944
Built By: Victoria Motor Boat & Repair Works Ltd., Victoria, British Columbia
In Service: 1946 - 1951
Dimensions: 48 x 13.6 x 5.3
Type: Harbour Defence Patrol Craft
Cost:
Power:
Displacement: 18 GT
Speed: 12 kts
Official Number: 195237
Radio Call Sign: CGPT
RCMP Number: MP 60
Code: 200-60

Name: Starnes
Year Built: 1942
Built By: Davie Shipbuilding and Repairing Co. Ltd., Lauzon, Quebec
In Service: Not taken into service
Dimensions: 162 x 28 x 8.3
Type: Commissioner class
Cost: $200,000
Power: Diesel
Displacement: 592 GT
Speed: 16 kts
Armament: 1-12 pounder, 2-20 mm
Official Number: 177879
Radio Call Sign:
RCMP Number: MP 17
Code: 200-17

Courtesy RCN

STARNES

HMCS LACHINE, was a Bangor class minesweeper that was transferred to the RCMP from the RCN on August 3, 1945 and renamed RCMP *Starnes*. She was not commissioned by the RCMP but turned over to War Assets on August 21, 1946 and sold. She became a salvage tug and was renamed *Lachine*.

Name: Tagish (2)
Year Built: 1944
Built By: Palmer & Williams, Summerside, Prince Edward Island
In Service: 1946 - 1956
Dimensions: 48 x 13.6 x 5.3
Type: Harbour Defence Patrol Craft Detachment Class
Cost:
Power: Twin 225 hp Kermath Seawolf engines
Displacement: 18 GT
Speed: 12 kts
Official Number: 156429
Radio Call Sign: CGPQ
RCMP Number: MP 71
Code: 200-71

TAGISH (2)

Harbour defence patrol craft HPC-24 was transferred to the RCMP from the RCN on January 14, 1946 and renamed RCMP PB *Tagish*. She served on the Great Lakes out of Windsor, Ontario until 1956 when she was turned over to CADC. She is seen in the photograph, right.

Library and Archives Canada e010764893

Courtesy RCMP Historical Collections Unit

Name: Willow Bunch
Year Built: 1942
Built By: Dartmouth Lumber Co., Dartmouth, Nova Scotia
In Service: 1946 - 1958
Dimensions: 48 x 13.6 x 5.3
Type: Harbour Defence Patrol Craft Detachment Class
Cost:
Power: Twin 225 hp Kermath Seawolf engines
Displacement: 18 GT
Speed: 12 kts
Official Number: 314049
Radio Call Sign: CGPW
RCMP Number: MP 72
Code: 200-72

WILLOW BUNCH

Harbour defence patrol craft HPC-6 was transferred to the RCMP from the RCN on January 30, 1946 and renamed RCMP PB *Yellowknife*. When it was discovered, however, that there was another vessel of the same name, they changed it to *Willow Bunch*. She served on the East Coast out of Halifax, Nova Scotia until 1958 when she was turned over to CADC. She was sold and renamed *Poco Temp* in 1960.

It can be a lonely life for RCMP crews on patrol. The Aklavik II *at anchor in remote northern waters.*

Vessels added to the RCMP fleet of former Navy ships from 1947 to 1970

Courtesy RCMP Historical Collections Unit

No longer having a need to build military vessels on the same scale as during the war, many shipyards turned to pleasure craft and patrol vessel building after the Second World War.

Courtesy RCMP Historical Collections Unit

Name: Acadian (2)
Year Built: 1959
Built By: Harley S. Cox & Sons, Shelburne, Nova Scotia
In Service: 1960 – 1976
Dimensions: 65 ft
Type: Detachment class
Cost: $125,934
Power: Single 600 hp GM turbo-charged Series 71 diesel
Displacement: 48 GT
Speed:
Crew: 4
Official Number:
Radio Call Sign: CGMV
RCMP Number: MP 52
Code: 200-52

ACADIAN (2)

PB *Acadian* was the second boat of this name for the RCMP, the first one being transferred to the Royal Canadian Navy in 1939. This vessel was commissioned on February 9, 1960. Mrs. D.A. McKinnon, wife of RCMP Assistant Commissioner McKinnon, acted as the sponsor for the launching. The vessel departed Halifax NS on May 01, 1960 for her base at Harbour Breton, Newfoundland and was replaced by the *Centennial*. The *Acadian* was later transferred to Fortune Newfoundland, where she served until March 17, 1976. She was later turned over to CADC. They sold her to the Canadian Forces who renamed her CFAV ACADIAN, pennant PB194 until 1996.

Courtesy RCMP Historical Collections Unit

ADVANCE (2)

MB *Advance* was the first fibreglass vessel constructed by Canoe Cove Manufacturing in British Columbia, and was one of 45 similar hulls. She was the second vessel of this name and was commissioned in August 1961. She served on the West Coast out of Gibsons and Vancouver, British Columbia until 1986 then turned over to CADC. The *Advance* was replaced by the S*tikine* in 1986. The *Advance* had her cabin design changed later in her life.

Courtesy RCMP Historical Collections Unit

Name: Advance (2)
Year Built: 1961
Built By: Canoe Cove Mfg, Sidney, B.C.
In Service: 1961 – 1986
Dimensions: 35 ft
Type: Motor boat
Cost: $21,775
Power: Single 240 hp Ford Meteor engine
Displacement:
Speed:
Crew: 2
Official Number:
Radio Call Sign:
RCMP Number: MP 59
Code: 200-59

Courtesy RCMP Historical Collections Unit

Name: Adversus (2)
Year Built: 1958
Built By: Harley S. Cox & Sons Ltd., Shelburne, Nova Scotia
In Service: 1959 – 1976
Dimensions: 65 ft
Type: Detachment class
Cost: $119,930
Power: Single 400 hp Cummins turbo charged diesel engine
Displacement: 45.43 GT
Speed:
Crew: 4
Official Number:
Radio Call Sign: CGJG
RCMP Number: MP 99
Code: 200-99

ADVERSUS (2)

PB *Adversus* was the second vessel of this name used by the RCMP, the first one having been turned over to the RCN in 1939. She was a wood-hulled vessel built in Shelburne, Nova Scotia and was commissioned May 19, 1959. She served in the Halifax area until March 17, 1976 when she became a vessel of the Canadian Forces and was renamed CFAV Adversus, pennant number PB191. There she served until 1996.

Courtesy RCMP Historical Collections Unit

ALERT (2)

PB *Alert* (2) was a wood-hulled vessel built in British Columbia and launched on December 6, 1958. She was the second vessel to be named so with the original having served on Prince Edward Island in 1936. The *Alert* served the west coast of B.C. out of Alert Bay until declared surplus to requirements and turned over to CADC in October 1975.

Name: Alert (2)
Year Built: 1958
Built By: McKay-Cormack Ltd., Victoria, British Columbia
In Service: 1958 – 1975
Dimensions: 65 x 15 x 5.5
Type: Detachment class
Cost: $136,785
Power: Single 400 hp turbo charged Cummins diesel
Displacement: 44 GT
Speed:
Crew: 4
Official Number:
Radio Call Sign:
RCMP Number: MP 98
Code: 200-98

Name: Athabaska
Year Built: 1967
Built By: Canoe Cove Mfg. Ltd., Sidney, British Columbia
In Service: 1967 – 1990
Dimensions: 26 x 9.9 x 2.3
Type: Detachment class
Cost: $16,354
Power: Twin 150 hp Mercruiser gas engines
Displacement: 4.38 GT
Speed: 32 mph
Crew: 2
Official Number:
Radio Call Sign:
RCMP Number: MP 48
Code: 200-48

Courtesy RCMP Historical Collections Unit

ATHABASKA

PB *Athabasa* was a fibreglass-hulled vessel built for EXPO 67. After duty at EXPO she was transferred to Fort Chipewyan (Lake Athabasca) and then in August 1969 she was transferred to Nanaimo, British Columbia. She was declared surplus in 1990 and transferred to CADC.

Courtesy RCMP Historical Collections Unit

BATTLEFORD (2)

PB *Battleford (2)* was a wood-hulled vessel specially built for off-shore patrol duties at Expo 67 in Montreal, Quebec. After Expo she was transferred to Marine Sub-Division, Esquimalt, B.C. In November 1972, the boat was declared surplus to Force requirements and turned over to CADC for disposal. She was a sister ship to the *Slideout*.

Name: Battleford (2)
Year Built: 1966
Built By: J.J. Taylor & Sons Ltd., Toronto, Ontario
In Service: 1966 – 1972
Dimensions: 29 ft
Type: Detachment class
Cost: $22,100
Power: Twin Volvo Penta gas engines
Displacement:
Speed:
Crew: 1
Official Number:
Radio Call Sign:
RCMP Number: MP 42
Code: 200-42

Courtesy RCMP Historical Collections Unit

BEAVER (2)

PB *Beaver* was a wood-hulled vessel and the second one of this name to be used by the RCMP. This vessel operated out of Fort William, Ontario, conducting border patrol and enforcement duties at the head of Lake Superior until June 1971 when she was no longer required and released to Crown Assets Distribution Centre (CADC). She was replaced by two 17.5 foot fibreglass vessels, each with 100 hp Johnson outboard engines.

Name: Beaver (2)
Year Built: 1962
Built By: J.J. Taylor & Sons Ltd., Toronto, Ontario
In Service: 1962 – 1971
Dimensions: 35 ft
Type: Detachment class
Cost: $27,569
Power: Single 240 hp Interceptor engine
Displacement:
Speed:
Crew: 2
Official Number:
Radio Call Sign:
RCMP Number: MP 61
Code: 200-61

Courtesy RCMP Historical Collections Unit

Name: Blue Heron
Year Built: 1956
Built By: Hunter Boat Works, Orillia, Ontario
In Service: 1957 - 1968
Dimensions: 92 x 17.5 x 6.6
Type: Fort class
Cost: On loan from RCN
Power: Twin 550 hp Cummins diesel
Displacement: 85 GT
Speed: 14 kts
Crew: 16
Official Number:
Radio Call Sign: CGZH
RCMP Number: MP 32
Code: 200-32

BLUE HERON

ML *Blue Heron* was a wood-hulled vessel built for the RCN and was one of the four Bird class seaward defence patrol craft. She was launched as HMCS Blue Heron with naval pennant number 782. After six months of service she was turned over to the Marine Section of the RCMP February 28, 1957 on loan. She replaced the RCMP *Fort Pitt* and her patrol area was Halifax, Nova Scotia. On May 6, 1968 the *Blue Heron* was returned to the RCN and sold in 1970.

Courtesy Gilles Gagne

Name: Brule (2)
Year Built: 1967
Built By: D. Mason Boats Ltd., Smith Falls, Ontario
In Service: 1967 – 1976
Dimensions: 29 x 10
Type: Detachment class
Cost: $22,533
Power: Twin Volvo Penta gas engine
Displacement:
Speed:
Crew: 2
Official Number:
Radio Call Sign:
RCMP Number: MP 46
Code: 200-46

Courtesy RCMP Historical Collections Unit

BRULE (2)

The PB *Brule* was built for Expo 67. After duty at Expo she was transferred to Long Sault, Ontario area on the Great Lakes where she served until declared surplus and sent to CADC in October 1976.

Above: PB Brule *(2) in the Great Lakes. Left: This was the* Brule *(1), an earlier vessel by the same name.*

Name: Burin
Year Built: 1955
Built By: David A. Mason, Tancook Island, Nova Scotia
In Service: 1955 - 1971
Dimensions: 48 x 12 x 4.3
Type: Detachment class
Cost: $48,700
Power: Single 175 hp Cummins diesel
Displacement: 18 GT
Speed:
Crew: 4
Official Number:
Radio Call Sign:
RCMP Number: MP 84
Code: 200-84

Courtesy RCMP Historical Collections Unit

BURIN

The PB *Burin* was a wood-hulled vessel constructed for Marine Division in June 1955. She served out of Harbour Breton, Newfoundland until 1959 when she was transferred to Shelburne, then North Sydney and finally Halifax, Nova Scotia until September 14, 1971 when she was sent to CADC.

Courtesy RCMP Historical Collections Unit

CAPTOR (2)

PB *Captor* (2) was the second vessel of this name used by the RCMP with the first one being turned over to the RCN in 1939. The *Captor* (2) was a wood-hulled vessel built in Lunenburg, Nova Scotia. On March 10, 1959 the Force took possession of the vessel and christened her *Captor*. The sponsor for the christening was Mrs Howe, wife of Assistant Commissioner J. Howe, Officer Commanding 'H' Division. *Captor* served in the Bagotville, Quebec area until March 17, 1976 when she was turned over to the Canadian Forces who renamed her CFAV Captor, pennant number PB193. She served until 1993.

Name: Captor (2)
Year Built: 1958
Built By: Smith & Rhuland, Lunenburg, Nova Scotia
In Service: 1959 – 1976
Dimensions: 65 x 15 x 5.5
Type: Detachment class
Cost: $124,300
Power: Single 400 hp Cummins turbo-charged diesel engine
Displacement:
Speed:
Crew: 4
Official Number:
Radio Call Sign: CGLN
RCMP Number: MP 50
Code: 200-50

Name: Carnduff II
Year Built: 1957
Built By: Grew Boat, Penetanguishene, Ontario
In Service: 1957 – 1971
Dimensions: 50.3 x 13 x 3.2
Type: Detachment class
Cost: $56,650
Power: Twin 350 hp Scripps gas engines
Displacement: 28 GT
Speed:
Crew: 4
Official Number:
Radio Call Sign:
RCMP Number: MP 88
Code: 200-88

Courtesy Don Klancher

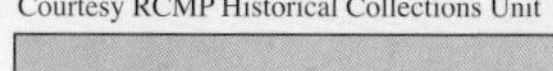
Courtesy RCMP Historical Collections Unit

CARNDUFF II

PB *Carnduff II* was a wood-hulled vessel built to replace the original *Carnduff*. She was built in 1957 and is a sister ship to the *Tagish II*. The *Carnduff II* served out of Sault Ste Marie, Ontario. She was declared surplus on May 17, 1971 and turned over to CADC.

Courtesy RCMP Historical Collections Unit

CHILCOOT II

PB *Chilcoot II* was a wood-hulled vessel built to replace the original *Chilcoot* received from War Assets in 1946. She served in the Windsor, Ontario area of the Great Lakes until September 1971 when she was turned over to CADC.

Name: Chilcoot II
Year Built: 1954
Built By: J.J. Taylor & Sons Limited, Toronto, Ontario
In Service: 1954 - 1971
Dimensions: 50.2 x 13 x 3.2
Type: Detachment class
Cost: $54,950
Power: Twin 350 hp Scripps gas engines
Displacement: 28 GT
Speed: 30 mph
Crew: 4
Official Number:
Radio Call Sign:
RCMP Number: MP 81
Code: 200-81

Name: Cutknife II
Year Built: 1955
Built By: J.J. Taylor & Sons Limited, Toronto, Ontario
In Service: 1955 - 1972
Dimensions: 50.2 x 13 x 3.2
Type: Detachment class
Cost: $59,128
Power: Twin 350 hp Scripps gas engines
Displacement: 28 GT
Speed: 30 mph
Crew: 4
Official Number:
Radio Call Sign:
RCMP Number: MP 82
Code: 200-82

Courtesy RCMP Historical Collections Unit

CUTKNIFE II

PB *Cutknife II* was a wood-hulled vessel built to replace the original *Cutknife* received from War Assets in 1946. Mrs G.B. McClellan, wife of the Officer Commanding 'O' Division, christened her July 6, 1955. She served in the Kingston, Ontario area of the Great Lakes until June 1972 when she was turned over to CADC.

Courtesy RCMP Historical Collections Unit

DAUPHIN

PB *Dauphin* was the last vessel constructed specially for Expo 67. She was a wood-hulled vessel and after Expo 67 served out of the Montreal, Quebec area until May 3, 1971 when she was turned over to CADC for disposal. She was a sister ship to the *Lac La Ronge*.

Name: Dauphin
Year Built: 1967
Built By: Cliff Richardson Boats Ltd., Meaford, Ontario
In Service: 1967 – 1971
Dimensions: 34 ft
Type: Detachment class
Cost: $34,500
Power: Twin 290 hp Chrysler engines
Displacement:
Speed:
Crew: 2
Official Number:
Radio Call Sign:
RCMP Number: MP 45
Code: 200-45

Name: Detector (2)
Year Built: 1957
Built By: Shelburne Shipbuilders Ltd., Shelburne, Nova Scotia.
In Service: 1957 – 1976
Dimensions: 64.9 x 15.4 x 5.4
Type: Detachment class
Cost: $97,248
Power: Single 400 hp Cummins diesel
Displacement: 44 GT
Speed:
Crew: 4
Official Number:
Radio Call Sign: CGKE
RCMP Number: MP 86
Code: 200-86

Courtesy RCMP Historical Collections Unit

DETECTOR (2)

PB *Detector* was a wood-hulled vessel built for the RCMP and officially launched by Mrs S.A. Beanlands, wife of Staff Sergeant Beanlands, on June 28, 1957. This vessel served in the Saint John, New Brunswick area until she was turned over to CADC on March 17, 1976 then to the Canadian Forces as the CFAV Detector, pennant number PB192 until 1988.

Courtesy RCMP Historical Collections Unit

Name: Fort Erie
Year Built: 1959
Built By: J.J. Taylor & Sons., Toronto, Ontario
In Service: 1959 – 1971
Dimensions: 34 ft
Type: Motor boat
Cost: $24,277
Power: Single 240 hp Interceptor engine
Displacement:
Speed:
Crew: 2
Official Number:
Radio Call Sign:
RCMP Number: MP 54
Code: 200-54

FORT ERIE

MB *Fort Erie* was a wood-hulled vessel purchased from J.J. Taylor & Sons in March 1959. She served in the Niagara Falls, Ontario area until August 1971 when she was declared surplus and sent to CADC.

Name: Fort Frances
Year Built: 1947
Built By: Canadian Power Boat Co.
In Service: 1947 - 1956
Dimensions: 24 x 8 x 2.5
Type: Motor boat
Cost:
Power: Single 95 hp Chrysler Marine gasoline engine
Displacement: 1.6 GT
Speed: 18 kts
Crew: 2
Official Number:
Radio Call Sign:
RCMP Number: MP 91
Code: 200-91

FORT FRANCES

RCMP MB *Fort Frances* was built for the RCMP on March 27, 1947. She served out of Fort Frances, Ontario on the Great Lakes until February 20, 1956 when she was turned over to CADC.

Courtesy RCMP Historical Collections Unit

Name: Fort Frances II
Year Built: 1956
Built By: J.J. Taylor & Sons Limited, Toronto, Ontario
In Service: 1956 - 1971
Dimensions: 25 x 8.6 x 1.7
Type: Motor boat
Cost: $9,120
Power: Single 215 hp Dearborn Interceptor engine
Displacement: 12 GT
Speed:
Official Number: 12E 1219
Radio Call Sign:
RCMP Number: MP 92
Code: 200-92

FORT FRANCES II

The MB *Fort Frances II* was a wood-hulled vessel purchased on February 10, 1956 to replace the original *Fort Frances*. She served in the Great Lakes out of Fort Frances, Ontario. The patrol area for this vessel was Rainy River and her main duties were to patrol the international boundary. On April 5, 1971 Lakehead Marina, Fort Frances, purchased the *Fort Frances II* for $3,000 on a trade-in for a 19-ft Comoro fibreglass boat replacement.

The Kenora II *(right) was a sister ship to the* Fort Frances II.

Courtesy RCMP Historical Collections Unit

FORT ST JAMES

MB *Fort St James* was a wood-hulled vessel built for 'E' Division. She was transferred to the Marine Division on March 22, 1962 and was in operation out of Fort St James, British Columbia. She served until January 8, 1968 when she was turned over to CADC.

Name: Fort St James
Year Built: 1953
Built By: Star Shipyards, (Mercer's) Ltd., New Westminster, British Columbia
In Service: 1953 - 1968
Dimensions: 30 ft
Type: Detachment class
Cost: $9,615
Power: Single100 hp inboard engine
Displacement: 25 GT
Speed:
Crew: 1
Official Number:
Radio Call Sign:
RCMP Number: MP 60
Code: 200-60

Name: Fort Steele (2)
Year Built: 1958
Built By: Canadian Shipbuilding and Engineering Ltd., Kingston, Ontario
In Service: 1958 – 1973
Dimensions: 118 x 21 x 7
Type: Fort class
Cost: $908,171
Power: Twin 2,500 hp Napier Deltic
Displacement: 164 GT
Speed: 21 kts
Crew: 17
Official Number:
Radio Call Sign: CGMQ
RCMP Number: MP 34
Code: 200-34

Courtesy RCMP Historical Collections Unit

FORT STEELE (2)

ML *Fort Steele* was a welded steel-hulled vessel built for the RCMP and launched July 18, 1958. She was the second vessel of this name to be used by the RCMP although the first one, a Fairmile, was never commissioned. Mrs L.H. Nicholson, wife of the Commissioner, christened her July 18, 1958. This vessel served out of Halifax, Nova Scotia until she was turned over to CADC. She was transferred to the Canadian Forces Naval Reserve where she was renamed HMCS Fort Steele, a training vessel, pennant number PB140. Fort Steele served from 1974 to 1994 in Halifax, Nova Scotia. In 2008 she was called the *Lady Rosella Regina B* and was based in Newfoundland.

Courtesy RCMP Historical Collections Unit

Name: Ganges
Year Built:1958
Built By: Star Shipyard (Mercer's) Ltd., New Westminster, British Columbia
In Service: 1958 – 1977
Dimensions: 65 x 15 x 4.5
Type: Detachment class
Cost: $135,251
Power: Single 600 hp G.M. turbo-charged Series 71 engine
Displacement: 48 GT
Speed: 10.5 kts
Crew: 4
Official Number:
Radio Call Sign:
RCMP Number: MP 97
Code: 200-97

GANGES

The PB *Ganges* was built in New Westminster, British Columbia and launched November 27, 1958. Mrs Lett, wife of Chief Justice Sherwood Lett, was the sponsor for the launching. The vessel served in the Tofino area (photo left) until May 1962 when she was transferred to Port Alberni, B.C. She was found to have dry rot and was sent to CADC for disposal on January 7, 1977.

Courtesy RCMP Historical Collections Unit

Name: Interceptor (2)
Year Built:1955
Built By: Shelburne Shipbuilders Ltd., Shelburne, Nova Scotia
In Service: 1955 - 1974
Dimensions: 65 x 15 x 5.4
Type: Detachment class
Cost: $81,703
Power: Single 350 hp Cummins diesel
Displacement: 44 GT
Speed: 12 kts
Crew: 4
Official Number: 370980
Radio Call Sign:
RCMP Number: MP 83
Code: 200-83

INTERCEPTOR (2)

PB *Interceptor* was the second boat of this name to be built and used by the RCMP Marine Division. This vessel was a wood-hulled vessel built to replace the aging *Big Bend*. Mrs A.R. Ascah, wife of Officer Commanding 'H' Division, christened her August 8, 1955. She served out of Harbour Breton, Newfoundland until 1961 when she was moved to North Sydney, Nova Scotia. In 1973 she was replaced by the *Centennial*. On April 30, 1974 she was declared surplus and transferred to CADC. In 1977 CADC transferred her to the Department of Indian and Northern Affairs. Note the similarity of her design to the *Ganges*.

Courtesy RCMP Historical Collections Unit

Name: Kenora
Year Built: 1947
Built By: Canadian Power Boat Co., Montreal, Quebec
In Service: 1947 - 1957
Dimensions: 24 x 8 x 2.5
Type: Motor boat
Cost
Power: Single Chrysler Marine gasoline 95 hp
Displacement: 1.6 GT
Speed: 18 kts
Crew: 2
Official Number:
Radio Call Sign:
RCMP Number: MP 90
Code: 200-90

Name: Kenora II/Fraser
Year Built: 1957
Built By: Kingston Shipyards, Kingston, Ontario
In Service: 1957 – 1969
Dimensions: 26 x 9.3 x 2.3
Type: Motor boat
Cost $17,632
Power: Twin 185 hp Dearborn Interceptor engines
Displacement: 12 GT
Speed: 10 kts
Crew: 2
Official Number:
Radio Call Sign:
RCMP Number: MP 94
Code: 200-94

KENORA

The MB *Kenora* served out of Kenora, Ontario until February 19, 1957 when she was replaced by the *Kenora ll* and turned over to CADC.

Courtesy RCMP Historical Collections Unit

Above: The Fraser, *also shown to the right and below, was formerly the MB* Kenora II.

KENORA II/FRASER

MB *Kenora II* had a steel hull and a wood superstructure. She was built in 1957 to replace the *Kenora* and served in Kenora, Ontario until June 15, 1960 then transferred to 'G' Division for use at Inuvik. In August 1962 she was transferred to the Marine Section in Vancouver. To avoid confusion with *Kenora III*, she was re-named *Fraser* October 15, 1962. On October 31, 1969 she was turned over to CADC and sold on January 12, 1970.

Courtesy RCMP Historical Collections Unit

Name: Kenora III
Year Built: 1960
Built By: J.J. Taylor & Sons Ltd., Toronto, Ontario
In Service: 1960 – 1971
Dimensions: 26 ft
Type: Motor boat
Cost: $12,099
Power: Single 215 hp Interceptor engine
Displacement:
Speed:
Crew: 2
Official Number: 20E 5730
Radio Call Sign:
RCMP Number: MP 57
Code: 200-57

KENORA III

MB *Kenora III* was a wood-hulled vessel purchased on January 19, 1960. She served out of Kenora, Ontario until September 7, 1971 when she was declared surplus to Force requirements and sent to CADC for disposal.

Name: Lac La Ronge
Year Built: 1967
Built By: Cliff Richardson Boats Ltd., Meaford, Ontario
In Service: 1967 – 1972
Dimensions: 34 ft
Type: Detachment class
Cost: $34,500.
Power: Twin 290 hp Chrysler engines
Displacement:
Crew: 2
Official Number:
Radio Call Sign:
RCMP Number: MP 44
Code: 200-44

Courtesy Gilles Gagne

LAC LA RONGE

PB *Lac La Ronge* was a wood-hulled vessel constructed specially for Expo 67. After Expo she served out of the Chamblay, Quebec area until 1972 when she was turned over to CADC for disposal. She was a sister ship to the *Dauphin*.

Courtesy RCMP Historical Collections Unit

LITTLE BOW II

PB *Little Bow II* was a wood-hulled vessel built in 1958 in British Columbia to replace the original *Little Bow*. She was launched and christened *Little Bow II* by Mrs W.H. Nevin, wife of Superintendent Nevin, Officer Commanding Vancouver Sub-Division, on March 20, 1958. She served in Vancouver until 1963 when she was moved to Powell River, British Columbia until 1972.

Name: Little Bow II
Year Built: 1958
Built By: Star Shipyards (Mercer's) Ltd., New Westminster, British Columbia
In Service: 1958 – 1972
Dimensions: 55 x 14 x 4
Type: Detachment class
Cost: $123,754
Power: Twin 300 hp G.M. turbo-charged diesel engines
Displacement: 39 GT
Speed:
Crew: 4
Official Number:
Radio Call Sign:
RCMP Number: MP 95
Code: 200-95

Name: Masset
Year Built: 1958
Built By: McKay-Cormack Ltd., Victoria, B.C.
In Service: 1958 – 1974
Dimensions: 65 x 15 x 5.5
Type: Detachment class
Cost: $136,983
Power: Single 400 hp turbo-charged Cummins diesel
Displacement: 52.44 GT
Speed: 11 kts
Crew: 4
Official Number: 370044
Radio Call Sign:
RCMP Number: MP 93
Code: 200-93

Courtesy RCMP Historical Collections Unit

MASSET

PB *Masset* was a wood-hulled vessel. She was launched and christened RCMP *Masset* by Mrs G. Pearkes, wife of the Honourable George R. Pearkes, Minister of National Defence, on February 15, 1958 in B.C. This is another of the new type single engine Detachment Class Patrol Boats built for operating in rough waters, where considerable debris from logging and fishing may be encountered. She served in Campbell River on Vancouver Island in British Columbia until turned over to CADC in 1974 and sold. She was subsequently renamed *Great Escape*.

Courtesy Kenn Haycock

Name: ML 2/Tahsis
Year Built: 1954
Built By: Fosters Shipyard, Victoria, British Columbia
In Service: 1954 - 1971
Dimensions: 33 x 9.2 x 4.8
Type: Detachment class
Cost: $10,678
Power: Single 105 hp Chrysler Crown M47
Displacement: 25 GT
Speed: 10 kts
Crew: 2
Official Number:
Radio Call Sign:
RCMP Number: MP 80
Code: 200-80

ML 2/TAHSIS

PB *ML 2* was a wood-hulled vessel built for the RCMP as part of the reconstruction process in 1954 for 'E' Division (British Columbia). She operated out of Powell River. In 1962 the *ML 2* was transferred to the RCMP Marine Division, and had her name changed to *Tahsis*. At the time she was serving in the Port Alice area, but in August 1964 she was moved to Tahsis on the west coast of Vancouver Island. She served in the area until December 13, 1971 when she was declared surplus and went to CADC for disposal. *Tahsis* was a sister ship to *ML 1/Westview*.

Name: ML 6
Year Built: 1928
Built By: Hoffar Beaching Shipyards Ltd., Vancouver, British Columbia
In Service: 1950 - 1959
Dimensions: 45 x 11 x 5.5
Type: Patrol boat
Cost:
Power: 75 hp Buda diesel
Displacement: 22 GT
Speed: 9 kts
Crew: 2
Official Number: 154828
Radio Call Sign:
RCMP Number: MP 73
Code: 200-73

ML 6

PB *ML 6* was a British Columbia Provincial Police boat, opposite page, that served in the Gulf Islands. In 1950 she was taken over by the RCMP and assigned the number MP 73. She served out of Ganges on Salt Spring Island on the west coast of British Columbia until declared surplus and sold in 1959. She was renamed *Dali-Anne*.

Courtesy Don Klancher

Courtesy Don Klancher

Name: ML 9
Year Built: 1930
Built By: John Stockland, New Westminster, B.C.
In Service: 1950 - 1958
Dimensions: 41 x 10.5 x 5.2
Type: Patrol boat
Cost:
Power: 145 hp Norberg Knight Marine 6 cyl gasoline
Displacement: 17 GT
Speed: 9 kts
Crew: 2
Official Number: 156473
Radio Call Sign:
RCMP Number: MP 74
Code: 200-74

ML 9

RCMP PB *ML 9* was a British Columbia Provincial Police boat that served at Ocean Falls, British Columbia and was taken over by the RCMP in 1950 and assigned the number MP 74, then served out of Campbell River and Powell River on the west coast of B.C. She was turned over to CADC June 4, 1958 and sold. She was renamed *Redcoat* and moved by her owner to Kamloops, British Columbia around 1993. She was renamed *Sea Viper* at a later date.

Name: ML 10
Year Built: 1932
Built By: W.R. Menchions, Vancouver, B.C.
In Service: 1950 - 1957
Dimensions: 29 x 9 x 5
Type: Patrol boat
Cost:
Power: Single Marlin Norberg, 6 cyl 110 hp gasoline engine
Displacement: 9 GT
Speed: 7 kts
Crew: 1
Official Number: 157108
Radio Call Sign:
RCMP Number: MP 75
Code: 200-75

ML 10

RCMP PB *ML 10* was a British Columbia Provincial Police boat that served in B.C. and was taken over by the RCMP in 1950. She served out of Port Alice on Vancouver Island until around 1957.

Courtesy BC Archives e-04176

Courtesy Doug Scattergood

Name: ML 15
Year Built: 1939
Built By: Armstrong Brothers, Victoria, B.C.
In Service: 1950 - 1959
Dimensions: 63 x 15.5 x 6
Type: Patrol boat
Cost:
Power: 120 hp Vivian 6 cylinder gasoline engine
Displacement: 49 GT
Speed: 10 kts
Crew: 3
Official Number: 171629
Radio Call Sign:
RCMP Number: MP 76
Code: 200-76

ML 15

RCMP PB *ML 15* was a British Columbia Provincial Police boat that served at Alert Bay, B.C. and was taken over by the RCMP in 1950. She served out of Port Alice on Vancouver Island in B.C. until around 1957. She was turned over to CADC on March 5, 1959. They sold her to a private owner who operated her as a pleasure yacht out of Ladysmith, British Columbia under the name *Blue Fjord*.

Courtesy BC Archives b-09521

ML 16

PB *ML 16* was a British Columbia Provincial Police boat that served in Tofino, B.C. and was taken over by the RCMP in 1950. She served out of Port Alberni on the west coast of Vancouver Island until around 1957 then moved to Prince Rupert on the north coast of the province. She was turned over to CADC in 1959 and sold. Subsequently she was renamed *Sea Comet*.

Name: ML 16
Year Built: 1944
Built By: Star Shipyards (Mercers Ltd.), New Westminster, B.C.
In Service: 1950 - 1959
Dimensions: 60 x 16 x 5
Type: Patrol boat
Cost:
Power: Vivian diesel 6 cyl 150 hp
Displacement: 51 GT
Speed:
Crew: 4
Official Number: 177994
Radio Call Sign:
RCMP Number: MP 77
Code: 200-77

Name: ML 17
Year Built: 1948
Built By: W.R. Menchion's Shipyard, Vancouver, B.C.
In Service: 1950 - 1959
Dimensions: 50 x 13.5 x 5.5
Type: Patrol boat
Cost:
Power: Vivian diesel 6 cyl 105 hp
Displacement: 31 GT
Speed: 9 kts
Crew: 2
Official Number: 312838
Radio Call Sign:
RCMP Number: MP 78
Code: 200-78

Courtesy Vancouver Maritime Museum

ML 17

PB *ML 17* was a British Columbia Provincial Police boat that served in British Columbia and was taken over by the RCMP in 1950. She served out of Ocean Falls, B.C. until she was turned over to CADC on December 30, 1959. She was taken over by the Provincial Fish and Game Branch of the Department of Recreation and Conservation then by the B.C. Forest Service in Prince Rupert and renamed *Otter*. At a later date she was renamed *Poplar III*.

Courtesy RCMP Historical Collections Unit

MOOSE JAW

PB *Moose Jaw* was one of five vessels constructed specially for Expo 67. Other vessels used in Expo 67 included *Dauphin, Lac La Ronge, Brule, Wood* and *Athabaska*. She was a wood-hulled vessel and after Expo 67 was stationed at Hamilton, Ontario. In June 1970 she was transferred to the West Coast where she served out of the Pender Harbour, British Columbia area until September 28, 1972 when she was turned over to CADC for disposal.

Name: Moose Jaw
Year Built: 1966
Built By: J.J. Taylor & Sons Ltd., Toronto, Ontario
In Service: 1967 – 1972
Dimensions: 36 ft
Type: Detachment class
Cost: $35,500
Power: Twin 290 hp Chrysler engines
Displacement:
Speed:
Crew: 2
Official Number:
Radio Call Sign:
RCMP Number: MP 43
Code: 200-43

Name: Moosomin II
Year Built: 1958
Built By: J.J. Taylor & Sons Ltd., Toronto, Ontario
In Service: 1958 – 1979
Dimensions: 50.3 x 13 x 3.3
Type: Detachment class
Cost: $65,970
Power: Four 215 hp Dearborn Interceptor engines
Displacement: 28 GT
Speed:
Crew: 4
Official Number:
Radio Call Sign:
RCMP Number: MP 96
Code: 200-96

Courtesy RCMP Historical Collections Unit

MOOSOMIN II

PB *Moosomin II* was a wood-hulled vessel built in 1958 in Toronto, Ontario and served the Montreal, Quebec area until she was disposed of in 1979. There was a major engine change from the original gas engines to diesel in 1967, thereby increasing her patrol range and safety.

Courtesy RCMP Historical Collections Unit

Name: Nanaimo
Year Built: 1956
Built By: McKay-Cormack Limited, Victoria, British Columbia
In Service: 1957 – 1973
Dimensions: 64.9 x 15.4 x 5.4
Type: Detachment class
Cost: $139,535
Power: Single 400 hp Cummins diesel engines
Displacement: 44 GT
Speed:
Crew: 4
Official Number:
Radio Call Sign:
RCMP Number: MP 87
Code: 200-87

NANAIMO

PB *Nanaimo* was a wood-hulled vessel commissioned on March 7, 1957 and launched by Mrs C.W. Harvison, wife of Assistant Commissioner Harvison. The vessel operated mainly out of Prince Rupert and Campbell River, British Columbia as a floating detachment and patrolled from the Alaska Border to Caamano Sound. She was declared surplus July 11, 1973 and turned over to CADC for disposal. Photograph on opposite page.

Courtesy Gilles Gagne

Name: Nicholson
Year Built: 1968
Built By: Smith & Rhuland Limited, Lunenburg, Nova Scotia
In Service: 1968 – 1976
Dimensions: 75 ft
Type: Class 1
Cost: $244,339
Power: Twin Cummins VT 12-700 M diesel engines
Displacement:
Speed: 14 kts
Crew: 4
Official Number:
Radio Call Sign: CGRA
RCMP Number: MP 49
Code: 200-49

NICHOLSON

PB *Nicholson* was a wood-hulled vessel built in Nova Scotia and served on the East Coast out of Charlottetown, Prince Edward Island until 1976. Her commissioning, June 5, 1968 was sponsored by Mrs L.H. Nicholson, wife of Commissioner Nicholson (Retd). This was the second Centennial vessel built. She was declared surplus to requirements and disposed of through CADC following the 1976 Olympics. She was transferred to the Canadian Forces as CFAV Nicholson, pennant PB196, and served as such until 1992.

MP 49

Opposite: Patrol boat Nicholson *was built of wood in Lunenburg, Nova Scotia and served on the East Coast from 1968 to 1976.*
Far right: Tahsis Narrows, B.C. in the patrol area of the Port Alice.

Name: Point May
Year Built: 1934
Built By: John Kendell, Morrisville Bay d'Espoir, Newfoundland
In Service: 1949 (not commissioned)
Dimensions: 53 x 15.9 x 5.6
Type: Motor boat
Cost:
Power: 88 hp Kelvin diesel
Displacement: 30.87 GT
Speed:
Official Number: 159122
Radio Call Sign:
RCMP Number:

Name: Port Alice
Year Built: 1960
Built By: Star Shipyard (Mercer's) Limited, New Westminster, B.C.
In Service: 1960 – 1968
Dimensions: 26 x 9 x 2.5
Type: Motor boat
Cost: $9,830
Power: Single 215 hp Interceptor engine
Displacement: 5 GT
Speed:
Crew: 1
Official Number: 14K-11140
Radio Call Sign:
RCMP Number: MP 58
Code: 200-58

POINT MAY

When the RCMP took over the policing duties in Newfoundland April 1, 1949 they inherited two vessels from the government. The *Point May* was one of those vessels but was never commissioned by the RCMP and rather turned over to CADC for disposal on June 1, 1949. She was transferred to the Minister of Fisheries on September 3, 1949.

Courtesy RCMP Historical Collections Unit

PORT ALICE

MB *Port Alice* was a wood-hulled vessel, She served on the West Coast out of Tahsis, British Columbia. Her patrol area was from Zeballos to Gold River. In August 1964 she was transferred to Port Alice. She was declared surplus on February 2, 1968 after which she was sold by CDAC on March 29, 1968.

Courtesy RCMP Historical Collections Unit

Name: Reliance (3)
Year Built: 1966
Built By: Canoe Cove Mfg Ltd., Sidney, B.C.
In Service: 1966 – 1975
Dimensions: 26 x 9.9 x 2'3
Type: Detachment class
Cost: $14,675
Power: Twin 150 hp Mercruiser gas engines
Displacement: 4.38 GT
Speed: 32 mph
Crew: 2
Official Number: 14K 26857
Radio Call Sign:
RCMP Number: MP 47
Code: 200-47

Name: Shaunavon II
Year Built: 1955
Built By: J.J. Taylor & Sons Limited, Toronto, Ont
In Service: 1956 - 1972
Dimensions: 50.2 x 13 x 3.2
Type: Detachment class
Cost: $61,115
Power: Twin 350 hp Scripps gas engines
Displacement: 28 GT
Speed:
Crew: 4
Official Number:
Radio Call Sign:
RCMP Number: MP 85
Code: 200-85

RELIANCE (3)

PB *Reliance* was a fibreglass-hulled vessel purchased on August 12, 1966 that served in the Sicamous area of British Columbia until May 1968 when she was transferred to Fort St James. The detachment at Fort St James used her to visit the isolated First Nations reserves and lodgings on Stuart, Trembleur and Takla Lakes in B.C. until 1975 when she was sent to CADC. She was a sister ship to the vessel *Athabaska*.

Courtesy RCMP Historical Collections Unit

SHAUNAVON II

PB *Shaunavon II* was a wood-hulled vessel built to replace the original vessel by the same name. *Shaunavon II* served in the Great Lakes out of Toronto, Ontario until June 1, 1972 when she was turned over to CADC for disposal.

SHULAMITE

When the RCMP took over the policing duties in Newfoundland in 1949 they inherited two vessels from the government. The *Shulamite* was one of those vessels and was never commissioned by the RCMP but rather turned over to CADC for disposal in June that year. When she was sold she was renamed *Norsyp*. She was a former rum runner and a sister ship to a vessel called *Marvita*. She was beached and scrapped in 1965.

Name: Shulamite
Year Built: 1930
Built By: John McLean & Sons Ltd., Mahone, Nova Scotia
In Service: 1949 (not commissioned)
Dimensions: 105 x 20 x 8.4
Type: Motor boat
Cost:
Power: Fairbanks diesel 420 hp
Displacement: 122 GT
Speed:
Official Number: 156692
Radio Call Sign:
RCMP Number:
Code:

Name: Sidney
Year Built: 1959
Built By: A.C. Benson Shipyard, Vancouver, British Columbia
In Service: 1959 – 1976
Dimensions: 55 x 13.8 x 7.7
Type: Detachment class
Cost: $120,751
Power: G.M. Model 6022T & 6023T engines
Displacement: 22 GT
Speed: 11 kts
Crew: 4
Official Number: 819426
Radio Call Sign: CGQT
RCMP Number: MP 53
Code: 200-53

Courtesy RCMP Historical Collections Unit

SIDNEY

PB *Sidney* was a wood-hulled vessel built in 1959 in Vancouver, British Columbia and served in the Ganges, Salt Spring Island, B.C. area. She was launched and christened by Mrs Bordeleau, wife of Superintendent J.R.W. Bordeleau August 3, 1959. On March 17, 1976 she was turned over to the Canadian Forces who renamed her CFAV SIDNEY, pennant number PB195. There she served until 1993.

Right: Ganges Harbour and the adjacent town on Salt Spring Island, B.C., where the Patrol Boat Sidney *served.*

Courtesy RCMP Historical Collections Unit

Name: Slideout (2)
Year Built: 1966
Built By: J.J. Taylor & Sons Ltd., Toronto, Ontario
In Service: 1966 – 1976
Dimensions: 29 x 9.5 x 3
Type: Detachment class
Cost: $22,100
Power: Twin Volvo Penta gas engines
Displacement: 8 GT
Speed:
Crew: 2
Official Number:
Radio Call Sign:
RCMP Number: MP 41
Code: 200-41

SLIDEOUT (2)

PB *Slideout* was a wood-hulled boat specially built for Expo 67 in Montreal, Quebec. After Expo the *Slideout* was transferred to Kelowna, British Columbia for duties on Okanagan Lake. In 1976 she was declared surplus to requirements and transferred to CADC and sold. She was a sister ship to the *Battleford*. This was the second vessel of the same name.

Name: Sorel
Year Built: 1959
Built By: Norse Boat Co., Penetanguishene, Ontario
In Service: 1959 – 1971
Dimensions: 26 ft
Type: Motor boat
Cost: $13,130
Power: Single 240 hp Interceptor
Displacement:
Speed:
Crew: 2
Official Number:
Radio Call Sign:
RCMP Number: MP 55

Courtesy RCMP Historical Collections Unit

SOREL

MB *Sorel* was a wood-hulled vessel that served in Sorel, Lachine and Ìsle Perrot, in the Quebec area under command 'C' Division until August 4, 1971 when she was declared surplus and sent to CADC.

Courtesy Gilles Gagne

Opposite: Patrol Boat Standoff *(2), accompanied by RCMP helicopter CF-MPZ, on patrol off the Newfoundland coast.* Standoff *was based in Burin, Newfoundland to carry out Customs and Excise patrols to limit liquor being smuggled from the French island of St Pierre.*

STANDOFF (2)

PB *Standoff* was a wood-hulled vessel built in Nova Scotia and served on the East Coast out of Charlottetown, Prince Edward Island until 1978. She was considered the first Centennial boat and was a sister ship of the *Nicholson* and *Centennial*. Mrs R.C. Butt, wife of Inspector Butt, sponsored her christening June 26, 1966. She served out of Halifax, Nova Scotia and Burin, Newfoundland until 1978. She was turned over to the Canadian Forces on March 11, 1980. They renamed her CFAV Standoff, pennant number PB199 and used her as tender to HMCS Cabot. She was paid off May 14, 1997. She was the second vessel of this name.

Name: Standoff (2)
Year Built: 1966
Built By: Smith & Rhuland Limited, Lunenburg, Nova Scotia
In Service: 1966 – 1980
Dimensions: 75 x 17
Type: Class 1
Cost: $224,414
Power: Twin Cummins VT12 – 700 M diesel engines
Displacement: 69.69 GT
Speed: 14 kts
Crew: 4
Official Number:
Radio Call Sign: CGMU
RCMP Number: MP 40
Code: 200-40

Opposite page: RCMP vessel MP 51 Tofino. *The small photo shows it and MP 87* Nanaimo, *on patrol on the west coast of British Columbia.*

Name: Tagish II
Year Built: 1957
Built By: Grew Boat Works Ltd., Penetanguishene, Ontario
In Service: 1957 – 1971
Dimensions: 50.3 x 13 x 3.3
Type: Detachment class
Cost: $56,650
Power: Twin 350 hp Scripps gas engines
Displacement: 28 GT
Speed:
Crew: 4
Official Number:
Radio Call Sign:
RCMP Number: MP 89
Code: 200-89

Courtesy RCMP Historical Collections Unit

TAGISH II

PB *Tagish II* was a wood-hulled vessel built to replace the original *Tagish*. She was built in 1957 and is a sister ship to the *Carnduff II*. The *Tagish II* served out of Sarnia, Ontario for patrol work from the St Clair River to Tobermory. She was declared surplus on May 7, 1971 and sent to CADC.

TOFINO

PB *Tofino* was another 65-foot wood-hulled vessel constructed for the RCMP in British Columbia, and launched on July 7, 1959. Her launch and christening was sponsored by Mrs Lemieux, wife of A/Commissioner J.R. Lemieux. The *Tofino* served out of Ocean Falls on the central coast from Caamano Sound to Margaret Bay until December 10, 1976 when she was turned over to CADC and replaced by the 25-foot *Outlook*.

Courtesy RCMP Historical Collections Unit

Name: Tofino
Year Built: 1959
Built By: Star Shipyard (Mercer's) Ltd., New Westminster, B.C.
In Service: 1959 – 1976
Dimensions: 65 x 15 x 6.5
Type: Detachment class
Cost: $132,257
Power: Two 600 hp GM turbo charged Series 71 diesel, single screw
Displacement: 47.5 GT
Speed: 16 kts
Crew: 4
Official Number:
Radio Call Sign:
RCMP Number: MP 51
Code: 200-51

Courtesy RCMP Historical Collections Unit

Courtesy RCMP Historical Collections Unit

Name: Valleyfield
Year Built: 1959
Built By: Grew Boat Works Ltd., Penetanguishene, Ontario
In Service: 1959 – 1968
Dimensions: 26 ft
Type: Motor boat
Cost: $13,304
Power: Single 240 hp Interceptor
Displacement:
Speed: Crew: 1
Official Number:
Radio Call Sign:
RCMP Number: MP 56
Code: 200-56

VALLEYFIELD

MB *Valleyfield* was a wood-hulled vessel that served in the Valleyfield/Île Perrot, Quebec area until July 10, 1968 when she was declared surplus and sent to CADC.

Opposite: RCMP vessel MP 51 Tofino *on the West Coast. Details on page 235. Right: This historic photograph of the* Tofino *was taken at Ocean Falls, British Columbia.*

Courtesy Gilles Gagne

VALLEYFIELD II

PB *Valleyfield II* was a wood-hulled vessel built to replace the smaller, 26-foot *Valleyfield*. She was accepted by the Force at Valleyfield, Quebec on June 26, 1968. She served in the Valleyfield/Ville de l 'Île-Perrot, Quebec area until 1976 when she was declared surplus and transferred to CADC for disposal.

Name: Valleyfield II
Year Built: 1968
Built By: J.J. Taylor & Sons Ltd., Toronto, Ontario
In Service: 1968 – 1976
Dimensions: 36 x 9
Type: Detachment class
Cost: $39,500
Power: Twin 290 hp Chrysler engines
Displacement: 16.98 GT
Speed:
Official Number:
Radio Call Sign:
RCMP Number: MP 35
Code: 200-35

Name: Victoria
Year Built: 1957
Built By: Yarrows Shipyard Ltd., Victoria, British Columbia
In Service: 1957 – 1970
Dimensions: 92 x 17.5 x 6.6
Type: Fort class
Cost: $415,000
Power: Twin 550 hp Cummins diesel engines
Displacement: 85 GT
Speed:
Crew: 14
Official Number:
Radio Call Sign: CGMS
RCMP Number: MP 31
Code: 200-31

Courtesy Don Klancher

VICTORIA

PV *Victoria* was built for the RCMP as a steel-hulled version of the Bird Class patrol boats designed and used by the RCN when they built the *Blue Heron* (MP 32 shown at right). She was the first vessel to pass over the infamous Ripple Rock in Seymour Narrows on the Alaska cruise ship route after the blast that removed a large section of the tip of the reef. She served on the west coast of British Columbia until turned over to CADC on March 12, 1970.

Courtesy RCMP Historical Collections Unit

WESTVIEW/ML 1

The PB *ML 1* was a wood-hulled vessel built for the RCMP as part of the reconstruction process in 1953 for 'E' Division. Mrs NcNaught, wife of Special Constable McNaught, mechanical supervisor for 'E' Division (British Columbia), commissioned her September 16, 1954. In 1961 the *ML 1* was transferred to the RCMP Marine Division. In 1962 her name was changed to *Westview*. At the time she was serving in the Zeballos area, but was moved to the Westview and Gibsons area until November 5, 1970 when she was declared surplus and sent to CADC for disposal.

Name: Westview/ML 1
Year Built: 1953
Built By: McKay- Cormack Ltd., Victoria, British Columbia
In Service: 1953 - 1970
Dimensions: 33 x 9.2 x 4.8
Type: Detachment class
Cost: $10,678
Power: Single 105 hp Chrysler Crown M47
Displacement: 25 GT
Speed: 10 kts
Crew: 2
Official Number:
Radio Call Sign:
RCMP Number: MP 79
Code: 200-79

Opposite: The Quebec-built MP 17 Wood *ended up being used by a private owner for illegal activities.*

WOOD

PV *Wood* was a steel-hulled vessel built for the RCMP and was based out of Halifax, Nova Scotia. Mrs S. T. Wood, wife of Commissioner Wood (Rtd), christened her June 28, 1958. She served the RCMP Marine Division until January 16, 1970 when she was transferred to the Coast Guard and renamed *Daring*. She patrolled the East Coast waters for the Coast Guard until she was sold in 1985. Her new owner got involved in the illicit drug trade and she was seized in 1987 in Guatemala for drug importation.

The *Wood* was the largest vessel constructed by the RCMP.

Name: Wood
Year Built: 1958
Built By: George T. Davie & Sons Ltd., Lauzon, Quebec
In Service: 1958 - 1970
Dimensions: 178 x 29 x 9.5
Type: Commissioner class
Cost: $1,350,833
Power: Twin 1330 hp Fairbanks Morse
Displacement: 700 GT
Speed: 16 kts
Crew: 37
Armament: 3 PDR Hotchkiss guns
Official Number: 331714
Radio Call Sign: CGMW
RCMP Number: MP 17
Code: 200-17

MP 17
XVII
XVI
XV
XIV

An RCMP offficer of the Marine Services goes ashore during a patrol off Haida Gwaii, B.C. to view the totems at SGang Gwaay World Heritage Site.

Chapter Five

The RCMP Marine Services

The RCMP Marine Section controlled most of the Marine assets of the RCMP from 1932 to 1939 and 1945 to 1946, as did the RCMP Marine Division from 1947 to 1970. They focused on patrols for rum runners, contraband, search and rescue, boating safety, detachment assistance and special event security in the Great Lakes and on both of Canada's coasts. Before 1932 there was a small fleet of vessels that patrolled the Arctic, lakes and rivers of Canada's north, and these played an important role in supplying outposts of the RCMP. These vessels carried on throughout the formation of the Marine Section and Marine Division. They were not part of these larger departments but were managed by them and considered Divisional assets.

Many of these Divisional vessels were very small runabouts and not remarkable in any way, but there were a few larger vessels that should be listed. Wear and tear on these craft was considerably less than on the ocean-going vessels so they lasted years longer. After the RCMP Marine Division was well established, the vessel replacement program also considered replacements for Division vessels. In the early 1950s new vessels were being built, mainly in Nova Scotia, for many of the Divisions.

Seven vessels built in Nova Scotia for service in the Arctic were the 32-footers *Alexander Fiord*, *Herschel Island* and *Fort Chimo*, the 45-foot *Aklavik* (2), the 30-foot *Craig Harbour*, the 24-foot *Liard* and the 47-foot *Eskimo Point*. These were suitable additions to the old MV *Bylot*, already in the north.

Some of the vessels built for 'B' Division in Newfoundland included the 35-footers *St Anthony*, *Hawke Bay, Battle Harbour, Hampden, Cartwright, Red Bay, Hopedale* and *Port Saunders*.

One vessel built for 'A' Division in 1958 was the 35-footer called *Moose Factory* which served in Moose Factory, Ontario.

In the Commissioner's Report for 1961, discussed in the previous chapter, there was a total of 73 vessels within the RCMP, operated by 232 members. The Northwest Territories which had the largest contingent of Division vessels, had its resources cut almost in half from 27 vessels to 14 by 1965.

Shortly after the RCMP Marine Division was terminated in 1970 its vessels were turned over to the individual provinces which then became responsible for maintaining and crewing them. Soon the number of vessels diminished. Beginning with the largest and most expensive, the vessels were turned over to other departments such as the Canadian Coast Guard or the Royal Canadian Navy and others were just sold off. By the end of 1972, of the 41 vessels in service in 1970, there were 31 remaining in the various RCMP divisions throughout Canada. Of these 31 vessels, nine had been built within the previous two years.

The 31 former Marine Division vessels scattered throughout the country were distributed as follows:

'A' Division (Ottawa, Ontario): *Brule, Outlook* and *Yellowknife*

'B' Division (Newfoundland): *Acadian* and *Standoff*

'C' Division (Quebec): *Captor, Lac La Ronge* and *Valleyfield*

'D' Division (Manitoba): *Moosomin II*

'E' Division (British Columbia): *Athabasca, Slideout, Tofino, Advance, Reliance, Dufferin, Alert, Ganges, Pearkes, Regina, Little Bow II, Masset,* and *Sidney*

'H' Division (Nova Scotia): *Fort MacLeod, Fort Steele, Adversus* and *Interceptor*

'J' Division (New Brunswick): *Detector*

'L' Division (Prince Edward Island): *Nicholson*

'O' Division (London, Ontario): *Dawson, Whitehorse* and *Manyberries*

Five new vessels were constructed in 1973 (RCMP Centennial Year). These were the *Harvison, Centennial, Duncan, McClellan,* and *Rivett Carnac* which would be the last new vessels until 1986. As vessels became older it appears most Divisions were not prepared to pay for replacements of the larger craft, but were satisfied with utilizing the smaller one- and two-man vessels for local needs. These boats did not require specially trained officers or skippers with Transport Canada certificates of competency. Most detachments sent interested members on a special in-house 'Basic Water Transport' course to introduce them to the skills of small boat operations. The RCMP provided members with small vessels which met most detachment needs for patrol work in their duty area. Search and rescue missions were now carried out by the rapidly expanding Canadian Coast Guard and their auxiliary vessels. Rum running was a crime of the past and other government agencies like Canada Customs and Excise and the Department of Fisheries had their own resources.

From 1970 to 1973 the administration and implementation of RCMP policy was still maintained by RCMP Headquarters under a Marine Services Directorate. In 1974 the Directorate's responsibilities were transferred to the new Transport Management Branch of the Services and Supply Directorate. This negated the RCMP policy of issuing 'MP' numbers to vessels and explains why all vessels after that date did not display such identification.

By 1983 the Divisional Marine Services of the RCMP had only 12 patrol vessels over eight metres in length. Two of these were on the East Coast, one was in the Great Lakes and eight were on the West Coast. The patrol vessels were rated as Class I, II, and III. The *Centennial* was a 75-foot Class I wood-hulled ship on the East Coast. The *Pearkes* and *Rivett Carnac* were 53-foot Class II fibreglass vessels on the West Coast. Additional 41-foot Class II fiberglass vessels were the *McClellan*, *Harvison*, *Regina* and *Manyberries* on the West Coast and the *Fort McLeod* on the East Coast. There were also the old 35-foot *Advance* and the 28-foot *Duncan* on the West Coast. On the Great Lakes there was a 25-foot boat, *Outlook,* which was the smallest of the craft.

The Divisions had over 300 small vessels to operate on the lakes, rivers and ocean shorelines. These were 15- to 30-foot rigid hulled inflatables (RHIBs), fibreglass runabouts and aluminum-hulled coastal vessels.

Since 1973 only one vessel of a notable size had been built for RCMP Marine functions, the *Stikine*. She was built in 1986 for operations during Expo '86 in Vancouver, B.C.

Soon a new dimension in vessel size and type was to take place. This saw the introduction of the aluminum catamaran police patrol boat. In the early 1990s it was decided to replace the numerous coastal vessels with even fewer but slightly larger, aluminum catamarans. This was to take place mainly in 'E' Division on the West Coast of Canada since most other Divisions had lost many of their large marine assets.

The new aluminum catamarans were named after former commissioners of the RCMP. They were approximately 65 feet long (about19 metres) and had about a three-foot draft, meaning they could travel in water as shallow as five feet. Powered by two 820 horsepower MAN diesel engines they had a cruising speed of over 30 knots. With a beam of 22 feet they were a stable platform for operations requiring large amounts of equipment or personnel like dive teams or Emergency Response Teams. Instead of rudders these ships had surface piercing propellers on Arneson articulating drives. This made maneuvering easy and produced the recognizable rooster tail when running at speed.

Four catamarans were based on the west coast of British Columbia. The first catamaran was the Patrol Vessel (PV) *Nadon* which was built in 1991 and stationed in Port McNeil. The second was the PV *Higgitt* built in 1992 and stationed in Prince Rupert. Shortly afterwards the PV *Lindsay* was built and based in Vancouver. When the PV *Inkster* was built it was 10 feet longer and more suitable for open water than its sister ships, so it went to Prince Rupert to replace the *Higgitt* which moved to Port Alberni, B.C.

The East Coast had the catamaran PV *Simmonds*, based in Marystown, Newfoundland. She patrolled the waters of the Gulf of St Lawrence, the fishing banks and waters close to the French islands of Saint-Pierre and Miquelon. In 2005 she was turned over to the Canadian Coast Guard who operated her with RCMP officers on board as the enforcement body on the Great Lakes. The next one, built in 2003, was called the PV *Murray* which replaced the PV *Simmonds* in Newfoundland.

Responsibility for the RCMP Marine assets changed over the next few years. In 1994 the Transport Management Branch was incorporated as Fleet Program Administration, Material & Services Management Branch. By the year 1997 the Marine Services of the RCMP consisted of only four catamarans for the west coast of Canada and one catamaran for the East Coast. On the West Coast these vessels operated independently in their zones.

In September 1998 one West Coast catamaran, the *Nadon*, was removed from service, taken out of the water and placed on shore blocks. The crews were reduced by half, with many of the members reassigned to shore detachments. The West Coast Marine Services now consisted of three vessels with one crew of four members per vessel. The four catamarans then represented the entire police marine assets on the oceans and Great Lakes of Canada. This was considerably smaller than the former 33 vessels of the RCMP Marine Section or the 48 vessels of the RCMP Marine Division.

A 22-foot Titan aluminum detachment transport vessel at Pender Islands in B.C.

Courtesy RCMP West Coast Marine Services

The RCMP patrol vessel Nadon *in Kingcome Inlet, British Columbia, supporting the Kids Don't Float water safety program. L-R: Cst Mike Schmeisser, Cst Paul McIntosh and Cst Greg Hepner. Photograph courtesy of Cpl John May.*

During the next few months several major events occurred which taxed the assets of the RCMP Marine Services. First a Swissair Flight 111 jumbo aircraft crashed in the water off the east coast of Nova Scotia in September 1998. RCMP investigators assisted Transport Canada with their investigation and the recovery of numerous exhibits and aircraft parts. Secondly a large quantity of drugs was seized from the ocean-going fishing vessel *Blue Dawn* in November 1998 on the West Coast. The third incident involved the capture on August 1999, on the West Coast, of several Asian vessels with illegal immigrants aboard. These events led to the formation of a new RCMP West Coast Marine Detachment located in Nanaimo, B.C. in February 2000.

In the year 2000 the Vancouver Maritime Museum and the RCMP joined in a fund-raising venture to help preserve the original RCMP *St Roch* schooner on display at the museum. The *Nadon*, also referred to as the *St Roch II*, for the duration of the voyage, circumnavigated North America and brought international awareness of the RCMP marine operations, its cherished history, and its presence on all three coasts of Canada.

In September 2001 a world event which is now referred to as '9/11' occurred in the United States. The threat of international terrorism was now present in North America. This event reinforced the need for an operational marine presence on the three coasts, the St Lawrence Seaway and the Great Lakes of Canada. New and additional vessels were scheduled to add to the inventory for use in joint border patrols. In 2003 Fleet Program Administration, Material & Services Management Branch was incorporated into the new Assets & Procurement Branch, Corporate Management & Comptrollership.

RCMP West Coast Marine Services 2006

Courtesy RCMP West Coast Marine Services

Front Row sitting (L-R): Cpl John May, Sgt Mike Lariviere, Cheryl Dean, Ken Bedell, S/Sgt Bryan Gordon, Superintendent Byron Boucher, Wendy McLeod, Sandy Machan, Sgt Peter Attrell, Sgt Andy Brinton, Cpl Richard Harry. Rear Row standing: Cst Greg Hepner, Cst Mark Futter, Cst Rob Pikola, Cst John Stringer, Cst Chris Pillsworth, Cst Carl-Eric Lippke, Cst Clarence Dykema, Cst Carl Tulk, Cst Cal Keir, Cst Todd Eppler, Cst Mike Schmeisser, Cst Gene Kikcio, Cst Blake Ward, Cst Dave Kokesch, Cst Chris Caldwell, Missing: Cst Paul McIntosh, Cst Trevor Murray, Cst Kenn Haycock, Cst Bryan Valentine, Cst Ryan Scrase, Cst Sean Phillip.

Divisional Vessels of the RCMP 1945 to 2005

As wood made way for the new construction material—fibreglass and aluminum—modern patrol boats as we have come to know them today emerged from the shipbuilding yards. A well-appointed police patrol boat appears on the scene as one with good engineering, high speed capabilities, modern electronics and relative comfort for its crews.

Name: Aklavik II/Jennings
Year Built: 1954
Built By: W.W. Robar, Upper LaHave, N.S.
In Service: 1954 – 1969
Dimensions: 45 x 11 x 5
Type: Schooner
Cost: $19,000
Power: Single 83 hp General Motors
Displacement: 19.36 GT
Speed: 9 kts
Official Number: 810532
Radio Call Sign:
Code: 7311

Name: Alexandra Fiord
Year Built: 1954
Built By: W.W. Robar, Upper LaHave, N.S.
In Service: 1954 – 1964
Dimensions: 32 ft
Type: Motor
Cost: $5,477.00
Power: 1-35 hp Acadia Marine
Displacement:
Speed:
Official Number: 2H-4885

AKLAVIK II/JENNINGS

The *Akalavik II* was a wood-hulled motor/sail boat built in 1954 that served in Aklavik in the Northwest Territories. She was a 'G' Division vessel. Superintendent Henry Larsen supervised her construction. She was taken by train to Hay River in the Northwest Territories where she was launched. In 1960 she was renamed *Jennings* and in 1965 sent to the Coppermine Detachment. She was declared surplus in 1969 and sent to CADC where she was sold and re-named *Amoulik*. In 1982 she was purchased by a Mr Larry Whittaker and renamed *Fort Hearne* (seen in the photograph above). In 2000 Captain Whittaker used the *Fort Hearne* to escort the *St Roch II* in and out of Coppermine as part of the 'St Roch II-Voyage of Rediscovery.' She was still in service as a private cargo vessel in April 2010.

ALEXANDRA FIORD

The *Alexandra Fiord* was a wood-hulled motor boat built for 'G' Division and based out of Alexandra Fiord, Northwest Territories until 1964. She was in service for 10 years.

BYLOT

Name: Bylot
Year Built:
Year Built:
In Service: c. 1970
Dimensions:
Type: Motor boat
Cost:
Power:
Displacement:
Speed:
Official Number:
Radio Call Sign:

The photographs opposite and far right are of the RCMP MV Bylot *in Pond Inlet.*

The MV *Bylot* was probably a Division vessel and operated out of Pond Inlet in the Northwest Territories. The photographs of her, opposite and right, were taken about 1970.

Courtesy Don Klancher

CARTWRIGHT

Name: Cartwright
Year Built: 1955
Built By: Nova Scotia Yacht & Boat Builders Ltd., Mahone Bay, N.S.
In Service: 1955 – 1969
Dimensions: 35 x 9.3 x 4
Type: Raised deck motor boat
Cost: $7,177
Power: Single 35 hp Acadia Marine
Displacement:
Speed:
Official Number:
Radio Call Sign:
Code: B513-2

The *Cartwright* was a wood-hulled vessel constructed for 'B' Division and served out of Cartwright Detachment in Labrador. By the summer of 1969 she was no longer serviceable and was sold through CADC. She was replaced by a boat hired locally. The *Cartwright* is shown in the above photograph.

Library and Archives Canada e010764878

Courtesy Gary Dalton

PV Centennial *operated as a RCMP patrol vessel on the East Coast in the 1970s and 1980s.*

Name: Centennial
Year Built: 1973
Built By: A.F. Theriault & Son, Meteghan River, Nova Scotia
In Service: 1973 – 1988
Dimensions: 75 x 17
Type: Class 1
Cost: $355,040
Power: Twin Cummins VT-12-700 M Turbo Charged diesels (509 hp each)
Displacement: 70 GT
Speed: 16 kts
Crew: 6
Official Number:
Radio Call Sign:
RCMP Number: MP 76/MP100
Code: 200-100

Courtesy RCMP Historical Collections Unit

Courtesy RCMP Historical Collections Unit

CENTENNIAL

PV *Centennial* was the third and last of the Class l wood-hulled vessels constructed for the RCMP centennial year. Mrs W. L. Higgitt, wife of Commissioner Higgitt, sponsored her christening on November 15, 1973. The ship was stationed in 'B' Division in Fortune, Newfoundland. The *Centennial* was the last single-hulled vessel of this size constructed in the 20th century and was a replacement vessel for the *Interceptor*. She was turned over to CADC in 1988.

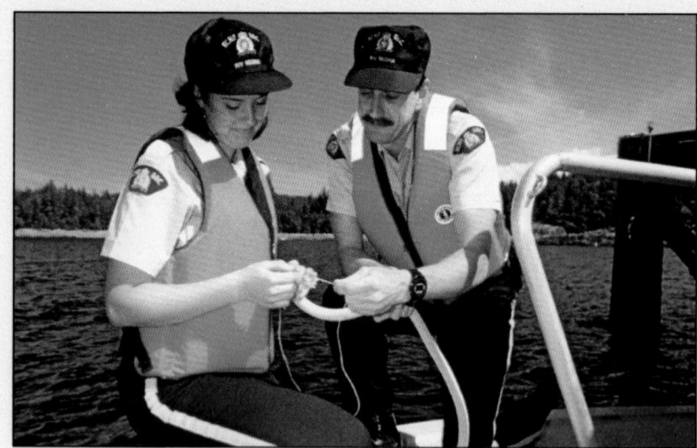

Left, top: Constable Mark Peers & summer student Sherri Campbell aboard PV Regina *at Lasquiti Island, West Coast, circa 1990.*

CRAIG HARBOUR (2)

The *Craig Harbour* was a wood-hulled motor boat built in 1956. She served in 'G' Division at Craig Harbour. She was placed on board the Department of Transport Arctic Patrol vessel *C.D. Howe* and transported to Craig Harbour in the Northwest Territories in June 1956. She was sent to Crown Assets December 15, 1969.

Name: Craig Harbour (2)
Year Built: 1956
Built By: Stright-McKay, Pictou, N.S.
In Service: 1956 - 1969
Dimensions: 30 ft
Type: Whaler
Cost: $4,042
Power: Single 35 hp Acadia Marine
Displacement:
Speed:
Official Number: 2H 4907
Radio Call Sign:
Code: G513-3

Courtesy RCMP Historical Collections Unit

DAWSON (2)

MB *Dawson* had a fibreglass Bertram hull. She was built in British Columbia but was sent east to be stationed in Sarnia, Ontario on the Great Lakes. She was the sister ship to the *Outlook*.

Name: Dawson (2)
Year Built: 1971
Built By: Canoe Cove Mfg Ltd., Sidney, British Columbia
In Service: 1971 - 1973
Dimensions: 25 ft
Type: Detachment Class
Cost: $24,091
Power: Twin 160 Mercruiser inboard/outboard motors
Displacement:
Speed:
Official Number:
Radio Call Sign:
RCMP Number: MP 38
Code: 200-38

Name: Dufferin
Year Built:
Built By: Canoe Cove Mfg Ltd., Sidney, British Columbia
In Service: 1972 - 1981
Dimensions: 41 x 14 ft
Type: Class II
Cost: $72,156
Power: Twin 210 hp Cummins diesels
Displacement: 25.01 GT
Speed:
Official Number:
Radio Call Sign:
RCMP Number: MP 74
Code: 200-74

DUFFERIN

PV *Dufferin* was a fibreglass vessel built in British Columbia. She worked out of Sidney, B.C. for a while, then in 1980 was moved to Port Alberni. She appears to be a sister ship to the *Manyberries*. The *Dufferin* was stolen February 1981 while docked in Ucluelet, British Columbia and sunk. She was salvaged but not put back into service. She was turned over to CADC and sold in 1981.

Courtesy Gary Dalton

Name: Duncan (2)
Year Built: 1973
Built By: Calgan Marine, North Vancouver, British Columbia
In Service: 1973 - 1993
Dimensions: 28 x 10 ft
Type: Class III
Cost: $37,657
Power: Single 375 hp gas engine with 1300 series Hamilton Jet
Displacement: 11 GT
Speed: 25 kts
Official Number:
Radio Call Sign:
RCMP Number: MP 20
Code: 200-20

DUNCAN (2)

PV *Duncan* was a fibreglass vessel built for 'E' Division in British Columbia and served on the West Coast near Tahsis on Vancouver Island. The *Duncan* originally had jet propulsion rather than a propeller. She was the second vessel of this name operated by the RCMP. In the summer of 1975 she was partially destroyed by fire. She was repaired and the engines changed to two 318 cubic inch Chrysler inboard engines. She served out of Tahsis, B.C. until taken out of service and turned over to CADC in 1993.

EAGLE RIVER

PV *Eagle River* was a fiberglass boat purchased for Mary's Harbour Detachment. The name Eagle River is that of the Electoral District covering the Labrador Coast and also the designated patrol area for the vessel. The area contained many isolated temporary fishing communities that were accessible only by boat. In 1982 she was declared surplus to requirements and sent to CADC.

Name: Eagle River
Year Built: 1978
Built By: Guilfords Ltd., Dartmouth N.S.
In Service: 1978 - 1982
Dimensions: 41 ft
Type: Cape Island boat
Cost:
Power:
Displacement:
Speed:
Official Number:
Radio Call Sign:
RCMP Number:
Code: 200-94

Below: Belcher, *once* Eskimo Point, *being launched from a work yard.*

Courtesy NWT Archives N-1979-002-0505

ERWIN STONE

The *Erwin Stone* was purchased from the Department of National Health and Welfare in 1961. She was sold October 6, 1965.

Name: Erwin Stone
Year Built: 1958
Built By: Purvis Brothers, Selkirk, Manitoba
In Service: 1961-1965
Dimensions: 39 x 10.1 x 4
Type:
Cost:
Power:
Displacement: 11.72 GT
Speed:
Official Number: 188249

Name: Eskimo Point/Belcher
Year Built: 1956
Built By: W.W. Robar, Upper LaHave, Nova Scotia
In Service: 1956 – 1969
Dimensions: 47 x 13 x 4.5
Type: Sail/motor cargo
Cost: $34,240
Power: Single 87 hp G.M. diesel
Displacement:
Speed: 9 kts
Official Number: 2H-4897
Radio Call Sign:
Code: G 513-1

Courtesy Vancouver Maritime Museum

ESKIMO POINT/BELCHER

The *Eskimo Point* was a wood-hulled vessel built in 1956. She served in 'G' Division, Eskimo Point in the Northwest Territories as a cargo and supply vessel. She sailed from Halifax, Nova Scotia to Eskimo Point with skipper Cst W.F. Gallagher and crew members S/Cst J. Gibbons, S/Cst N.H. Brownell and Cpl R.E. Moore. This vessel was specifically designed for northern work, and was of extremely rugged construction. She had accommodation for six, and a sizable hold amidships. She was renamed *Belcher* in 1962. She was transferred to Rankin Inlet Detachment July 14, 1967 and on November 17, 1969 declared surplus and transferred to CADC.

Library and Archives Canada e010764890

Far left: Art Tomsett in the RCMP Marine Services catalogue circa 1950s and in 2000 on the Simon Fraser *accompanying* St Roch II.

FORT CHIMO (1)/GAGNON

During her time of service, the *Fort Chimo* (1) was renamed *Gagnon*. On October 6, 1969 she was declared surplus and transferred to CADC then sold to the Department of Indian Affairs and Northern Development.

Name: Fort Chimo (1) / Gagnon
Year Built: 1951
Built By: John Etherington, Shelburne, N.S.
In Service: 1951 – 1969
Dimensions: 40 x 10 x 6
Type: Peterhead
Cost:
Power: Acadia engine
Displacement:
Speed:
Official Number: 2H-4912
RCMP Number:
Code: 7285

FORT CHIMO (2)

The *Fort Chimo* (2) was a wood-hulled motor boat built for 'G' Division and based out of Fort Chimo, Quebec. She was delivered September 13, 1954. On October 5, 1958 she was completely wrecked in a severe storm at Chimo Post. She dragged her anchor, the crew was unable to start the engine and the storm drove her ashore. The motor was saved but the hull was condemned and scrapped.

Name: Fort Chimo (2)
Year Built: 1954
Built By: J.T. Thorpe, Kingsport, N.S.
In Service: 1954 – 1958
Dimensions: 32 ft
Type: Motor boat
Cost: $4,000
Power: Single 35 hp Acadia Marine
Displacement:
Speed:
Official Number:
Radio Call Sign:
Code: G4/3-1

Below: The Regina, *similar hull to the* Fort MacLeod *but with a very different superstructure.*

Name: Fort MacLeod
Year Built: 1971
Built By: Canoe Cove Mfg. Ltd., Sidney, British Columbia
In Service: 1971 – 1984
Dimensions: 41 x 14
Type: Class II
Cost: $72,665
Power: Twin Cummins V470 diesel engines (185 hp ea.)
Displacement: 25.01 GT
Speed: 21 kts
Official Number:
Radio Call Sign:
RCMP Number: MP 73
Code: 200-73

Courtesy Gilles Gagne

FORT MACLEOD

PV *Fort MacLeod* was a fibreglass-hulled vessel built similarly to the *Regina* but with a design change to the cabin. She was transferred to the East Coast and served in Halifax, Nova Scotia until 1984 when she was turned over to CADC. She was the second vessel with the MP 73 markings. The first was the old *ML 6* of the Marine Division.

Library and Archives Canada e010764884

GRISE FIORD

The *Grise Fiord* was an RCMP vessel that worked out of Grise Fiord in the Northwest Territories. She was wrecked in a storm September 6, 1968 and as she was damaged beyond economical repair the hull was destroyed by burning September 24, 1969.

Name: Grise Fiord
Year Built: 1952
Built By: John Etherington Ltd., Shelburne, N.S.
In Service: 1952 – 1969
Dimensions: 29 x 9 x 4.5
Type: Utility boat
Cost: $3,850
Power: 20-35 hp Acadia WXAH
Displacement:
Speed:
Official Number: 2H-4906
Radio Call Sign:
Code: 7298

NWT Archives N-1979-051:1208S

HAMPDEN/HOPEDALE (2)

The *Hampden* was a wood-hulled vessel constructed for 'B' Division and served out of Hampden Detachment in Labrador. She was transferred to Hopedale on February 9, 1966 and renamed *Hopedale*. She was declared surplus to requirements September 5, 1967 and transferred to CADC.

Name: Hampden/Hopedale (2)
Year Built: 1955
Built By: Nova Scotia Yacht & Boat Builders Ltd., Mahone Bay, N.S.
In Service: 1955 – 1967
Dimensions: 35 x 9.3 x 4
Type: Raised deck motor boat
Cost: $7,177
Power: Single 35 hp Acadia Marine
Displacement:
Speed:
Official Number:
Radio Call Sign:
Code: B513-1

Courtesy Vancouver Maritime Museum

Name: Harvison
Year Built: 1973
Built By: Canoe Cove Mfg. Ltd., Sidney, B.C.
In Service: 1973 – 1991
Dimensions: 41 x 14
Type: Class II
Cost: $96,585
Power: Twin model 636 Caterpillar diesel engines
Displacement: 25.01 GT
Speed: 21 kn
Official Number:
Radio Call Sign:
RCMP Number: MP 21
Code: 200-21

HARVISON

PV *Harvison* was a fibreglass-hulled vessel built in British Columbia and stationed in Port Alberni. In 1981 she worked out of Sidney, B.C. where she served until 1991. She was a sister ship to the *McClellan*.

The Hawke's Bay *lying at anchor near Port Hope, Labrador, c 1958. Aboard are S/Cst H. Spearing and his dog Bill.*

Courtesy Don Klancher

Name: Hawke's Bay
Springdale/Hopedale (3)
Year Built: 1954
Built By: John Etherington Ltd., Shelburne, N.S.
In Service: 1954 - 1970
Dimensions: 35 x 9.3 x 4
Type: Raised Deck motor boat
Cost: $6,798
Power: Single 35 hp Acadia Marine
Displacement:
Speed:
Official Number:
Radio Call Sign:
Code: 7308

HAWKE'S BAY/SPRINGDALE/HOPEDALE (3)

The *Hawke's Bay* was wood-hulled and built for 'B' Division to serve out of Hawke's Bay, Newfoundland. She was transferred to the Springdale Detachment in 1962 and renamed *Springdale*. In 1969 she was transferred to the Hopedale Detachment and renamed *Hopedale*. She was condemned April 9, 1970 and sold by CADC September 23, 1970

Name: Heron
Year Built: 1965
Built By:
In Service: 1990
Dimensions: 24 ft
Type: Motor boat
Cost:
Power:
Displacement:
Speed:
Official Number: 32E12909
Radio Call Sign:
RCMP Number:

HERON

The *Heron* was a 24-foot runabout that was given to the RCMP by the Department of Fisheries after 25 years of service. On her first run things started falling apart, only the engine, horn and wipers worked reliably. Two weeks later she sank (photo right) while tied to the dock. She was salvaged and repaired but two weeks after her return she went missing – stolen – and was recovered. Two weeks later, while on patrol, the vessel failed to go forward after the crew stopped to conduct a vessel inspection. It was decided to go the few hundred yards back to base in reverse but soon the engine just stopped. After being towed into dock and secured the members said goodbye to the *Heron* and retired her.

Name: Herschel (3)
Year Built: 1956
Built By: Stright-MacKay, Pictou, N.S.
In Service: 1956 - 1966
Dimensions: 32 x 9
Type: Motor
Cost: $5,335
Power: Single 35 hp Acadia Marine
Displacement:
Speed:
Official Number:
Radio Call Sign:
Code: G513-4
RCMP Number:

HERSCHEL (3)

The *Herschel* was a wood-hulled motor boat built in 1956. She served at Herschel Island in 'G' Division as a supply vessel. In 1966 she dragged her anchor during a storm, the hull was breached and she sank. She was beached and remained inoperative until destroyed in 1969. The above photograph at Herschel Island, was taken by Sgt Ken Burton during his Voyage of Rediscovery in 2000. At right is the *Herschel* (2) on the ways.

904
RESCUE
SAUVETAGE
RC
GRC
POLICE
HIGGITT

Opposite: Higgitt *on an air-sea rescue mission in rough conditions on the West Coast. Right: At scenic Princess Louisa Inlet and the Chatterbox Falls in British Columbia. Below: At Langara in Haida Gwaii.*

Name: Higgitt
Year Built: 1992
Built By: Shore Boat Builders Ltd., Richmond, B.C.
In Service: 1992 - Still in service (SIS)
Dimensions: 58 x 22 x 6
Type: Commissioner class catamaran
Cost: $1,100,632
Power: Twin 820 hp MAN diesel engines
Displacement: 61.23 GT
Speed: 35 kts
Official Number: 827166
Radio Call Sign:
RCMP Number:

Courtesy Kenn Haycock

HIGGITT

PV *Higgitt* was the second catamaran built for the RCMP, and was named after Commissioner William L. Higgitt. She was a sister ship to the PV *Nadon* and like her, was stationed on the west coast of British Columbia.

HOPEDALE (1)

Library and Archives Canada e010764887

The *Hopedale* was a wood-hulled vessel based out of Hopedale, Newfoundland. On October 1, 1964 a freighter arrived at Hopedale carrying new housing units. As the landing of the units was urgent the local Detachment had been instructed to assist. While aiding the freighter tie up alongside, *Hopedale* was extensively damaged by the freighter's propeller. She was beyond economical repair and was declared surplus and sent to CADC May 26, 1965

Name: Hopedale (1)
Year Built: 1953
Built By: John Etherington Ltd., Shelburne, N.S.
In Service: 1953 - 1965
Dimensions: 35 x 9.3 x 4
Type: Raised deck motor boat
Cost: $4,224
Power: Single 25 hp Acadia gas engine
Displacement:
Speed:
Official Number:
Radio Call Sign:
Code: 7300

Courtesy RCMP West Coast Marine Services

INKSTER

PV *Inkster* was built on the West Coast and incorporated a new cabin design. Although still a catamaran she was 10 feet longer than the previous cats and had a lower profile cabin. She worked out of Prince Rupert on the north coast of British Columbia and patrolled to Haida Gwaii (the Queen Charlotte Islands). Her longer water line gave her better stability in the open ocean. She was named after former Commissioner Norman Inkster.

Name: Inkster
Year Built: 1996 – still in service (SIS)
Built By: Allied Shipbuilders Ltd., Vancouver, B.C.
In Service: 1996 - Still in service
Dimensions: 65 x 22 x 7
Type: Commissioner class catamaran
Cost: $1,860.589
Power: Twin 820 hp MAN diesel engines
Displacement: 63.83 GT
Speed: 35 kts
Official Number: 827167
Radio Call Sign:

Courtesy Vancouver Maritime Museum

Above: RCMP St Roch *at Lake Harbour, N.W.T., 1943. The smaller vessel is the H.B.C. schooner. At lower left are the Anglican buildings. The RCMP detachment is on the opposite shore.*
Right: The Lake Harbour *at Baffin Island, N.W.T., in 1948.*

Courtesy RCMP Historical Collections Unit

Name: Lake Harbour
Year Built: 1935
Built By: Montreal Boat Builders Ltd., Lachine, Quebec
In Service: 1948 – 1959
Dimensions: 40 ft
Type: Schooner
Cost:
Power: Chrysler Marine engine
Displacement: 18 GT
Speed:
Official Number: 2H-4909
Radio Call Sign:
Code: 7113

LAKE HARBOUR

The *Lake Harbour* was purchased by the RCMP in June 1948 and was operated out of Lake Harbour Detachment. In 1959 she was reportedly declared surplus. Another report states she was renamed *Ryan* in 1960, and continued to operate out of Lake Harbour until she was destroyed by fire August 07, 1966.

Name: Liard
Year Built: 1953
Built By: Russel-Hipwell, Owen Sound, Ontario
In Service: 1953 - 1960
Dimensions: 24 ft
Type: Motor
Cost: $6,197
Power: Single 35 hp Acadia
Displacement:
Speed:
Code: 7305

LIARD

The *Liard* was a wood-hulled motor boat built in 1953 and served in Liard in the Northwest Territories as a 'G' Division vessel. She was declared surplus in July 1960.

Courtesy Kenn Haycock

LINDSAY

PV *Lindsay* was the third catamaran built for the RCMP. She was named after Commissioner Malcolm F. Lindsay and was a sister ship to the PV *Nadon* and PV *Higgitt*. Like these two, she was stationed on the west coast of British Columbia.

Insets: Cst Doug Cleough and Cst John May preparing for water rescue practice in Pender Harbour, B.C.

Name: Lindsay
Year Built: 1992
Built By: Shore Boat Builders Ltd., Richmond, B.C.
In Service: 1993 - Still in service
Dimensions: 58 x 22 x 6
Type: Commissioner class catamaran
Cost: $1,100,632
Power: Twin 820 hp MAN diesel engines
Displacement: 61.23 GT
Speed: 35 kts
Official Number: 827165
Radio Call Sign:
RCMP Number:
Code:

Overleaf: RCMP patrol boat Inkster *was commissioned to duty at Port Hardy on Vancouver Island as security for a visit by two past presidents of the United States in 2004. Below: Cst Larry Burden at the helm of the police vessel* Manyberries *in 1984.*

Courtesy Vancouver Maritime Museum

Name: Manyberries
Year Built: 1969
Built By: Canoe Cove Manufacturing Ltd., Sidney, B.C.
In Service: 1969 –
Dimensions: 41 x 12.7 x 6.4
Type: Class II
Cost: $73,812
Power: Twin 210 hp Cummins diesel engines
Displacement: 15.8 GT
Speed: 21 kts
Official Number: 824519
Radio Call Sign:
RCMP Number: MP 75
Code: 200-75

MANYBERRIES

The *Manyberries* was a fibreglass vessel built in British Columbia but sent back to Ontario and worked out of Toronto. She was returned to B.C. and served on the West Coast. In 1980 she was based out of Vancouver. Her cabin and hull were later modified by Canoe Cove Manufacturing Ltd. She was eventually turned over to the Ministry of Fisheries and Oceans (right) and was still in service April 2010.

NOVA SPIRIT

21489
ROYAL VIKING

Name: McClellan
Year Built: 1973
Built By: Canoe Cove Mfg. Ltd., Sidney, B.C.
In Service: 1973 – 1992
Dimensions: 41 x 14
Type: Class II
Cost: $97,388
Power: Twin model 636 Caterpillar diesel engines
Displacement: 25.01 GT
Speed: 21 kts
Official Number:
Radio Call Sign:
RCMP Number: MP 22
Code: 200-22

Left: The PV McClellan *is seen off the Vancouver Convention Centre, and opposite, out on patrol.*

McCLELLAN

The PV *McClellan* was a fiberglass-hulled vessel built in British Columbia in 1973 and sent to Port Alberni, then in 1980 to Vancouver where she served until after 1991. She was a sister ship to the *Harvison*.

Courtesy BC Archives F-03478

ML 11

The *ML 11* was a British Columbia Provincial Police boat that served in West Kootenay, B.C. and was purchased by the RCMP in 1951. She continued to serve in West Kootenay, as a RCMP detachment vessel.

Name: ML 11
Year Built: 1934
Built By:
In Service: 1951 -
Dimensions: 30 ft
Type: Patrol boat
Cost: $7,000
Power:
Displacement:
Speed:
Official Number:
Radio Call Sign:
Code:

Courtesy RCMP Historical Collections Unit

Library and Archives Canada e010764880

MOOSE FACTORY (1)

The *Moose Factory* was a wood-hulled vessel built for 'A' Division and served out of Moose Factory in Ontario.

Name: Moose Factory (1)
Year Built: 1946
Built By: W.W. Robar, Upper LaHave, N.S.
In Service: 1946 – 1957
Dimensions: 35 ft
Type: Peterhead
Cost:
Power:
Displacement:
Speed:
Official Number:
Radio Call Sign:
Code: 7275

MOOSE FACTORY (2)/ST LAWRENCE

The *Moose Factory* (2) was built for 'A' Division and went into service out of Moose Factory, Ontario in 1958. She was a wood-hulled vessel and her hull was painted blue with light grey topsides. In April 1962, she was transferred to St Lawrence Detachment 'B' Division (Newfoundland). She was renamed *St Lawrence* and her code was changed to B713-1. The vessel was sold November 7, 1966.

Name: Moose Factory (2)/St Lawrence
Year Built: 1958
Built By: W.W. Robar, Upper LaHave, N.S.
In Service: 1958 – 1966
Dimensions: 35 x 9.3 x 4
Type: Detachment class raised deck motor boat (Modified)
Cost: $9,699
Power: Single 125 hp V8 Interceptor engine
Displacement:
Speed: 10 kts
Official Number:
Radio Call Sign: Code: A713-1/B713-1

Courtesy RCMP West Coast Marine Services

Name: Murray
Year Built: 2003
Built By: A.F. Theriault & Son Limited, Meteghan River, N.S.
In Service: 2005 - SIS in 2010
Dimensions: 65 x 22 x 6.5
Type: Commissioner class catamaran
Cost: $3,600,000
Power: Twin 1000 Caterpillar diesels
Displacement: 72.07 GT
Speed: 25 kts
Official Number: 827160
Radio Call Sign:

MURRAY

PV *Murray* was yet another design variance of the original aluminum catamarans and was built on the East Coast to serve there. She took over the duties of the *Simmonds* out of Newfoundland. The *Murray* was named after Commissioner Philip Murray.

Courtesy Kenn Haycock

Courtesy Vancouver Maritime Museum

Opposite page: Nadon *as she nears the completion of her Voyage of rediscovery in 2000. Above: The original* St Roch *in the Arctic.*

Name: Nadon
Year Built: 1991
Built By: Shore Boat Builders Ltd., Richmond, B.C.
In Service: 1991 - SIS
Dimensions: 58 x 22 x 6
Type: Commissioner Class catamaran
Cost: $1,151,238
Power: Twin 820 hp MAN diesels
Displacement: 61.23 GT
Speed: 35 kts
Official Number: 827164
Radio Call Sign:

NADON

PV *Nadon* was the first aluminum catamaran built for the RCMP and was designed by Robert Allen Ltd. of Vancouver, British Columbia. She was the first police vessel of this type in North America. She operated with a crew of four police officers, and having two crews meant she could be in service 365 days a year. This vessel served as the *St Roch II* during the 'Voyage of Rediscovery' in the year 2000 and sailed around North America in 165 days to raise funds towards restoration of the original *St Roch*. The *Nadon* was named after Commissioner Maurice Nadon.

POLICE
NADON
Voyage of Rediscovery
ST. ROCH II
KOBELT
KONGSBERG
VANCOUVER
MARITIME

NAUJA

This vessel was on loan from the Department of Mines and Technical Surveys. She was accepted May 15, 1951 and was employed at Chesterfield Inlet until she was returned to her owner August 10, 1963.

Name: Nauja
Year Built: 1949
Built By: W.W. Robar, Upper LaHavre N.S.
In Service: 1951 - 1963
Dimensions: 42.8 x 12.4 x 6
Type: Peterhead (modified)
Cost: (Loan)
Power: Series 85 bhp G.M. 71 diesel
Displacement: 18.04 GT
Speed: 8 kts
Official Number: 190546
Radio Call Sign:

Library and Archives Canada e010764896

OUTLOOK

MB *Outlook* was a fibreglass Bertram hulled boat that was sent east to be stationed at Sault Ste Marie in Ontario on the Great Lakes. In 1977 she was sent west to Prince Rupert, to be a replacement vessel for the two 65-foot vessels *Ganges* and *Tofino*. The *Outlook* was a sister ship to the *Dawson* (photo right) and served on the West Coast until 1990 when she was turned over to CADC.

Name: Outlook
Year Built: 1971
Built By: Canoe Cove Mfg. Ltd., Sidney, British Columbia
In Service: 1971 – 1990
Dimensions: 26 x 10
Type: Detachment Class
Cost: $24,539
Power: Twin 160 Mercruiser inboard/outboard motors
Displacement: 4.5 GT
Speed:
Official Number:
Radio Call Sign:
RCMP Number: MP 37
Code: 200-37

In recent years the RCMP has moved towards the use of many smaller inland water transport vessels (IWTs) such as that pictured above.

Name: Pearkes
Year Built: 1972
Built By: Canoe Cove Mfg. Ltd., Sidney, British Columbia
In Service: 1972 – 1996
Dimensions: 52 x 14 x 7.5
Type: Class II
Cost: $104,600
Power: Twin Cummins 300 diesel engines (185 hp ea.)
Displacement: 34.29 GT
Speed: 21 kts
Official Number: 819005
Radio Call Sign:
RCMP Number: MP 90
Code: 200-90

Courtesy Gilles Gagne

PEARKES

PB *Pearkes* was a fibreglass-hulled vessel constructed in British Columbia as a replacement vessel. She served on the west coast of British Columbia beginning in Port Alberni then moving to Alert Bay from 1980 to 1996. She was later replaced by the PV *Inkster*. Her registry was closed October 9, 2008

Courtesy Mark Lowe

POND INLET

This boat was used at Pond Inlet for patrol purposes and for long hunting trips to secure dog food. She was ideally suited for this work and was equipped with a mast and sails for emergency use. She was declared surplus November 5, 1969 and sold by CADC.

Name: Pond Inlet
Year Built: 1954
Built By: W.W. Robar, Upper LaHave, N.S.
In Service: 1954 – 1969
Dimensions: 31 x 9.7 x 4.5
Type: Motor boat (Walrus Hunter)
Cost: $5,477.89
Power: Single 35 hp Acadia gas
Official Number: 2H-4885
Code: 7302

PORT SAUNDERS/BURGEO

The *Port Saunders* (pictured left) was a wood-hulled motor boat built in 1956 for 'B' Division. She served in Port Saunders and later Burgeo, Newfoundland. *Burgeo* was declared surplus August 28, 1969 and sold by CADC November 17, 1969.

Name: Port Saunders/Burgeo
Year Built: 1956
Built By: W.W. Robar, Upper LaHave, N.S.
In Service: 1956 – 1969
Dimensions: 35 x 9.3 x 4
Type: Raised deck motor boat
Cost: $6,919
Power: Single 35 hp Acadia gas
Code: B513-3

PREVENTOR

In Halifax, July 10th, 2010 was perhaps a milestone day for maritime police work as the Royal Canadian Mounted Police, Federal Policing, Coastal Watch Program launched their newly refurbished Police Vessel *Preventor*. She is 42 feet in length and her engine produces 375 horsepower. She has a range of up to 25 miles offshore in winds of up to 33 knots and carries a crew of three.

The *Preventor* was a Canadian Coast Guard research vessel (6C-4828) that the RCMP acquired and rebuilt. She was outfitted to patrol and provide enforcement along the Nova Scotia coastline, gather intelligence during marine patrols reinforcing border integrity, provide a visible RCMP presence on the water and enhance community and coastal policing initiatives. She was also equipped to gather intelligence and combat organized crime-led smuggling and drug trafficking and provide security of coastal waters and shorelines. Marine enforcement partners along with RCMP veterans from the former Marine Division, joined RCMP Deputy Commissioner, Atlantic, and Commanding Officer of Nova Scotia, Steve Graham in launching the vessel at The Maritime Museum of The Atlantic.

Name: Preventor
Year Built: 2009
Built By: Les Bateaux Demes Ltd., New Brunswick
In Service: 2010 -
Dimensions: 42 ft
Speed: 18 kts
Power: single engine 375 hp 3208 Caterpillar diesel
Displacement: 18 GT
Speed: 33 kts

Courtesy RCMP Historical Collections Unit

The Preventor, *a former Canadian Coast Guard vessel, making its debut in Halifax Harbour.*

Library and Archives Canada e010764886

RED BAY/NAIN

The *Nain* was originally built for Red Bay Detachment and consequently was initially named *Red Bay*. She was sent to Nain so the name was changed to *Nain*. The newly named vessel worked out of Nain Harbour. She was sold by CADC October 13, 1967.

Name: Red Bay/Nain
Year Built: 1953 - 1967
Built By: John Etherington Ltd., Shelburne, N.S.
In Service: 1953 - 1967
Dimensions: 35 x 9.3 x 4
Type: Raised Deck Motor Boat
Cost: $3,840.
Power: 15-45 hp Acadia model H1xB gasoline engine
Displacement:
Speed: 25 kts
Official Number:
Radio Call Sign:
RCMP Number:
Code: 7299

REGINA (2)

PV *Regina* was christened by Inspector (Retd) K.S. Crease at Canoe Cove in Sidney, British Columbia, on September 29, 1970 and first stationed in Victoria, B.C. Later she was transferred to Tahsis, B.C. and worked the west coast of Vancouver Island out of that station.

In 1980 she was in Prince Rupert. Part way through her service she had a cabin design change. She was turned over to CADC in 1995 when she was replaced by the 58' catamaran PV *Higgitt*.

Name: Regina (2)
Year Built: 1970
Built By: Canoe Cove Mfg. Ltd., Sidney, B.C.
In Service: 1970 – 1995
Dimensions: 41 x 14
Type: Class II
Cost: $48,750
Power: Twin Cummins 470 diesel engines (170 hp ea.)
Displacement: 21.78 GT
Speed: 21 kts
Crew: 2
Official Number:
Radio Call Sign:
RCMP Number: MP 60
Code: 200-60

Left, bottom left, and opposite page: the Patrol Vessel Regina *after, and before alterations. Below: Crew member Erika Missfeldt. Bottom right: PV* Regina *on patrol in British Columbia.*

Name: Reliance (2)
Year Built: 1951
Built By: Alberta Motor Boat Co. Ltd., Edmonton, Alberta
In Service: 1951 – 1966
Dimensions: 33 x 9 x 4.9
Type:
Cost: $9,968.60
Power: Kermath engine
Displacement:
Speed:
Official Number:
Radio Call Sign:
Code: 7280

Courtesy RCMP Historical Collections Unit

RELIANCE (2)

The *Reliance* (2) was purchased September 29, 1951 and was sent to Reliance Detachment. She was transferred to Coppermine Detachment circa 1958. She saw service until 1966 when she was transferred by CADC to the Department of Northern Affairs and Natural Resources on April 19 that year.

Courtesy RCMP Historical Collections Unit

RIVETT CARNAC

PV *Rivett Carnac* was built in British Columbia and originally sent to Ocean Falls on the north coast. In 1980 she was located in Campbell River, B.C. Her original cabin design (seen in inset photograph, right) was changed to the above configuration after a few years service. She served until sent to CADC in 1991.

Name: Rivett Carnac
Year Built: 1973
Built By: Canoe Cove Mfg Ltd., Sidney, B.C.
In Service: 1973 - 1991
Dimensions: 52 x 14
Type: Class II
Cost: $140,689
Power: Single model 903 Cummins diesel
Displacement: 34.29 GT
Speed: 21 kts
Official Number:
Radio Call Sign:
RCMP Number: MP 23
Code: 200-23

RODDICKTON/ST ANTHONY

The *St Anthony* was wood-hulled and built for 'B' Division. She served out of St Anthony, Newfoundland. She was transferred to Roddickton January 12, 1965 and had the name changed to *Roddickton*. The ship was totally destroyed by fire on July 6, 1965.

Name: Roddickton/St Anthony
Year Built: 1954
Built By: John Etherington Ltd., Shelburne, N.S.
In Service: 1954 - 1965
Dimensions: 35 x 9.3 x 4
Type: Raised deck motor boat
Cost: $6,798
Power: Single 35 hp Acadia gas engine
Displacement:
Speed:
Official Number:
Radio Call Sign:
Code: 7309

Wearing the colours and insignia of the Canadian Coast Guard and the RCMP, the PV Simmonds *is used on border patrols on the East Coast, where she was built.*

Name: Simmonds
Year Built: 1995
Built By: Chantier Naval Matane Inc., Matane, Quebec
In Service: 1995 - 2005
Dimensions: 58 x 22 x 6
Type: Commissioner Class catamaran
Cost: $1,300,000
Power: Twin 820 hp MAN diesels
Displacement: 61.23 GT
Speed: 35 kts
Official Number: 828052
Radio Call Sign:

Courtesy Kenn Haycock

SIMMONDS

PV *Simmonds* was the fourth RCMP catamaran and was named after Commissioner Robert H. Simmonds. Unlike most of her sister ships, she was built on the East Coast. She was meant to serve the Federal Government and was based out of Marystown, Newfoundland. Her main duties involved Customs enforcement around the French Islands of St Pierre and Miquelon. In 2005 she was moved to the Great Lakes and worked out of Hamilton, Ontario where she was transferred to the Ministry of Public Safety and Emergency Preparedness and became part of a joint effort in border patrols with the Canadian Coast Guard.

Courtesy Joseph Parsons

SPALDING

The *Spalding* was a motor vessel that served out of Inuvik and Cambridge Bay, Northwest Territories from 1960 to 1969. She was declared surplus June 4, 1969 and sold October 16, that year.

Name: Spalding
Year Built: 1960
Built By: W.W. Roper, Upper LaHavre, N.S.
In Service: 1960 - 1969
Dimensions: 40 x 11 x 4.5
Type: Motor
Cost: $10,774.40
Power: 8 Cyl. Chrysler gas engine
Displacement:
Speed: 7 kts
Official Number: 32E 6478
Radio Call Sign:
Code: G913-1

Courtesy Spud Roscoe

The RCMP vessel Spalding *docked at Cambridge Bay in 1962.*

Name: Stikine
Year Built: 1986
Built By: West Bay Boat Builders Ltd., Delta, B.C.
In Service: 1986 - 1995
Dimensions: 45 x 15.3 x 3
Type: Class II
Cost: $360,000
Power: Twin 300 hp Volvo Penta TAMD70E diesel engines
Displacement: 14.99 GT
Speed: 23.6 kts
Official Number:
Radio Call Sign:

STIKINE

The *Stikine* was launched and commissioned on January 31, 1986 at HMCS Discovery in Stanley Park, Vancouver, British Columbia. She was christened by Mrs Lynn Venner, wife of Deputy Commissioner Venner. This vessel was constructed for Expo 86 to replace the 25-year-old *Advance*. She was based out of Steveston, B.C. at the mouth of the Fraser River. Her patrol area was the Fraser River to Mission, British Columbia and the Strait of Georgia from the mouth of the Fraser River to the Canada–USA Border. This vessel served on the West Coast until 1995 when she was turned over to CADC for disposal.

TWILLINGATE

The *Twillingate* was stationed at Harbour Breton, Newfoundland. The vessel was declared surplus on June 14, 1965.

Name: Twillingate
Year Built:
Built By:
In Service: - 1965
Displacement:
Official Number:
Code: B013-1

W. FERGUSON

The *W. Ferguson* was a fibreglass-hulled vessel on loan to the RCMP from the Department of Fisheries on the East Coast about 1990 and served out of Pugwash Harbor, Nova Scotia until about 2005 when she was sold. She was still in service as a private fishing boat April 2010.

Name: W. Ferguson
Year Built: 1990
Built By: Bateaux De Mer Ltd., Cocagne, New Brunswick
In Service: 1990 – 2005
Dimensions: 35 x 12 x 5
Type: Fishing vessel
Cost: $34,240
Power: Single 325 hp diesel engine
Displacement: 18.27 GT
Speed: 17 kts
Official Number: 813722
Radio Call Sign:

Library and Archives Canada e010764876

WHITEHORSE

The *Whitehorse* was built in British Columbia and transported to Windsor, Ontario where she worked on the Great Lakes until 1978 before being turned over to CADC and sold. She was the sister ship to the *Yellowknife*, opposite.

Name: Whitehorse
Year Built: 1972
Built By: Canoe Cove Mfg. Ltd., Sidney, B.C.
In Service: 1972 – 1978
Dimensions: 30 x 14
Type: Detachment Class
Cost: $36,535
Power: Twin 270 hp Mercruiser inboard/outboard engines
Displacement: 14.94 GT
Official Number:
Radio Call Sign:
RCMP Number: MP 39
Code: 200-39

Courtesy Gilles Gagne

Name: Yellowknife
Year Built: 1972
Built By: Canoe Cove Mfg. Ltd., Sidney, B.C.
In Service: 1972 – 1978
Dimensions: 30 x 14
Type: Detachment Class
Cost: $36,535
Power: Twin 270 hp Mercruiser inboard/outboard engines
Displacement: 14.94 GT
Speed: 30 kts
Official Number:
Radio Call Sign:
RCMP Number: MP 63
Code: 200-63

YELLOWKNIFE

PV *Yellowknife* was built in British Columbia and transported to Kingston, Ontario where she worked on the Great Lakes until 1978 when she was turned over to CADC and sold. She was the sister ship to the *Whitehorse*.

POLICE
Canada
NADON

Chapter Six

The St Roch II–Voyage of Rediscovery

Several men sat around a table, heavily involved in shop talk. Considering they shared an interest in the marine environment, it is no surprise that the conversation was about ships. The topic turned to the condition of the *St Roch*, a retired RCMP schooner that sat in great disrepair at the Vancouver Maritime Museum. Little funding could be found to restore this vessel, which was suffering from dry rot to its heavy wood construction. To make matters worse, the roof above it leaked badly when it rained, a common state of the weather in Vancouver, British Columbia. It was at this meeting an idea was born that in a few years would become reality.

The *St Roch* is a 104-foot schooner that plied the waters of the Canadian Arctic for over 25 years and established herself in the annals of Canadian history by being the first vessel to travel the North West Passage from west to east in 1940-1942. She then became the first vessel to travel the Passage in both directions in 1944 when she returned to Vancouver. Another maritime record was set in 1950 when she sailed from Vancouver to Halifax through the Panama Canal thus becoming the first vessel to ever circumnavigate North America.

In 1954 she returned to Vancouver via the Panama Canal and set a fourth record by being the first vessel to circumnavigate North America in both directions. In 1958 she was moved to a dry dock on the south shore of False Creek in Vancouver, B.C. In 1962 she became a National Historic Site and in 1966 a building was constructed over top of her to protect her from the elements. Parks Canada assumed control of her destiny at that time.

Above: In the Arctic aboard St Roch II–Nadon. *Opposite: The* Nadon *in Bellot Strait on her epic voyage through the North West Passage in the year 2000. Photographs by Constable David Johns (Retd).*

The RCMP patrol vessel Nadon, *re-named* St Roch II *for the duration of the Voyage of Rediscovery in 2000.*

Troubles for the vessel began in 1995 when a major funding cutback to Parks Canada undermined the preservation of the *St Roch*. The Vancouver Maritime Museum staff debated ideas on how to generate some interest in this preservation effort. When someone suggested that a fund raising-trip following the historic travels of the *St Roch*, a kind of re-enactment of its voyages, might accomplish this, Cpl Ken Burton of the RCMP PV *Lindsay* started to research the viability of such a proposal. With funding from the Millennium Partnership Program offered by the Federal Government of Canada in 1998 this became a very real possibility. It would be a joint venture between the Vancouver Maritime Museum and the Royal Canadian Mounted Police and became known as the 'St Roch II—Voyage of Rediscovery.'

A *St Roch* Preservation Campaign was initiated with the purpose of establishing an endowment fund. This would provide funding for the *St Roch* for years to come and would also contribute funds for the RCMP drug awareness program called 'Vision Quest.' For the price of a 30-second television commercial, a corporation could get their logo painted on the side of the *St Roch II*, thus receiving all the publicity surrounding and during the voyage. Furthermore, the logo would appear in all advertising, documentaries and books published about the event in the future, plus have their name on display beside the *St Roch* in the Maritime Museum.

Many things had to fall into place before this project would become reality. The Vancouver Maritime Museum established the manpower to manage the project, including communications, managers, sponsorship, advertising, fund-raising, promotion, merchandising, media relations and education. A steering committee was made up which consisted of many retired and current RCMP officers, Coast Guard representatives and Vancouver Museum directors. The logistics of such an enterprise appeared to be overwhelming at first but slowly it began to come together. The departure date was set for July 1, 2000–Canada Day of the new millennium.

The St Roch Preservation Campaign had an objective of raising some $4.5 million of which $500,000 would be for repairing the dry rot in the *St Roch*, $2.5 million to building a new exhibit enclosure, and $1.5 million to a perpetual maintenance program to ensure the future existence of the *St Roch*. This fund-raising campaign consisted of two parts, a painting called 'Isumataq' and the 'Voyage of Rediscovery.'

The painting is a landscape demonstrating the beauty of the Arctic and its people. 'Isumataq' is the world's largest oil painting measuring 12 feet high by 152 feet long and consisting of 38 panels for a total area of 1,824 square feet. It was done by renowned painter Ken Kirkby. The name 'Isumataq' means 'an object or person in whose presence wisdom might show itself.' The general public were able to purchase square inches of this painting for $10 each with the funds going to the St Roch Preservation Campaign. Eventually the painting would be the surrounding background of the new home of the *St Roch*.

Sponsors would receive recognition through their donations by having their corporate name on display at the museum permanently, access to several special event receptions, complimentary museum passes and memberships, gifts, and a charitable tax receipt. The sponsorship levels were identified by the size of their donation. The 'Platinum Inukshuk' ($25,000), 'Gold Inukshuk' ($15,000), 'Silver Inukshuk' ($10,000), 'Bronze Inukshuk' ($5,000) and the 'Granite Inukshuk' ($2,500). Each level had its own defined benefit list.

The vessel to be used for the 'Voyage of Rediscovery' was an aluminum catamaran, the RCMP PV *Nadon*. She had been laid up due to mechanical problems and was not being used by the RCMP at the time. A Canadian Coast Guard ship was needed as a support vessel. The Coast Guard Ship (CGS) *Simon Fraser* from Halifax, Nova Scotia was finally chosen for this role. The crew of the *Nadon* would come from the ranks of the RCMP and the crew of the *Simon Fraser* would come from the Coast Guard and volunteers. Cpl Burton, later promoted to Sergeant and since to Inspector, would skipper the RCMP vessel *Nadon* and Captain Robert Mellis would command the Coast Guard Ship *Simon Fraser*.

For Canadian students and others worldwide to follow the adventures of the trip through the Arctic, a Vancouver School Board French Immersion teacher by the name of Carolyn Dymond was hired to spearhead an education program on the internet. Every day an entry was to be made with a photograph or two of the progress of the PV *Nadon*, which with increasing frequency was being referred to as the *St Roch II*. On this site anyone could see where the ship was, the latitude and longitude bearings, the temperature and weather, A question of the day was presented to students, lessons were recommended for teachers, and a journal of the crew's recent experiences was posted. Not only would this be a daily compilation of the trip, but also it would serve to make

St Roch II – Voyage of Rediscovery Steering Committee

Brian Watt, RCMP Deputy Commissioner Pacific Region

Frank Palmer, Retired RCMP Deputy Commissioner – Chair

Les Holmes, Retired RCMP Assistant Commissioner, RCMP Veterans

Don Saigle, RCMP Inspector OIC Marine Section

Don Davis, RCMP Inspector Community Policing

Roger Kembel, Retired RCMP Inspector

Don Van Dusen, RCMP OIC Fleet Program Administration

Jim Delgado, Executive Director of the Vancouver Maritime Museum

Linda Morris, Vancouver Maritime Museum Chair

Captain David Johns, Retired Canadian Coast Guard Captain

David Valpy, Vancouver Maritime Museum, President

Sergeant Ken Burton, RCMP Marine Services

John Grant, Vision Quest

Ron Defieux, Vancouver Maritime Museum

Katie Fitzgerald, Vancouver Maritime Museum, Community Relations Co-ordinator

Randall Graham, Vancouver Maritime Museum

Stephen Rybak, Vancouver Maritime Museum, Project Co-ordinator

Cathy Beaumont, Vancouver Maritime Museum, Media Contact

Donna Turner, Vancouver Maritime Museum, Director of Development

Gina Johanson, Vancouver Maritime Museum, Community Relations Co-ordinator

Tara Knight, Vancouver Maritime Museum, Communications Co-op Student

Salmia Virani, Vancouver Maritime Museum, Communications Co-op Student

The Canadian Coast Guard ship, Simon Fraser *with the* Nadon.

people aware of the historic significance of the role that the original *St Roch* played in the Arctic and the legacy it left, focusing on the need to preserve her as an important Canadian artifact.

Part of the trip would involve a science program. Aboard the CGS *Simon Fraser* was a bio-acoustic forward-scanning sonar which would scan sea life, sea bottom contours, Arctic ice, and search for wrecks. Another science program would be the launching of 2,000 sealed bottles at certain locations along the Canadian northern shores. These would assist in tracking Arctic currents and circulation patterns. Still other programs included the assessment of the ice coverage in the Arctic and a search for the wrecks of the ill-fated Franklin Expedition in the 1800s.

Fiddler Productions, a company located in Vancouver, British Columbia was given the rights to film the voyage. They planned to produce documentaries of various aspects of the trip and would have a film crew aboard the *Simon Fraser* to shoot film footage of the entire voyage. It was hoped that if enough world attention was attracted, there would be international interest in the broadcast rights held by Fiddler Productions. All aspects of the Voyage of Rediscovery had a potential for huge interest around the world through the discovery of historic remains, education and science of the north, re-enactments and social interest of the *St Roch* and the communities it served, as well as recognition of the new Nunavut Territory.

The logistics of putting together a timetable and arranging for numerous ports of calls, dignitaries, VIPs and meeting sponsors was an enormous task. This timetable had to be flexible because the weather was not. Stops were prescheduled in order to lessen the impact of a two- or three-day weather delay. The worst fear of all was the ice pack. An aluminum catamaran cannot come in contact with any ice as it could open up like a tin can and sink. The small draft of the *Nadon* allowed her to avoid the large icebergs by keeping close to shore in the shallow waters, but there was still the chance of ice being driven closer towards the shore by winds and currents.

It seemed everything was in order and with time running out, the Voyage of Rediscovery was about to begin as scheduled on July 1, 2000. In late April 2000 a serious problem surfaced: there was a possible hitch in obtaining the CGS *Simon Fraser* from the Coast Guard. She still had not left Halifax for Vancouver, a journey of over 7,000 nautical miles. After some extensive negotiations and compromises, the *Simon Fraser* with her volunteer crew departed Halifax, Nova Scotia on May 27, 2000. She arrived in Vancouver, British Columbia via the Panama Canal on June 26. This left her with four days to replenish her stores, bring her crew up to speed and prepare for the departure date of July 1.

The crew of the *Simon Fraser* consisted of volunteers. Over 161 applications were received for the 29 crew positions. The qualifications of these volunteers were very high and satisfied the needs of the Coast Guard. They signed on for the token pay of $1 per month, then departed for Halifax to begin the first leg of the voyage. Once in Vancouver the crew was joined by the documentary film crew, some scientists and the onboard educator. Due to the six-month commitment, some crew members found they could not stay on once they arrived in Vancouver, so they were replaced by new crew in late June for the Arctic return to Halifax.

Two crew members of note were Hugh Parry and Art Tomsett. Mr Parry was from Victoria, B.C., and had served as an electrician on the *Simon Fraser*, bringing with him 23 years of experience in marine electronics at HMC Esquimalt Dockyard. He is also the son of the original *St Roch* cook – Reg #7756 Cst W. J. 'Dad' Parry who served from 1928 to 1934 and 1940 to 1942. Mr Art Tomsett from Saanichton, B.C. was the Second Engineer on the *Simon Fraser* and had served 20 years with BC Ferries as an engineer. He is a retired member of the RCMP and also served as a crew member of the original *St Roch* from 1950 to 1951.

The RCMP PV *Nadon* (*St Roch II*), was crewed by RCMP members who applied for relief of their regular duties to participate in the Voyage of Rediscovery. Sgt Ken Burton was the master of the vessel at the time, and carried on that duty for the entire duration of the voyage. The other three crew members were rotated in and out at various destinations.

Throughout the whole voyage 16 members of the RCMP and two engineers

Crew of the Canadian Coast Guard Ship *Simon Fraser*

Capt R.J. Mellis – Master
Capt C. Mellis – Chief Officer
Capt Dave Johns – Director of Support Operations
Capt W. Dancer – Second Officer: Arctic
Capt Jack Bragg – Second Officer: Panama
Moody McKay – Third Officer
Bruce Landry – Boatswain: Panama, Seaman: Arctic
Paul Isserlis – Boatswain: Arctic
Dianne Simms – Bosun's Mate
Sue Sharp – Seaman
John Rooney – Seaman: Panama
Mike Mont – Seaman: Arctic
James Erlam – Seaman
Amie Gibbins – Seaman
Oscar Martens – Seaman: Arctic
Jacques Asselin – Chief Engineer
Hugh Parry – Electrician
Jack Lyngard – 1st Engineer: Panama
Vlodomir Syomin – 1st Engineer: Arctic
Art Tomsett – Second Engineer
James MacDougal – Third Engineer
Frank Eberlein – Oiler: Panama
Lyle Roberts – Oiler: Panama
Allan Weber – Oiler: Panama
Bill Robinson – Oiler: Arctic
Jasmin Sauvé – Oiler: Arctic
Laslo Bedocs – Oiler: Arctic
Gordon Gillis – Chief Cook
Thea Provost – Second Cook
Margo Wood – Steward: Panama
Mike Ferguson – Steward: Panama
Doreen Ferguson – Steward: Panama
Rena Patrick – Steward: Arctic
Peter Malacarne – Steward: Arctic
Naomi Franks – Steward: Arctic
Dr. Francis (Blackie) Forbes – Medical Officer
Diane Sauvé – Engineering Cadet: Arctic

Non-Crew Passengers

Carolyn Dymond – Learn-on-Board Educator
Lionel Johnston – Merchandise/Display Coordinator
Seth Berkowitz – Patron
Beth Berkowitz – Patron
Mark Abrahms – Documentary Film Crew
Norm Torp – Documentary Film Crew
Leann Parker – Documentary Film Crew
Colleen Corley – Documentary Film Crew

participated as crew. Changes of crew occurred at Prince Rupert, B.C.; Tuktoyaktuk, N.W.T.; Cambridge Bay, Nunavut; Pond Inlet, Nunavut; Goose Bay, Labrador; Halifax, N.S.; Fort Lauderdale, Florida; Panama; Acapulco, Mexico; and San Diego, California.

The departure date of Saturday, July 1, 2000 arrived. The farewell celebrations from Canada Place, Vancouver, were broadcast live on television by CBC NewsNet. Public speeches were made to the on site audience by representatives of the Vancouver Maritime Museum, sponsors of the voyage and the RCMP. Commissioner Phillip Murray and retired Commissioner Maurice Nadon, after whom the RCMP vessel was named, made a good wish blessing. Following a blessing by RCMP Chaplain Turner, a presentation was made of the original *St Roch* ship's bell by retired RCMP Deputy Commissioner Frank Palmer. Commissioner Maurice Nadon then presented the original *St Roch* 'Blue Ensign' flag. This was followed by a gun salute by the RCMP honour guard. The Voyage of Rediscovery had begun and the *St Roch II* set sail with Sgt Burton at the helm, Sgt Frank Lalear as mate and Cst John May as deckhand.

The first leg of the journey was brief as some dignitaries who had boarded the vessel for the official departure, had to return to Vancouver. The PV *Nadon* tied up in Gibsons, B.C., a short distance north of Vancouver, and participated in the first of many community events to celebrate the voyage. During the first few days the trips were short and the celebrations abundant as the PV *Nadon* stopped in Nanaimo, Campbell River, Port McNeill, Port Hardy, Bella Bella,

Crew of the RCMP PV *Nadon*

Captain:

Sgt Ken Burton – Vancouver to Vancouver – 169 days

Crew:

Insp Don Saigle – Tuktoyaktuk, N.W.T. to Cambridge Bay, Nunavut – 11 days
Insp Ken Gates – Fort Lauderdale, Florida to Panama – 15 days
Insp Roger Kembel – Cambridge Bay, Nunavit to Pond Inlet, Nunavut – 17 days
Insp John Henley – Cabo San Lucas, Mexico to Oceanside, California – 5 days
Sgt Frank Lalear – Vancouver, B.C. to Tuktoyaktuk, N.W.T. – 36 days
Sgt Gene Pinnegar – Panama to San Diego, California – 17 days
Cpl Michael Hartung – Tuktoyaktuk, N.W.T. to Goose Bay, Labrador – 40 days
Cpl Bob Currie – Halifax, N.S. to Panama – 31 days
Cst Bruno Ouellette – Goose Bay, Labrador to Halifax, N.S. – 28 days
Cst John May – Vancouver, B.C. to Tuktoyaktuk, N.W.T. – 36 days
Cst Kenn Haycock – Goose Bay, Labrador to Fort Lauderdale, Florida – 44 days
Cst Dan Cochlan – Halifax, N.S. to Fort Lauderdale, Florida – 16 days
Cst John Stringer – Fort Lauderdale, Florida to Acapulco, Mexico – 21 days
Cst Mike Schmeisser – Panama to San Diego, California – 17 days
Cst Anne Clarke – Acapulco, Mexico to Vancouver, B.C. – 28 days
Cst Vic Cunha – San Diego, California to Vancouver, B.C. – 19 days
Cst Richard Harry – San Diego, California to Vancouver, B.C. – 19 days
Mr Jack Soo (engineer) – Prince Rupert, B.C. to Goose Bay, Labrador – 67 days
Mr Jasmin Sauvé (engineer) – Vancouver, B.C. to Goose Bay, Labrador (Simon Fraser) – 76 days, Goose Bay, Labrador to Halifax, N.S. (PV Nadon) – 28 days
Mr Don Van Dusen – various parts of the voyage
Mr David Burton – Vancouver, B.C. to Prince Rupert, B.C. – 10 days

RCMP crew members with Alaska State Troopers. RCMP in front, L-R, Sgt Frank Lalear, Deputy Commissioner Brian Watt, Alaska State Trooper Commissioner Burton (Rtd), Sgt Ken Burton (in behind) and Cst John May.

A young pair of eyes–David Burton on watch aboard the PV Nadon.

Kitimat, and finally Prince Rupert, all along the coast of British Columbia.

The first foreign stop was at Ketchikan, Alaska on July 11, 2000. There was one more stop at Juneau and a tourist look at Glacier Bay before the *Nadon* headed across the Gulf of Alaska. About half way to Kodiak, Alaska, the *Nadon* met up with the *Simon Fraser* for their first refueling rendezvous. After the *Simon Fraser* had departed Vancouver on July 1 she turned back for some machinery repairs, then left again on July 14, arriving on time in the Gulf of Alaska on the 17th to meet the *Nadon* for the refueling process. Together they arrived in Kodiak on July 19, 2000.

After Kodiak there were two more stops in Alaska, Dutch Harbour (Unalaska) on the Aleutian Islands and across the Bering Sea to Point Barrow on the northern shores of Alaska. This involved crossing the Arctic Circle near the Diomedes Islands in the Bering Strait at latitude 66 degrees 33 minutes north and meant that the crew who had not previously passed by sea into the Arctic had to participate in the maritime initiation ritual. This entailed a court of Walrus King and his assistants Seal, Char and Narwhal, played by various crew members, who set out tasks for the newcomers to complete. Initiation is finalized with an oath to respect the Arctic. It was two months since departing Halifax, N.S. that the crew of the *Simon Fraser* eventually was able to join in the relaxing and enjoyable festivity of the commencement of the voyage.

Together, the vessels continued their voyage, arriving at Point Barrow, their final Alaskan port, on August 1, 2000. This is where ice flows were first spotted. The *Simon Fraser* is a light icebreaker which still had to be very wary of ice packs and navigate according to the thickness of the ice and the depth of the water. As previously mentioned, the *Nadon* kept close to shore to avoid the ice pack. The expected ice threat presented itself here, but fortunately not for long. Winds and current kept the ice pack from the shore and the *Nadon* was soon on its way. Now in the Northwest Territories, the patrol vessel began to experience engine problems, so had to make for Tuktoyaktuk for repairs and a crew change. After a quick stop at Herschel Island (due to water in the fuel) she arrived in Tuktoyaktuk on the 4th of August. Cst John May and Sgt Frank Lalear departed the *Nadon* for home and were replaced by Inspector Don Saigle and Cpl Mike Hartung. Also arriving for the Arctic portion of the voyage were retired Cst Bill Cashin who was a crew member on the original *St Roch* in 1944. Norm Torp and Leann Parker representing Fiddler Productions now joined the crew of the *Simon Fraser* replacing Colleen Corely.

After a delay of two days for repairs, refueling and re-crewing, the vessels were on their way to Kugluktuk, Nunavut (NU) formerly known as Coppermine. On arrival, due to hazardous harbour conditions, the *Nadon* was escorted into harbour by a former RCMP marine vessel *Jennings* now called the *Fort Hearne* and operated by her owner Larry Whittaker.

On August 12 they arrived in Cambridge Bay, NU where they stayed for about nine days while scientific research was conducted during a search for the remains of the famous ships *Erebus* and *Terror* of the lost Sir John Franklin expedition of 1845. To assist with the Franklin search the voyage was joined by James Delgado, David Woodman, Mark Asplin and Stephen Rybak from the Vancouver Maritime Museum, and Mr George Hobson.

For scientific research Gilles Arfeuille, and Mark Trevorrow of the Institute of Ocean Sciences in Victoria, B.C. were in attendance to conduct studies of fresh water movement, climatic changes, and distribution of fish and plankton in the Arctic.

Sgt Ken Burton with Helen Tologanak.

A small crew change took place at this stage when Inspector Don Saigle was replaced by Inspector Roger Kembel. Supplies were restocked on the *Simon Fraser* for the remainder of her voyage.

While at Cambridge Bay Sgt Burton met a met an elder woman. She told Sgt Burton the story of how when she was a very young girl she was on a hunting trip with her family. They found themselves on a piece of ice that broke away from shore and drifted out to sea. After a few days afloat they had lost hope of being rescued and were in dire straits as they waited for death. Suddenly out of the fog came a vessel, the *St Roch*, and saved them from a terrible death on the ice. The Voyage of Rediscovery had brought back special memories to the local people who shared many such stories of the original RCMP vessel.

The *Nadon* and the *Simon Fraser* conducted side scan sonar searches for the *Erebus* and *Terror* on the southern shores of King William Island about 250 km east of Cambridge Bay. While this was being done, some crew went ashore and walked the water's edge looking for artifacts. Although several promising images were presented on the sonar scan, a camera search revealed they were natural formations. A total of 18 square miles was thoroughly searched, not as large a coverage as hoped for, because weather conditions prevented further scouring of the area. Several small islands had been re-examined with no significant results, but the information is important in that now this area could be excluded from being searched, and researchers could concentrate their efforts elsewhere.

From the search area, the *Simon Fraser* returned the scientists and archeologists to Cambridge Bay for their trip home while the *Nadon* carried on to Gjoa Haven, NU, arriving there on August 23 where an interesting event occurred regarding the Franklin search. A local Inuit resident by the name of Louie Kamookak took Sgt Ken Burton to two sites of undisturbed skeletal remains. The remains were human and very old and thought to be those of one or two of Franklin's crew members. The sites were untouched but were reported to the Government of Nunavut for further investigation.

The next stop was at Taloyoak, NU, formerly known as Spence Bay. Here the crew met retired S/Cst Adam Totalik who served as an interpreter for Henry Larsen on the *St Roch*. He had received a Long Service medal on March 31, 1973, but was now presented by Inspector Roger Kembel with a new medal furnished by RCMP 'V' Division.

From Taloyoak the voyage carried on to another planned stop at Pasley Bay on the west side of Bellot Strait on the shore of Boothia Peninsula. Here lies the stone cairn of Cst Albert J. 'Frenchie' Chartrand who died of a heart attack in 1942 while he was a crew member on the *St Roch*. A plaque donated by the Nova Scotia Division of the RCMP Veterans' Association was placed on the cairn by Moodie McKay, the third mate of the *Simon Fraser*.

Heading north the *Nadon* responded to a mayday call from a group of stranded Inuit hunters near Pasley Bay. The eight men had experienced boat engine failure and needed parts and fuel. Weather was very bad and a local response could not be launched. They had already been stranded for many days. Fortunately the men were able to radio their needs and the crew of the *Nadon* responded to their location. A Zodiac from the *Nadon*, operated by Cpl Mike Hartung, with Jack Soo's assistance, took the hunters the fuel and parts they had requested.

Only two days later, on August 27, the *Nadon* responded to another call for assistance. Two Inuit hunters had been reported missing since August 20. Philip Kameypatok and John Anaija of Gjoa Haven had been stranded without food near Andreason Point, where a search and rescue aircraft had spotted them and advised the *Nadon*. Again Cpl Mike Hartung responded in freezing winds and high seas in the open Zodiac to deliver the necessary fuel and food. The RCMP Zodiac flooded and nearly capsized on the rocky shores. Once the hunters were given some food and fuel and were safe, the Zodiac was easily floated off the beach and the rescuers returned to the *Nadon*. The hunters remained behind

Sgt Burton and Louie Kamookak examine newly discovered human remains that may have been from the Franklin Expedition.

Inspector Roger Kembel places a plaque on Chartrand's cairn.

The RCMP patrol vessel Nadon *and CCG* Simon Fraser *meet up with the CCG* Henry Larsen *at Erebus and Terror Bay near Beechey Island. This is where Sir John Franklin's vessels wintered in 1845/46.*

until the seas were calm enough for a safe trip home.

During the passage through Bellot Strait, a narrow body of water that separates Boothia Peninsula from Somerset Island, the voyage recorded its coldest day. It measured a high of 1 degree Celsius and a low of -2 degrees Celsius on a sunny day, which brought to light a fact that became more apparent as the journey continued. There was very little ice and the North West Passage was virtually open to sea traffic. This took on international interest as the presence of ice and dangerous navigation has traditionally kept commercial vessel traffic out of the Passage. Now it takes on a whole new dimension as the world learns of this effect of climatic change.

Once through Bellot Strait the *Simon Fraser* stopped at Fort Ross and some crew members went ashore to restock and clean up a storage shed that had been ransacked by a polar bear. The storage shed is used as an emergency supply depot for mariners stuck in the ice nearby and is well known to sailors transiting the area. Many of the existing supplies had been damaged so the crew spent some time cleaning up and putting the depot back in order.

Still heading north towards Devon Island the *Nadon* and the *Simon Fraser* met up with the CGS *Henry Larsen* near Beechey Island. This Coast Guard Ship was named after the captain of the *St Roch*. The crews went ashore on Beechey Island for a short visit to the graves of some of the men of the Franklin expedition.

On August 30 both vessels had reached their northernmost position for the voyage. After crossing Lancaster Sound they were about 230 km east of Resolute on the southern shores of Devon Island at Latitude 74 degrees 43.1 minutes north and Longitude 91 degrees 47.7 minutes west.

The next stop was the abandoned RCMP post of Dundas Harbour on Devon Island. The post, of three members, was established in 1924 but closed permanently in 1951. After a short visit the vessels headed south across Lancaster Sound, between Bylot Island and Baffin Island to Pond Inlet where they arrived on September 2.

The night before their arrival in Pond Inlet, the *Nadon* was anchored and the anchor watch, Inspector Roger Kembel, had to awaken Sgt Burton during the night. A small iceberg had blown up against their bow and was stressing the anchor rode. The decision was made to cut the line but there was another problem. On the ice was a polar bear that was very interested in the ship. Since polar bears are well known to hunt and kill humans, it presented a very dangerous situation. Inspector Roger Kembel decided to make a quick dash to the bow and cut the line. His action was successful and the *Nadon* was free and clear of the ice, which visibly upset the polar bear. In the process of releasing the *Nadon* from the ice, Inspector Kembel injured his arm and had to be flown

The Canadian Coast Guard vessel Sir Wilfred Laurier *in the ice during the St Roch II Voyage of Rediscovery.*

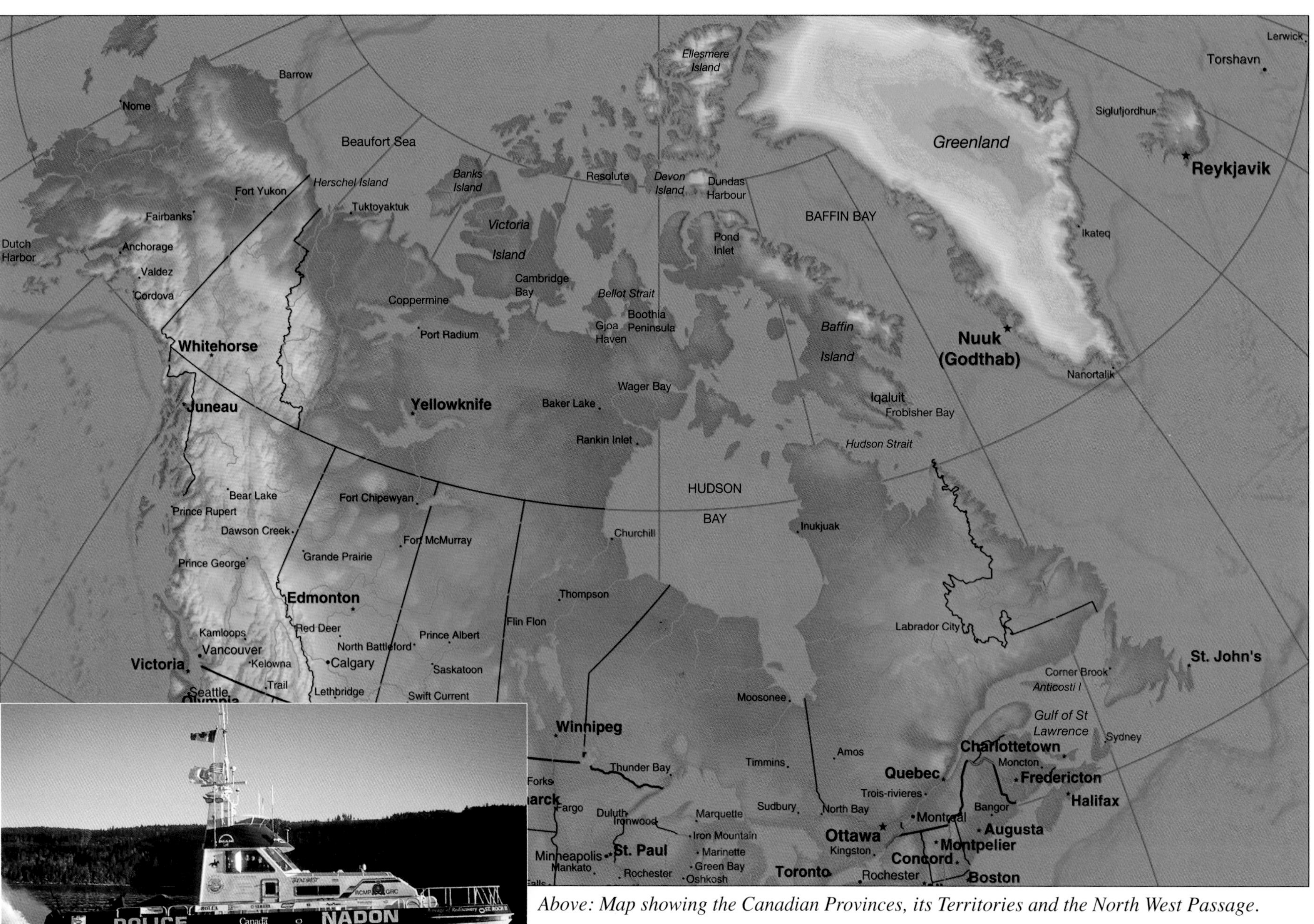

Above: Map showing the Canadian Provinces, its Territories and the North West Passage. Left: The RCMP patrol vessel Nadon/St Roch II, *nearing the end of her epic 169-day Voyage of Rediscovery. She was photographed here during a brief stop in Discovery Bay on the Olympic Peninsula immediately prior to arrival back in Vancouver.*

back to Vancouver from Pond Inlet the next day. An engineer aboard the *Simon Fraser,* Jasmin Sauvé was transferred to the *Nadon* to replace him.

Pond Inlet was the home of the Panipakichoo family who lived aboard the original *St Roch* during her voyages from Pond Inlet to Herschel Island acting as hunters, interpreters, and guides for the RCMP. Descendants of this family, Timothy Kadloo, Elijah and Eli Panipakichoo, Letia Kyak, Ningiuk Killiktee, Benjamin Arreak and their spouses were given a tour of the *Nadon*. The community held cultural performances and treated the crews to throat singing, games, drum dancing, Ajaja singing and storytelling. It was here that a disappointed Captain David Johns, Director of Operations aboard the *Simon Fraser* had to be airlifted to Vancouver with a medical condition.

On September 3 the vessels departed Pond Inlet and headed south along the eastern shores of Baffin Island, making stops at Broughton Island (Qikiqtarjuaq) NU, back across the Arctic Circle, Iqaluit (Frobisher Bay) then on to the coastal shores of Labrador, Newfoundland heading for Goose Bay. The Labrador Sea was very rough and numerous icebergs were spotted along the route. The northern lights were very bright and lit up the skies in the short nights. Finally, after a very rough ride, the vessels cruised up Hamilton Inlet into Lake Melville, at the head of which lies Happy Valley-Goose Bay, Labrador. They arrived there late Thursday, September 14, 2000.

At Happy Valley-Goose Bay there was a short reprieve as a crew change took place and some repairs were completed. Goose Bay is the home of 5 Wing Goose Bay and a rather large community that conveniently facilitated the access to parts and supplies that the far north communities lacked. Jack Soo, the chief engineer aboard the *Nadon* since leaving Prince Rupert, B.C. 67 days previously, and Cpl Mike Hartung who had been aboard for 40 days, departed for home and were replaced by Cst Bruno Ouellette as mate and Cst Kenn Haycock as deck hand. Jasmin Sauvé would continue as chief engineer. Norm Torp, Mark Abrahms and Leann Parker of Fiddler Productions also left from Goose Bay via RCMP Air Services to Montreal, Quebec, then to Vancouver, B.C.

The *Nadon* and CGS *Simon Fraser* continued on to St Anthony at the northern tip of Newfoundland. Crews from both vessels remarked that this passage probably had the worst sea conditions to date. Hurricane Florence was heading up the eastern seaboard and was creating huge swells as far north as Newfoundland. The *Nadon* had difficulty navigating during the night in the four to five metre swells and 65 kilometers per hour winds. With totally black skies and nothing to steer by, the *Nadon* crawled close to the stern of the *Simon Fraser* and followed her stern light throughout the night.

After a short stay at St Anthony, it was on through the Strait of Belle Isle to Isle de Gros Mecatina where the *Simon Fraser* refueled the *Nadon* for the last time. From there the ships would separate as the *Nadon* headed up the St Lawrence to Prescott, Ontario and the *Simon Fraser* carried on to Halifax, Nova Scotia, having completed her circumnavigation and escort duties. They separated on the morning of September 21 in very dense fog. The *Nadon* was now on her own.

The next portion of the Voyage of Rediscovery was not a repeat of any of the stops frequented by the original *St Roch* but rather a means to pay tribute to sponsors, government agencies and communities that had supported the project. This 3,000 kilometre trip in and out of the St Lawrence River also exposed the voyage to a larger audience and hopefully an increased financial response from other sponsors now that the Arctic part of the voyage was successfully completed.

Again weather became a critical factor as the remnants of Hurricane Gordon whipped up the seas of the Gulf of St Lawrence. The *Nadon* had to seek shelter at Havre St Pierre, Quebec, just north of Anticosti Island. The weather was hindering the schedule and soon they were behind by a day. After a quick

Crew of the CGS *Simon Fraser* and PV *Nadon*
Happy Valley, Goose Bay, Labrador
September 15, 2000

Front (L-R): Gord Gillis, Thea Provost, Laslo Bedocs, Robert Mellis, Jacques Asselin, Dianne Sauve, Dr Francis Forbes.

Second Row: Rena Patrick, Sue Sharp, Peter Malacarne, Bill Dancer, Lionel Johnston, Jim MacDougal.

Third Row: Naomi Franks, Aime Gibbons, Hugh Parry, Mike Mont, Cst Kenn Haycock, Sgt Ken Burton.

Fourth Row: Paul Isserlis, Carolyn Dymond, Art Tomsett, Bruce Landry (hidden), Jasmin Sauvé, Volodimir Syomin.

Back Row: Oscar Martens, James Erlam, Dianne Simms.

Missing: Cindy Mellis, Moody McKay, Bill Robinson, Cst Bruno Ouellette, Seth and Beth Berkowitz.

Photograph by Seth Berkowitz. Galleon's Lap Photography

refuelling at Rimouski the *Nadon* carried on, but had to bypass an important stop at Ville de la Baie on the Saguenay River where a major sponsor, Alcan Aluminum, was to be honoured. Instead of the *Nadon* attending, a volunteer crew travelled there on the vessel's behalf in an excursion vehicle being used as land support for the East Coast stops. The volunteers, Bill and Anna Vance and Carolyn Dymond, were responsible for merchandising and setting up displays regarding the Voyage of Rediscovery at the pre-determined destinations.

The *Nadon* continued along the St Lawrence. Even though it travelled continuously since leaving Havre St Pierre, the rough waters made progress slower than expected. This was due to the combination of the current of the St Lawrence River, the strong headwinds, and the effects of the tides, which made life pretty uncomfortable for the crew. After 42 hours of continual running the *Nadon* finally arrived at the Old Port in Montreal, Quebec on September 24 and secured to the float at Place Jacques Cartier, one day behind schedule.

The crew was joined in Montreal by the education coordinator Carolyn Dymond, the documentary film representative Mark Abrahms, and Don Van Dusen, OIC of RCMP Fleet Administration.

After a restful evening in Montreal and a much-needed night's sleep, the *Nadon* headed through the first of the seven locks of the St Lawrence Seaway. Each lock raised the *Nadon* anywhere from two to seven metres. The first two locks were at St Lambert and St Catherine, with two more at Beauharnois. Next were the Snell and Eisenhower locks which are operated by the United States, and then on to the last lock called Iroquois lock. Later that evening the ship arrived at Prescott, Ontario at approximately 2130 hours, an end to a very long and tiring day.

September 24, 2000 also marked the arrival date of the *Simon Fraser* in Halifax, Nova Scotia. This was the end of her journey of 119 days and circumnavigation of North America. The ship and crew were greeted by Vancouver Maritime Museum Director James Delgado, members of the RCMP Veterans' Association, and members of the Canadian Coast Guard. The volunteer crew was very tired but they still had a few days work ahead of them before they could return the *Simon Fraser* to the Canadian Coast Guard.

On the morning of Tuesday September 26, 2000 the *Nadon* headed out of its overnight mooring and picked up RCMP Commissioner Zaccardelli, the Prescott Mayor, the Commissioner's Executive Officer Dennis Constant, retired Commissioner Maurice Nadon, Mr Don Van Dusen and his wife Cheryl, Deputy Commissioner Paul Gauvin, Mr Fred Dupuis, and Mr Mitch Owens for a short trip to the Prescott Canadian Coast Guard Base where special events were to be held. They were escorted into the harbour by the CGS *Caribou Isle*.

After the arrival ceremonies the crew was greeted by approximately 14 bus loads of children from the Henry Larsen Elementary School in Ottawa. They viewed the *Nadon* then went to a nearby park for a barbecue. Speeches were

Top: RCMP on horseback welcome the Nadon *in Montreal. Right: Jasmin Sauvé prepares lines as the* Nadon *enters one of the locks on the St Lawrence Seaway.*

Children from Henry Larsen School sing along with the crew of the PV Nadon.

At Prescott, Ontario L-R: Cst Haycock, Sgt Ken Burton, Commissioner Maurice Nadon (rtd), Governor-General the Right Honourable Adrienne Clarkson, His Excellency John Ralston Saul, Cst Bruno Oullette, Jasmin Sauvé.

made by Sgt Ken Burton and the Mayor then the children swarmed around the crew and broke into a song that paid tribute to the man after whom their school was named, Henry Larsen. They were obviously very proud of their school and the *St Roch*.

Later in the evening the Governor General of Canada arrived. Her Excellency, the Right Honorable Adrienne Clarkson, with her husband His Excellency John Ralston Saul, toured the *Nadon* and paid tribute to the success of the voyage and the cause they were pursuing. Other special guests included members of Henry Larsen's family, (his children Doreen Riedel and Gordon Larsen), Mitch Owens (an original *St Roch* crew member), family of original crew members Chartrand and Dipplock, retired Commissioner Maurice Nadon, Mr Bert Walsh from Alcan Canada, and the Canadian Coast Guard.

At this event the Canadian Coast Guard spoke about the doubts they had had for the success of this passage through the Arctic in a small RCMP aluminum boat, citing the potential for danger and the numerous problems that could occur. They acknowledged that the relatively trouble-free voyage in the Arctic was remarkable and paid tribute to Sgt Burton, the skill and the luck which brought both his crew and vessel safely through the North West Passage.

Early the next day the *Nadon* departed Prescott and returned to Montreal where Carolyn Dymond and Don Van Dusen left the vessel. After a quick stop to refuel in Quebec City, it was on to Iles aux Coudres to overnight, then on to St Roch des Aulnaies, a small town on the southern shores of the St Lawrence after which the *St Roch* was named.

Since St Roch des Aulnaies did not have a harbour, the *Nadon* secured nearby, to the west, at St Jean Port-Joli. The crew was taken to the La Maree-Montante School, where they were interviewed by the students about the Voyage of Rediscovery and the *St Roch*. Carolyn Dymond and Cst Bruno Ouellette were both bilingual and could answer questions to the crew in both official languages. A tour of the area's cultural buildings and sites completed the remainder of the visit.

On September 30 the *Nadon* departed St Jean Port-Joli, Quebec and headed into rough waters again, for the next scheduled stop at Dalhousie, New Brunswick. Shortly after departure, the *Nadon* took a wave over the bow that was large enough to launch the emergency life raft and wash it overboard. It was recovered and had to be sent ahead to Halifax for repacking. After stopping at Matane and Paspediac, Quebec on the Gaspé Peninsula, the *Nadon* arrived in Dalhousie near the head of Chaleur Bay.

The community of Dalhousie had held a lottery to raise funds for the Voyage of Rediscovery and the prize was a short trip on the *Nadon*. RCMP Inspector Mike Woods, two guides and four draw winners were taken on a short tour around the bay. This event, which raised over $1,200, was one of several that helped contribute significantly to the campaign.

While en route from Dahousie to Shediac, New Brunswick the *Nadon* met up off the shores of Mirimachi at Point Escumine with her sister ship, the RCMP PV *Simmons*, and her crew. The skipper of the *Simmons*, Cpl Doug Cleough, was the former mate for Sgt Burton on the RCMP PV *Lindsay* when he was posted in Vancouver, B.C.

Nearing Shediac, New Brunswick late on October 3, the *Nadon* was greeted by a large contingent of people and resources. The RCMP helicopter and several vessels came out to escort her into harbour. The breakwater was covered with spectators waving to the crew, and on the docks numerous others were clamouring to witness their arrival. At the marina the Mayor of Shediac, Mr Raymond LeBlanc was presented with an invitation from the community of Gibsons, B.C. to be their East Coast sister city, which the Mayor accepted.

Also present was Mr Don Johnson who had sailed from Vancouver, B.C. to Halifax, N.S. via the Panama Canal as a member of the original *St Roch*.

Flag of the St Roch II.

Shediac is considered to be the lobster capital of the world, and the crew was treated to a fine lobster dinner that evening.

The next day there was a short break from formal activities as repairs and maintenance were done on the *Nadon*. The crew also checked out the vessel thoroughly from stem to stern to compile a list of repairs that would be needed when she was removed from the water after reaching Halifax. The crew had a short rest and joined in a 'meet and greet' barbecue with the local RCMP detachment.

The last day in Shediac was marked by the presence of the Moncton, New Brunswick RCMP Pipes and Drums Band that played to a gathering of people at the marina. Ms Kathleen Doyle Beaton presented the crew with her brother's parka that he wore while on the *St Roch*. Her brother, John Doyle, had replaced Cst Chartrand after his death in the Arctic in 1942.

The crew was joined by Carolyn Dymond, Cpl Mark Bridges and his wife for the short trip across Northumberland Strait to Charlottetown, Prince Edward Island. The winds were very strong and the seas rough, but that did not

PV Simon Fraaser *crew bids farewell to the PV* Nadon *in Atlantic Canada.*

The PV Nadon *in windswept waters on the Labrador coast.*

deter a small RCMP Boston Whaler from sitting under Confederation Bridge waiting for the *Nadon*. This 12.9 kilometre-long bridge ties the New Brunswick mainland to Prince Edward Island. Here Cst Greg Laturnus sat, hoping to get a good photograph of the vessel passing under the bridge.

In Charlottetown the *Nadon* was greeted by RCMP Inspector Steve Graham, Mayor George MacDonald and Attorney-General Jeff Lance. Informal events were conducted that evening and the next day. The crew was invited to Chief Superintendent Ken Burt's (Commanding Officer of 'L' Division) residence for a quiet and private dinner.

The plan was to arrive in Halifax, Nova Scotia on October 10, 2000. This was the anniversary date of the original *St Roch's* arrival in 1942. Leaving Charlottetown they passed through Georges Bay into the Canso Locks located between Cape Breton Island and the Nova Scotia mainland. Again the crew met up with the PV *Simmonds* as she was heading home to Newfoundland from Mirimachi. They had to move quickly as another storm was heading up the East Coast. With the weather getting much worse the *Nadon* had to take shelter at Stormont on the east coast of Nova Scotia. Early the next day they departed for Halifax and arrived one day early and secured to the Canadian Coast Guard base in Dartmouth on the other side of the harbour to await an appropriate moment to turn up for the following day's celebrations.

It was October 10, 2000, 58 years to the day that the *St Roch* had sailed into Halifax after taking two years to pass through the North West Passage from west to east. A rendezvous point outside the harbour off Black Point was where a convoy, including a Coast Guard vessel and a fireboat, escorted the *Nadon* into harbour. Aboard were some members of the CGS *Simon Fraser*, as well as former *St Roch* crew member Bill Cashin, Henry Larsen's daughter Doreen Reidel, and others.

While entering the harbour Cst Kenn Haycock raised the original Blue

Ensign flag that had been on the *St Roch* and provided by Mrs Reidel. It was dipped as they passed the Canadian Coast Guard Base, and Bill Cashin proudly rang the original *St Roch* bell that had been hanging off the mast of the *Nadon* since leaving Vancouver.

As they approached the dockside a gun salute was fired by the Royal Artillary 3rd Brigade from the Halifax Fortress on Citadel Hill and a Ceremonial Guard of the 78th Highlanders played on shore. Numerous RCMP veterans, members and previous *St Roch* crew were waiting dockside. The crew was greeted by Mike Murray of the Maritime Museum of the Atlantic, and Father Lloyd O'Neil offered a prayer of thanksgiving for the ship's safe arrival. RCMP Assistant Commissioner Dwight Bishop (Commanding Officer of 'H' Division), Deputy Commissioner Terry Ryan, Mr James Delgado, and retired Superintendent Clare Dent of the RCMP Veterans' Association were present.

This was a pivotal point in the Voyage of Rediscovery as the Canadian portion of the journey had been completed. It was time to refit the *Nadon* and prepare the vessel for the second half of the trip back home to Vancouver, B.C. Cst Bruno Ouellette had completed his portion of the trip, and left for home, as did Jasmin Sauvé who had been aboard both the CGS *Simon Fraser* and the *Nadon* as engineer for 104 days. They were replaced by Cpl Bob Currie and Cst Dan Cochlan.

The *Nadon* was hauled out of the water at the Halifax Naval Base. The trip had taken a toll on the vessel and she had to have her propellers replaced and some cracks in her hull welded. Jasmin Sauvé replaced a faulty transponder and carried out minor repairs on the decks and the electronics on the bridge. After 14,000 nautical miles the damage to the aluminum catamaran *Nadon* was actually rather minimal.

Stores and supplies which were needed for the remainder of the trip were removed from the CGS *Simon Fraser* and stowed aboard the *Nadon*. Oil

The PV Nadon *is taken out of the water at Halifax and refits are done to the hull and drives before the trip home to Vancouver, B.C.*

changes were completed, all the charts needed for the remainder of the trip were checked, and plans made for the next leg of the trip to New York City.

The evening was calm but the weather forecast called for deteriorating conditions. To safely cross the Gulf of Maine in calmer weather it was determined that the *Nadon* would leave Halifax on the evening of Friday, October 13 rather than wait until morning. Tropical Storm Leslie had just passed and Hurricane Michael was building off the Caribbean Islands. The *Nadon* departed Halifax on her 8,000 mile trip home at 1930 hours.

Except for a quick stop at Yarmouth for refueling, the overnight and daytime run across the Gulf of Maine to Cape Cod, Massachusetts was relatively smooth and continuous from Halifax. The vessel cleared US Customs in Provincetown Harbor and the next morning departed across Cape Cod Bay into Cape Cod Canal. Soon the *Nadon* was greeted by a New Bedford police vessel

The PV Nadon *at Ellis Island, New York.*

Taken from the PV Nadon *on the Intracoastal waterway, East Coast.*

and Sgt Jill Simmons, who escorted them into the New Bedford, Massachusetts Harbor for refueling and lunch. The next leg across Rhode Island Sound, Block Island Sound, and into the protected waters of Long Island Sound was completed as the *Nadon* arrived in New York City Harbor and secured there late in the evening of October 15.

The day of the official arrival of the *Nadon*, was scheduled for Monday, October 16. From Ellis Island the *Nadon* met up with the New York City fireboat and the New York Police Department police vessel that were to escort them around the Statue of Liberty, past the Staten Island Ferry terminal and to South Street Seaport Museum located just south of the Brooklyn Bridge. Halfway into the harbour the fireboat was called away to an emergency and had to abandon the escort. The New York City Maritime Museum covers 11 square blocks in Lower Manhattan, the largest facility of its type in the United States.

Canadian Consulate General representative Jennifer Kay held a reception that evening at the Melville Gallery where Mr James Delgado and Sgt Ken Burton made a presentation regarding the voyage. The next evening the same was done at the New York Explorers Club. Several media interviews were conducted with Sgt Burton while his crew attended maintenance and supply issues during their three day stay in New York.

The next stop was Norfolk, Virginia, the home of the United States Little Creek Naval Base. Leaving New York for the open seas the *Nadon* passed the states of New Jersey, Delaware and Maryland en route to Virginia. The official ceremonies that were to be conducted in Norfolk were cancelled due to the recent attack on the USS Cole in the Middle East. The whole base was on heightened alert, especially to foreign vessels.

From Little Creek Naval Base the *Nadon* headed into the Intracoastal Waterway (ICW) between Norfolk and Portsmouth on October 19. This Waterway is a continuous series of canals, rivers and bays that runs along the whole

United States eastern seaboard to facilitate a protected passageway for small vessels when the open seas become too rough due to frequent storms. The day was a short one, because the *Nadon* was experiencing steering problems and arrangements had to be made for a technician to attend. Repairs were made in Portsmouth but a whole day was lost in the process.

Progress was slow as the ICW dictated that the speed of all vessels must remain at about five to 10 knots, but with a scheduled five days to get to Fort Lauderdale, Florida, time did not seem crucial. The *Nadon* passed through the Big Bridge lock on the ICW, south of Portsmouth, and into the mouth of the North River, and the state of North Carolina. Here the *Nadon* continued through Albemarle Sound, Alligator-Pungo Canal and to the town of Bellhaven, North Carolina, just north of Pamlico Sound, where she moored at a small marina for the night. The voyage continued out into the open waters again as the vessel left the ICW at Morehead City and headed south across Onslow Bay, around Cape Fear, and into Southport, North Carolina, where she tied up at a local marina. Early the next day the *Nadon* headed out to open waters once more and continued along the South Carolina coast, finally arriving in Savannah, Georgia on Sunday, October 22. The weather had been cooperative, seas calm and winds light, but that was soon to change.

Weather had deteriorated as the remnants of Hurricane Michael and Tropical Storm Nadine whipped up the seas, even though their paths were many miles offshore. After a fuel stop at Thunderbolt Marina, the *Nadon* attempted to break out to open sea but was thwarted by the waves that broke over the shallow sand bars and threatened to bottom out the vessel. They returned to the ICW, obtained some charts and carried on south at a slow pace. Keeping to the speed restrictions of five to 10 knots, the 14-hour day produced only about 130 miles under the keel of the *Nadon*. This threatened to put them behind their expected arrival time in Fort Lauderdale, Florida.

It was a very windy evening when the *Nadon* secured overnight moorage at the US Kings Bay Naval Base in Georgia, just north of Cumberland Sound. The next day was no better. As they passed the mouth of St Mary's River on the ICW, the crew could see that the outside waters were still very rough, so they had to stick to the inside.

Passing into the state of Florida, they now experienced another passage-slowing phenomenon: bridges. From Fernandina Beach to Fort Lauderdale there were some 68 'open on demand' bridges. Each drawbridge over the ICW was controlled by an operator who would open it when requested, or at pre-determined time intervals. This hindered the speed of passage but was probably the lesser of the two evils considering the size of the three metre swells outside, which would have also slowed the *Nadon* and made it much more uncomfortable. They passed Daytona Beach and could see Cape Canaveral in the distance when they secured for the night at Titusville.

On October 25, 2000 the *Nadon* departed Titusville, Florida and had to run until it reached Fort Lauderdale. They were one day behind schedule, and sponsors and service technicians were awaiting their arrival. Finally, at 2100

hours they reached their mooring spot, the Fort Lauderdale Marriot Hotel Marina. This was the location of one of the largest boat shows in North America, and the *Nadon* was participating in it. Sponsors of the Voyage of Rediscovery were in attendance and technicians were ready to inspect their products. After a much-needed overhaul of some equipment they were ready to continue the journey home to Vancouver.

Before departing Fort Lauderdale there was another crew change. Cst Kenn Haycock departed after six weeks aboard and Cst Dan Cochlan also left for home. They were replaced by Cst John Stringer and Inspector Ken Gates for the next leg of the voyage while Sgt Ken Burton and Cpl Bob Currie continued.

After five days in Fort Lauderdale, the *Nadon* departed on October 31 in 30-knot winds, along the Florida Keys to Key West. Slowed by rough seas they arrived in Marina Hemingway, just outside Havana, Cuba three hours behind schedule. Refueling the *Nadon* was not allowed at Colony Marina on the west coast of Cuba and they had to travel 125 miles farther east to the southern Cuban port of Cayo Largo. This extra distance plus rough weather forced a change in the schedule, so a planned stop in Jamaica was cancelled as they forged ahead to the island of Grand Cayman. After 45 hours of travelling they arrived in Grand Cayman at noon on Saturday, November 4.

The arrival time presented its own problems as everything was closed until Monday and fuel, supplies, and cash were badly needed for the next long passage. There are not many places better than Grand Cayman to be forced to stay for a day or so.

On Monday, November 6, with five extra fuel tanks containing 1,000 liters of additional fuel strapped to the deck, the *Nadon* headed across the Caribbean Sea on a 26-hour run to Isle de San Andres, a small Columbian island about 140 miles off the coast of Nicaragua. Weather was relatively calm for a welcome change and the passage was uneventful. After a quick refueling the journey continued to Puerto San Cristobal at Colon, Panama on the Caribbean side of the Panama Canal.

On November 8 the *Nadon* was anchored off Colon while documents were prepared for the transit of the Canal. The crew travelled by car across the Panama Isthmus along Lake Gatun to Panama City to attend a reception hosted by Patty Goodfellow, the Canadian Consulate in Panama. Numerous embassies and the Canadian Association of Panama were represented. Sgt Brian Brasnett (RCMP Liaison Officer, Bogota), Jaime Sebastian and Andrew Wilkins of the Canadian Association of Panama, joined the *Nadon* for the canal transit.

Another crew change took place in Colon, Panama when Inspector Ken Gates departed as did Cpl Bob Currie after his 31-day journey from Halifax, N.S. Taking their places were Sgt Gene Pinnegar and Cst Mike Schmeisser. On leaving the canal the *Nadon* and her crew were back in the Pacific Ocean and heading north towards home.

Fuel was difficult to find on this stretch but with the extra fuel tanks on board the distance travelled could be extended, especially when speed was kept to a minimum. After refueling at Marina Flamingo, Bahia Potrero, in Costa Rica they ran up the coast passing Nicaragua, Honduras, El Salvador and Guatemala, then arrived in Mexico. Arrangements had been made by Sgt Daniel Goyette from the Canadian Embassy in Mexico for clearance to Mexican waters. Mexican Customs was cleared at Puerto Madero on Wednesday, November 15. Public events scheduled for Mexico were in Acapulco and Cabo San Lucas. Excellent weather made this leg of the voyage fast and comfortable.

The *Nadon* arrived at the Acapulco Yacht Club where another crew change took place. After three weeks on board Cst John Stringer went home and was replaced by Cst Anne Clarke who stayed aboard until Vancouver, British Columbia. With their newest crew member on board they departed on November 19. Travelling at night, the vessel entered Puerto Vallarta 24 hours later, refueled by tanker truck, then anchored about 12 miles off shore. Two days later they landed at Cabo San Lucas on the Baja California Peninsula in Mexico.

At Cabo San Lucas there were about 150 people present to meet them. One of the major sponsors, Trends West Resorts, provided a week-long holiday for contest winner Bernice Sharpe of North Vancouver, B.C. at their Coral Baja Resort in San Jose del Cabo. This was the result of promoting the Voyage of Rediscovery by the sponsor. The crew also had a break from living aboard the *Nadon* as they were treated to a stay at the air conditioned resort for two nights.

Vancouver was only three weeks away when they left Cabo San Lucas for San Diego, California, their first American stop on the Pacific coast. There was one more Mexican refueling stop, at Bahia Tortugas, about half way up the Baja coast, before crossing the Mexican-United States border.

The *Nadon* was met by the U.S. Customs Marine Unit and escorted into the Naval Air Station on North Island, San Diego, California, where customs was cleared. Less than 1,000 miles from home, they prepared for the final legs of the journey. Repairs were made and supplies loaded aboard while the last crew change took place. Sgt Gene Pinnegar and Cst Mike Schmeisser ended their 17-day stint and were replaced by Cst Vic Cunha and Cst Richard Harry. They were also met by John Henley of Trend West Resorts and Dean Hadley, a former crew member of the original *St Roch*. These two guests would be aboard the *Nadon* for the ride up to Oceanside Harbor, California from the San Diego Naval Air Station. Mr Hadley, age 81, shared many stories with the crew of the *Nadon* about the 1940-1942 *St Roch* trip through the Arctic.

There were approximately 50 VIPs, including the Mayor, the Honourable Mr Dick Lyon, to greet their Oceanside, California arrival. Over 300 people toured the *Nadon* and a presentation was made by Sgt Burton where he acknowledged the sponsorship of Trend West Resorts. Two television stations and two local newspapers gave prominent coverage to the now near-completed Voyage of Rediscovery. The *Nadon* departed Oceanside on Wednesday, November 29 heading for Santa Barbara, California.

After an overnight stay at Ventura Harbor the *Nadon* headed into Santa Barbara, only two hours away. A presentation was given by Sgt Burton at the Santa Barbara Maritime Museum that evening. Again, over 400 visitors toured the *Nadon*. It was now the beginning of December which would mark the end of the Voyage of Rediscovery, but several more stops had to be completed first.

In San Francisco, California the *Nadon* was secured at the San Francisco Maritime National Historic Park at Hyde Street Pier. This was a weekend stop with open boat tours but no scheduled events. Mr Howard Arneson, the owner and developer of Arneson Drive Systems met the crew and took them for a short ride on his turbine powered speed boat. Arneson drives are installed in RCMP catamarans and was the propulsion system in the *Nadon*.

The weather was much calmer than expected, so the next leg of the journey from San Francisco to Newport, Oregon, took only 28 hours. The schedule called for a stop at Depoe Bay. However, because of sea conditions that could hamper arrival and departure in that harbour it was decided to stay at Newport instead. From Oregon there was one last stop before the *Nadon* arrived home, and that was in Discovery Bay, Washington.

Ahead of schedule, the *Nadon* headed to Trend West Resorts at Discovery Bay in Port Townsend, Washington to prepare the vessel for the homecoming. No events were scheduled and the crew rested and cleaned up the vessel. Three representatives from the Ministry of the Attorney-General: Stephen Stackhouse, (Assistant Deputy Minister); Kevin Begg, (Director Police Services); and Barry Salmon (Policy Analyst), came aboard the *Nadon* for the ride into Victoria, B.C. Also joining them was James Delgado of the Vancouver Maritime Museum and Jeff Lee from the Vancouver Sun Newspaper.

The *Nadon* and her crew arrived in Victoria, B.C. on December 14, 2000. A

RCMP marine members and crew of the PV *Nadon* at the Welcoming Ceremonies on the return to Vancouver, British Columbia in December 2000.

Above, L–R back row: Sgt Peter Attrell, Cst John Stringer, Ceremonial Troop members, S/Sgt Vic Louks, Unknown–Ceremonial Troup, Inspector Don Saigle, Cst Dan Cochlan, Mr Don Van Dusen, Cst Kenn Haycock, Cst Vic Cunha. Middle row: Sgt Ken Burton, Mr Jack Soo, Cst Bruno Ouellette, Mr David Burton, Inspector Ken Gates, Cst Mike Schmeisser. Front row: Cst Richard Harry, Cpl Anne Clarke, Unknown–Ceremonial Troup, Cpl Mike Hartung.
Right: Former constable Dean Hadley (left), original member of the St Roch crew and Inspector John Henley (retired) representing Trend West Resorts on a visit to the St Roch II.

reception hosted by the Ministry of Attorney General, Police Services Division, was held at the Laurel Point Inn. In attendance were the Acting Mayor of Victoria the Honourable Helen Hughes, RCMP Deputy Commissioner Brian Watt, the Deputy Minister for the Ministry of Attorney General Cynthia Morton, and the Executive Director of the Vancouver Maritime Museum James Delgado. During the next day there was a presentation at the Maritime Museum of British Columbia in Victoria before the *Nadon* headed out to the small community of Sidney north of Victoria, where she was moored for the night at the Institute of Ocean Sciences.

The last day of the Voyage of Rediscovery had finally arrived. Weather conditions were rough so many of the guests who had planned to ride aboard the *Nadon* from Sidney to Vancouver chose to meet the vessel at its destination instead. They arrived at Heritage Harbour, home of the Vancouver Maritime Museum, on Saturday, December 16, 2000 at 1400 hours. The shores were lined with well-wishers standing in the rain. Many of the participants and crew were present in RCMP red serge to greet Sgt Burton and the *Nadon*. The vessel was escorted into harbour by the Vancouver City Police Marine Unit, the Canadian Coast Guard Ship *Osprey*, the Vancouver City Fireboat, the Vancouver Harbour Patrol, and Vision Quest canoes.

Many RCMP officers and dignitaries attended the event and congratulations were offered by RCMP Commissioner Giuliano Zaccardelli, Assistant Commissioner Bev Busson (CO of 'E' Division), Member of Parliament Hedy Fry, B.C. Attorney-General Graeme Bowbrick, and Vancouver Deputy Mayor Sandy McCormick. The deck of the original *St Roch* was the platform for welcome home speeches led by James Delgado Director of the Vancouver Maritime Museum and followed by Sgt Ken Burton who spoke of his gratitude and appreciation to all persons and sponsors who helped make the Voyage of

Above: The home team, Sgt Ken Burton, representative of Trend West, Cst Vic Cunha, Cpl Richard Harry and Cpl Anne Clarke. Below: Mr Howard Arneson meets up with Sgt Ken Burton and Cpl Anne Clarke in San Francisco Bay.

Courtesy Vancouver Maritime Museum

Left: Henry Larsen and crew of the St Roch *in Halifax, July 1944. L–R front row: Jim Diplock, Bill Peters, Pat Hunt, Rudy Johnsen, Henry Larsen. Missing from photo is Stan McKenzie and Lloyd Russel. Back row: Mitch Owens, G.B. Dickens, Frank Matthews, Bill Cashin, Ole Andreasen.*

Below, left: North Slope, Alaska, showing the ice-free waterway used by the Nadon/St Roch II. *This is very shallow but a stretch of ocean that allowed the ice-avoidance passage of the* Nadon *into the North West Passage.*

Below, right: St Roch II *crew near Herschel Island. L-R: Sgt Ken Burton, Sgt Frank LaLear, Cst John May and Mr Jack Soo.*

Rediscovery a success.

Despite the successes of the voyage, the bottom line for the project fell short of expectations. There were three goals at the outset with the first being to bring awareness to the historic value of the *St Roch* and the need to restore the vessel and provide a new home for her. The second goal was to provide an internet site for education purposes which could be followed by a world audience. The story of the *St Roch* and the Voyage of Rediscovery was told to an estimated world-wide audience of over 17 million people. The third goal was to raise an endowment fund that would provide for the existing and future needs of this historic vessel. Two of the first three goals were very successful but the fund-raising fell short. They were able to raise three million dollars in cash and contributions and spent 2.95 million dollars on the venture.

Although the project broke even by the end of the voyage, fund raising continued and a small endowment fund was established. Media attention to the project made it very difficult for anyone to totally ignore the *St Roch*. Although at the time of this writing, she does not yet have a new home. The original *St Roch* is still open to the public and draws 100,000 visitors annually.

The Voyage of Rediscovery came to an end taking 169 days to complete, and covering a distance of over 24,000 nautical miles. A list of accomplishments by the two RCMP vessels *St Roch*, and PV *Nadon* (*St Roch II*), and the CGS *Simon Fraser* is as follows:

Original *St Roch*
- First ship to travel the Northwest Passage from west to east 1940-1942
- First ship to sail the northerly deep-water North West Passage, 1944
- First ship to sail the North West Passage in both directions, 1944
- First ship to circumnavigate North America, 1950
- First ship to circumnavigate North America in both directions, 1954

PV *Nadon (St Roch II)*
- First vessel to reach Tuktoyaktuk from the west in 2000
- Smallest vessel ever to circumnavigate North America
- Circumnavigated North America in 169 days
- Sailed through the North West Passage in four weeks
- Participated in a major search for the lost Franklin Expedition
- Lead to a possible new grave site of the Franklin Expedition
- Was visited by over 15,000 people
- Generated over 1.1 million visitors to the *St Roch* web site
- Visited seven Canadian provinces, three Territories, seven foreign countries, and travelled in three oceans
- Brought international attention to the ice-free conditions of the Arctic and climatic change
- Participated in two Arctic rescues, a total of ten people rescued
- Reignited the kinship with the communities and elders of the Canadian North, following the legacy left by the *St Roch*
- Brought to the public's attention the current condition of and the need to preserve the *St Roch*

CGS *Simon Fraser* – Many of the above and:
- First vessel to circumnavigate North America in 2000 (started and ended in Halifax, N.S.) in 119 days
- Only Coast Guard Vessel ever to operate with a totally volunteer crew
- Participated in launching 2,000 bottles in the Arctic to provide scientific information on Arctic currents for years to come.

Top: Sgt Ken Burton, marine historian James Delgado and Inspector Roger Kimbel near Kirkwall Island. Above: Inspector Donald Saigle, Officer in Charge 'E' Division Marine Services, near Smoking Hills, Nunavut, 2000. Right: Nadon *in the ice.*

POLICE
Canada
NADON

Epilogue

The winds were howling down the channel, a waterway that usually affords protection against storms of this nature. At its head lay a harbour with 30 to 40 boats safely secured at their moorings but nevertheless suffering from the pounding of the waves as they smashed the hulls against the heavy timbers of the floats. One sailing vessel, unfortunate enough to be abeam of the winds, was heeled over so far that people struggling to get to their floating homes had to duck under the mast as it lay almost horizontal to the seas.

The Coast Guard Rescue boat had already left port, heading out into the Straits to assist a vessel that was taking on water. In the rough seas a through-hull fitting had been compromised and the vessel was slowly sinking as the bilge pumps could not keep up with the flooding. The local auxiliary Coast Guard in their 7.3-metre inflatable rescue craft was busy patrolling the harbour and assisting vessels resecure to the floats or move to better anchorages. Darkness was settling in, which made the situation even more tense, and owners looked warily out into the channel hoping no commercial or pleasure craft would cause damage to their much loved vessels.

The RCMP Marine Services vessel was tied up to these same floats, standing by on the radio emergency channel for the next call for assistance. Already they had secured a vessel that had taken on too much water and was in danger of sinking, by putting a salvage pump to work to keep it afloat. Then a call came in on the police radio.

An unoccupied vessel had dragged its anchor and had drifted into another boat causing some damage. The skipper of the RCMP vessel dispatched two deckhands in the 5.4-metre inflatable boat to investigate. They too were exposed to these elements and pounded their small craft over to the location in the harbour where the event had been reported.

When they arrived they found the unoccupied vessel had passed the point of collision, with the anchor secured to the bottom and holding firm. It was no longer a threat to anyone and a quick inspection of the boat indicated that it had suffered little damage and the anchor rode was strong enough to hold it. The members then attended to the occupied vessel and found there was a measureable amount of damage to the hull at the bow but nothing that threatened the boat's integrity. The owner stated he would go farther out in the channel and re-anchor for the night. Details and photographs would be taken in the daylight hours when it was safer to investigate in more detail. Meanwhile identification was obtained and assistance offered to relocate the damaged vessel.

A yacht owner stood leaning into the wind and driving rain, peering at a vessel that moments before seemed to be farther away. Protecting his eyes with his hands he stared at the boat and then became alarmed as he realized it too was dragging its anchor and was drifting towards his own craft. He ran and grabbed a Coast Guard auxiliary member who was busy tying up another vessel and informed him of the potential danger of this sailboat adrift. The three Coast Guard members jumped into their inflatable boat and bounced their way to the target. The bow of the sail boat was facing upwind with the taut anchor rode leading at a steep angle to the sea bottom. Lying bow to bow with the engines of the inflatable boat in reverse, the crew secured the anchor line and freed it from the bottom. Now it was just a matter of towing it farther away from the harbour and dropping the anchor again hoping it would hold this time.

Backing into the seas was not the best way to do this considering the size of the waves and the distance they had to travel, so the team decided to secure the boats side by side and face into the weather. This standard manoeuvre to tow an unmanned vessel to another location was practised regularly. To do so they had to reposition their rigid hulled inflatable boat (RHIB) and secure the two vessels together with mooring lines, then make way. However, in the process, with the RHIB almost in position, a huge wave rocked them violently just as two men were about to board the unmanned sail boat. Overboard they went into the icy cold waters, between the two hulls of the vessels.

The Coast Guard vessel operator had to keep his twin 150 horsepower outboard engines away from his crew mates, so he swung the stern back into the wind and seas but in doing so he could not assist his overboard crew. Both vessels had a high freeboard and it would have been difficult to get aboard either boat in optimum conditions let alone in a storm.

The RCMP inflatable craft had concluded its initial investigation and had finished assisting the damaged vessel move to a new location. They then spotted a 20-foot sailing boat about to smash onto the nearby shore and went to check it out. Even for a small inflatable, the waters were too shallow to get close enough to haul it off the beach. There was nothing they could do immediately so they turned around and that was when they heard shouts from the direction of the Coast Guard RHIB. The sight they saw was a rescuer's worst nightmare. Anyone falling into the water, at night, during a storm, and with their own vessel unable to help, was in a bad a situation. The RCMP responded immediately and manoeuvred into position. They too had to be concerned about their engine getting too close to the Coast Guard crew in the water. Even though their engine was a single 90 hp outboard it could still do real harm to anyone unfortunate enough to get struck by the propeller. The vessel's small size had a shallower freeboard which would make it easier to get the Coast Guard members on board, however they also had to be careful not to risk pinning them against the side of the sailboat.

Slowly the RCMP edged their way in and managed to pass them a heaving line from the bow. Once attached, they towed them a few feet away from the sailboat to reduce the danger of their being crushed. Then a RCMP crew member pulled both Coast Guard men aboard and delivered the wet and cold crew back to their very relieved skipper. Not missing a beat, although wet and cold, the Coast Guard continued with the task at hand and moved the sailboat to a safe mooring spot without any further incident. The RCMP assisted with the move to ensure the safety of everyone involved.

The night wore on but further patrols of the harbour indicated that only one vessel was damaged and one vessel was washed ashore. Considering the strength of the storm and the number of vessels seeking shelter in the harbour, both the RCMP and the Coast Guard were relieved it was not worse. The storm eventually abated and the RCMP walked the docks and floats talking with boat owners. They did not hide their relief that the storm had subsided and that the evening had become calm, although the seas were still quite rough. People were very grateful and expressed their thanks to the members for being there when needed.

This is the story of one small event in the service of a RCMP Marine member. Similar stories happen often, usually with no fanfare or notice. In stormy weather most people are safely at home. It has been noted by some that only fools and the police are out on the water in such bad conditions. The police are just doing the job they know must be done.

APPENDIX 'A'

Commissioners of the RCMP

1.	Lt Col W. Osborne SMITH	Sept 1873 – Oct 1873
2.	George Arthur FRENCH	Oct 1873 – Jul 1876
3.	James Farquharson MACLEOD	July 1876 – Oct 1880
4.	Acheson Gosford IRVINE	Nov 1880 – Mar 1886
5.	Lawrence William HERCHMER	Apr 1886 – Jul 1900
6.	Aylesworth Bowen PERRY	Aug 1900 – Mar 1923
7.	Cortlandt STARNES	Apr 1923 – Jul 1931
8.	Sir James Howden MACBRIEN	Aug 1931 – Mar 1938
9.	Stuart Taylor WOOD	Mar 1938 – Apr 1951
10.	Leonard Hanson NICHOLSON	May 1951 – Mar 1959
11.	Charles Edward RIVETT-CARNAC	Apr 1959 – Mar 1960
12.	Clifford Walter HARVISON	Apr 1960 – Oct 1963
13.	George Brinton McCLELLAN	Nov 1963 – Aug 1967
14.	Malcolm Francis Aylesworth LINDSAY	Aug 1967 – Sep 1969
15.	William Leonard HIGGITT	Oct 1969 – Dec 1973
16.	Maurice Jean NADON	Jan 1974 – Aug 1977
17.	Robert Henry SIMMONDS	Sept 1977 – Aug 1987
18.	Normand David INKSTER	Sept 1987 – Jun 1994
19.	Joseph Philip Robert MURRAY	June 1994 – Aug 2000
20.	Giuliano ZACCARDELLI	Sept 2000 – Dec 2006
21.	Beverley BUSSON	Dec 2006 – July 2007
22.	William ELLIOTT	July 2007 – Nov 2011
23.	Robert PAULSON	Nov 2011 –

APPENDIX 'B'

Last Roll Call of the RCMP Marine Division 1970 - 1973

DECK

Allen, R.B.	Cst	27908	H
Bain, C.R.	S/Sgt	19279	H
Bambury, G.R.	Cst	27887	J
Barr, H.W.	Cst	27857	J
Beazley, R.G.	Sgt	23734	D
Belanger, J.Y.L.M.	Cst	27902	H
Black, G.M.	Cpl	27865	B
Bowser, E.H.	Cpl	24721	H
Brown, T.M.	Cst	27972	E
Brownell, N.H.	Sgt	20569	H
Burns, J.R.	Cst	27897	L
Burns, R.	Cst	27974	E
Campbell, R.A.	Cst	27985	E
Carter, D.R.	Cst	27914	H
Castonguay, J.J.P.R.	Cpl	27911	L
Chiasson, E.J.	Cst	27849	D
Clarke, P.M.	Sgt	24224	H
Clements, R.A.	Cst	27904	O
Connell, R.W.	Cst	27830	D
Cook, G.A.	Cpl	24156	A
Copeland, R.G.	Cpl	23993	E
Cross, C.	Cpl	24717	E
D'Eon, R.J.	Cpl	22130	O
D'Entremont, L.M.	Cst	27975	C
Dalton, H.R.	Cst	28005	J
Davis, W.R.	Cst	27888	B
Dawe, S.H.	Sgt	24718	H
De St Remy, A.T.	Cpl	22897	E
De St Remy, C.E.	Cst	27969	E
Devison, J.O.	Sgt	22270	E
Duguid, W.G.	Cst	27173	E
Essiembre, J.C.H.	Cst	27912	C
Evans, A.P.	Cst	29219	E
Fowler, I.C.	Cst	28006	B
Frost, J.E.	Cst	28018	E
Gagne, J.E.G.	Sgt	24714	C
Gagne, O.G.	Sgt	20138	C
Gallant, J.V.	Cpl	24716	A
Gallant, P.E.	Cst	27849	H
Garbutt,G.W.	Cst	29004	E
Garton, W.	Cst	28023	E
Godreau, D.P.	Cst	27883	H
Grady, J.L.	S/Sgt	19639	H
Green, S.B.	Sgt	19794	E
Greeno, A.W.	S/Sgt	20319	B
Grovesw, R.B.	Cst	27864	H
Hall, R.G.S.	Cst	27988	E
Hansford, J.R.	Cst	27859	O
Hardiman, W.N.	Cst	27877	O
Harvey, J.N.L.C.	Cst	27843	C
Hiltz, D.A.	Cpl	24225	A
Himmelman, J.D.	Cpl	26693	H
Horne, C.V.	Cpl	24713	H

Houlihan, J.	Sgt	23426	E
Hunt, A.H.M.	S/Sgt	22754	B
Johnston, L.T.	Cpl	28024	E
Kearley, E.	Cst	27923	E
Keddy, J.N.	Cst	27870	E
Keefe, O.	Cst	27891	H
Kennedy, R.E.	Cst	27962	E
King, L.M.	Sgt	15818	O
Koehn, G.A.	Cst	27968	E
Laflamme, J.V.A.	Cpl	27873	C
Larocque, A.L.	Cst	27965	O
Leblanc, L.	Cst	27967	E
Lewis, G.E.	Sgt	19146	E
Lord, D.P.	Sgt	22855	H
Lowe, A.J.S.	Cst	27910	H
Luttrell, J.F.C.	Sgt	23991	E
Mackay, W.S.	Cst	27866	H
Mackeen, C.W.	Sgt	22757	J
Mason, B.	Sgt	24720	B
Mason, J.R.	Cst	27989	E
McCarthy, R.	Cst	28052	E
McGinis, J.L.	Cst	27889	B
McIntosh, I.D.	Cpl	23702	O
McPhail, K.S.	Cst	15896	H
Michaud, R.K.	Cpl	27405	O
Morris, K.J.	Cst	27963	E
Morrison, B.A.	Cst	27880	K
Musclow, L.D.N.	Sgt	20650	E
Nauss, D.F.	Cst	27124	L
Nickerson, K.E.	Cpl	26650	E
O'Reilly, M.F.	Sgt	22368	E

Parnell, A.R.	Cst	27879	J
Perley, G.D.	Cst	27896	F
Peters, D.L.	Cst	23198	E
Pettigrew, D.L.	Cst	27892	D
Phillips, K.M.	Cpl	26631	D
Pothier, C.G.	Cpl	22132	C
Prest, F.S.	Cst	27986	E
Rapacz, A.	Cpl	22755	C
Reid, R.W.	Cst	28019	J
Richard, J.R.	Cst	27884	O
Richardson, A.L.	Cst	27913	H
Riddle, J.A.	Cpl	21073	E
Roache, A.L.	S/Sgt	16036	HQ
Rose, C.A.	Cpl	24715	J
Russell, K.	Cst	27858	L
Samson, L.G.	Cst	27922	C
Scattergood, D.A.	Cst	28354	O
Smith, G.A.	Sgt	19841	D
Smith, R.D.	Cst	28017	E
Spears, E.D.	Sgt	15965	H
Sperry, D.R.	Cst	28325	B
Spurrell, A.N.	Cst	26695	J
Thornber, R.M.	Cst	27990	E
Unsworth, D.A.	Cpl	27086	E
Van De Braak, W.A.	Cpl	27668	E
Van Zant, G.G.	Cst	27987	E
Vance, W.F.	S/Sgt	20690	L
Veinott, G.W.	Cpl	27181	B
Veinotte, J.D.	Cst	27905	H
Walker, E.E.	Cpl	25757	E
Watters, W.D.	Cst	27893	H

Wells, E.H.	Cpl	27861	A
Welsh, M.E.	Sgt	23701	E
White, G.H.	Cst	28004	H

ENGINEERS

Bayers, R.W.	S/Sgt	19683	E
Budge, T.	Cpl	24257	C
Cantelope, D.F.	Cst	27894	H
Christison, G.J.	Cst	27898	K
Clarke, K.	Cst	27438	A
Cole, E.	Cpl	24158	E
Companion, J.G.	Cpl	24027	E
Creaser, B.B.	Cst	27869	A
Dalton, J.W.	Cst	27881	J
Davis, G.E.	Cst	27961	E
Dodds, R.E.	Cpl	19705	E
Doney, A.P.	S/Sgt	19110	H
Dunphy, C.M.	Sgt	22271	B
Durling, C.E.	Cst	27960	E
Fairn, D.R.	Cst	27973	E
Fleurie, R.E.	Cst	26867	E
Furlong, R.B.	Cst	27876	H
Gallant, G.S.	Cst	27860	HQ
Gardner, W.F.	Cpl	27867	E
Grant, H.B.	Cpl	22269	E
Hanton, L.J.	Cst	28680	E
Hill, W.R.	Cst	27874	H
Isnor, R.S.	Cpl	20301	H
Jesso, W.V.	Cpl	20203	H
Landers, A.B.	Cpl	23992	D
Leadbetter, H.M.	Cpl	23603	E
Leet, G.M.	Cst	26211	H
Long, G.P.	Cst	27895	K
Lowe, G.S.	Cst	26845	H
MacAulay, G.A.	Cst	27915	O
MacDouguall, R.G.J.	Cst	27819	E
Mackenzie, J.E.	Cst	27886	O
MacMillan, J.A.	S/Sgt	21649	H
Martel. J.A.J.F.	Cst	28864	C
McDonald, A.J.	Cpl	22756	A
McGarry, P.J.T.	Cpl	26651	L
McIntyre, T.L.	Cpl	21582	E
Moss, N.C.	Cpl	25758	E
Norman, F.J.	Cst	27372	C
Northcott, T.D.	Sgt	24026	L
Outhouse, W.E.	Cst	27890	E
Penny, L.E.	Cst	27959	E
Pheifer, C.A.	Cst	27901	A
Pierce, G.W.	Cpl	20310	E
Pryde, L.E.	Cpl	25519	H
Richards, J.M.	Cpl	19281	O
Rooke, J.E.	Cpl	22236	E
Sherman, P.M.	Cst	27875	E
Smith, D.L.	Cst	27970	E
Taylor, C.	Cpl	25365	B
Thorne, G.	Cpl	24719	B
Tucker, W.J.	Cpl	26844	O
Wesley, D.C.	Cst	27903	C
Winters, R.G.	Cpl	24157	J

Glossary of Abbreviations

ASDIC	Anti Submarine Detection Investigation
CADC	Crown Assets Distribution Centre
CCG	Canadian Coast Guard
CFAV	Canadian Forces Auxiliary Vessel
CFB	Canadian Forces Base
CGP	Canadian Government Police
CGS	Canadian Government Ship
FLIR	Forward Looking Infra Red
GT	Gross Tonnage
HMCS	Her Majesty's Canadian Ship
HP	Horsepower
ICW	Intracoastal Waterway
ML	Motor Launch
MV	Motor Vessel
NWMP	Nort West Mounted Police
PB	Patrol Boat
PL	Patrol Launch
PV	Patrol Vessel
RCMP	Royal Canadian Mounted Police
RCN	Royal Canadian Navy
RCNR	Royal Canadian Naval Reserve
RCNVR	Royal Canadian Naval Volunteer Reserve
RNWMP	Royal North West Mounted Police
RCAF	Royal Canadian Air Force

APPENDIX 'C'

Roll Call of RCMP West Coast Marine Services from February 2000

Name	Date	Name	Date
S/Sgt Vic Loucks	2000 - 2002	Cst John May	*2000 -
S/Sgt Frank Shedden	2002 - 2003	Cst Blake Ward	*2000 -
S/Sgt Bruce Morrison	2003 - 2005	Cst Calvin Keir	*2000 -
S/Sgt Bryan Gordon	2006 -	Cst Kenneth Haycock	*2000 -
Sgt Peter Attrell	*2000 -	Cst L.R. Newton	2000 - 2001
Sgt Kim McDonald	*2000 - 2006	Cst Jamie Taplin	2000 - 2002
Sgt Frank Lalear	*2000 - 2002	Cst Paul McIntosh	2000 -
Sgt Gene Pinnegar	*2000 - 2002	Cst Trevor Murray	2000 -
Sgt Andy Brinton	*2006 -	Cst Bryan Valentine	2000 -
Cpl/Sgt Ken Burton	*2000 - 2005	Cst Chris Caldwell	2000 -
Cpl/Sgt Mark Peers	*2000 - 2004	Cst Dave Campbell	2002 - 2003
Cst/Cpl/Sgt Mike Lariviere	*2000 -	Cst Alain Beaulieu	2002 - 2003
Cpl Richard Hartigan	*2000 - 2000	Cst Shane Meisner	2002 - 2005
Cpl Mike Hartung	*2000 - 2001	Cst Jeanne Vestergaard	2003 - 2005
Cpl Doug Scattergood	*2000 - 2002	Cst Todd Eppler	2003 -
Cpl Jim Vardy	*2000 - 2005	Cst Gene Kikcio	2003 -
Cpl Stan Mowez	*2000 - 2006	Cst Carl Lippke	2003 -
Cpl Kirby Anderson	*2003 - 2006	Cst Rob Pikola	2003 -
Cst/Cpl Ray Kobzey	*2000 - 2006	Cst Greg Hepner	2004 -
Cst/Cpl Richard Harry	*2000 -	Cst Therese Cochlin	2005 - 2006
Cst Pete Marsden	*2000 - 2000	Cst Clarence Dykema	2005 -
Cst Roy Nishimura	*2000 - 2000	Cst Mark Futter	2006 -
Cst Gerry Desaulniers	*2000 - 2004	Cst Sean Phillip	2006 -
Cst Ian Saul	*2000 - 2006	Cst Carl Tulk	2006 -
Cst Mike Schmeisser	*2000 -		
Cst John Stringer	*2000 -		

* Members of the Marine Service prior to its reorganization in 2000

APPENDIX 'D'

Chronology of the RCMP Marine Services

1841 - Ministry of Customs established.

1867 - Department of Marine and Fisheries established.

1868 - Dominion Police established.

1873 May - An Act Respecting the Administration of Justice and for the Establishment of a Police Force in the Northwest Territories marks the beginning of the NWMP, with the purpose of policing the territory from the western boundary of Manitoba to the Rocky Mountains, under the control of the Ministry of Justice.

1874 - First posts established in Fort MacLeod and Fort Pelly and NWMP HQ established at Swan River.

1876 - NWMP under the control of Department of the Secretary of State.

1878 - NWMP under the control of Department of Interior.

1879 - NWMP HQ moved to Fort MacLeod then to Fort Walsh.

1882 Dec 6 - NWMP HQ moved from Fort Walsh to Pile of Bones Creek at Regina.

1883 - NWMP under the control of Department of Indian Affairs.

1885 - Fisheries Protection Service established from Department of Marine and Fisheries.

1886 - Gold discovered in the Yukon.

1887 - NWMP under the control of president of Privy Council.

1889 - NWMP expanded into the Keewatin District at the request of Manitoba and the Northwest Territories with control turned over to Department of Railways and Canals.

1890 - First vessel purchased for the NWMP–the *Keewatin*.

1891 - NWMP control returned to the President of Privy Council.

1895 - First NWMP post established in Fort Constantine, Yukon Territory.

1897 - The Preventive Service of the Department of Customs and Excise established from Ministry of Customs.

1901 - NWMP sends total of 18 officers and 160 men to the 2nd Canadian Mounted Rifles and Lord Strathcona's Horse Corps for the Anglo Boer War in South Africa.

1903 - A detachment established at Herschel Island to proclaim Canada's Sovereignty over the Arctic to stave off Norwegian interest in the Arctic and to control whalers and explorers from America and Europe.

1903 - A dispute arises between Canada and the USA over the boundaries with Alaska.

1904 - NWMP expands into Hudson Bay area to open 'M' Division.

1904 June 24 - The prefix 'Royal' conferred on the North West Mounted Police becoming Royal North West Mounted Police.

1905 March - 'N' Division established for Athabasca District. Also new provinces of Alberta and Saskatchewan to use services of RNWMP.

1910 May 4 - The Royal Canadian Navy established.

1914 - First World War starts, RNWMP members refused entry into war effort.

1917 - Police duties in Manitoba, Saskatchewan and Alberta suspended for WW1.

1918 - Members of RNWMP allowed to enlist in war effort.

1918 Nov 11 - WW1 ends in Europe.

1919 Nov 10 - The RNWMP Act amended and provided for a name change to the Royal Canadian Mounted Police–RCMP, the Dominion Police Service was absorbed, RCMP authority extended to all of Canada with four branches, Criminal Investigation, Intelligence, Finance and Supply, and Adjutants Office. Headquarters moved from Regina to Ottawa.

1921 - Ministry of Customs becomes Customs and Excise, RCMP control to the Department of Justice.

1922 - RCMP control to Department of Militia and Defence temporarily then returned to the Department of Justice.

1927 - Customs and Excise becomes National Revenue.

1928 - RCMP takes over Provincial Policing for Saskatchewan 'F' Division.

1928 - The *St Roch* built in Vancouver for Arctic Patrols.

1930 - Department of Marine and Fisheries separated into Department of Marine and Department of Fisheries.

1932 - RCMP takes over Provincial Policing for Alberta ('K' Div.), Manitoba ('D' Div.), Nova Scotia ('H' Div), New Brunswick ('J' Div), Prince Edward Island ('L' Div), and the Department of National Revenue Preventive Service establishes the Marine Section with 35 vessels.

1936 - The Department of Transport established from Department of Railways and Canals (1879) and the Department of Marine (1930).

1938 - Yukon Territories 'B' Division HQ at Dawson, and Yukon Territory 'G' Division, with HQ at Edmonton amalgamated with HQ in Ottawa.

1939 Sep - World War II declared, RCMP Marine Section terminates as all assets and manpower moved to the RCN and RCAF. The RCN had 13 ships at the start of the war.

1939 - RCMP Criminal Investigation Department changed to RCMP Security Service.

1945 - RCMP Marine and Air Sections re-established.

1946 - The Canadian Naval Auxiliary Service formed.

1947 - RCMP Marine Section becomes the RCMP Marine Division with HQ in Halifax.

1950 Aug - British Columbia ('E' Div) and Newfoundland ('B' Div) comes under provincial contract with the RCMP.

1962 - The Canadian Coast Guard established from the Department of Transport Canadian Marine Service fleet.

1966 - RCMP control to Solicitor General of Canada.

1970 - The RCMP Marine Division terminated and assets turned over to their respective Provincial Divisions, management and control falls under the Divisional Criminal Operations Branch. Administration maintained by Marine Services Directorate at Headquarters.

1971 - Department of Fisheries becomes part of the Department of Environment then renamed Department of Fisheries and Environment in 1976.

1974 - RCMP Marine policy and administration goes to Transport Management Branch, Services and Supply Directorate.

1974 - 'M' Division established at Whitehorse in the Yukon.

1979 - Department of Fisheries and Environment split and becomes Department of Fisheries and Oceans and Environment Canada.

1984 Canadian Security Intelligence Service formed.

1994 - RCMP Marine Service Administration to Fleet Program Administration, Material & Services Management Branch.

1995 - Canadian Coast Guard becomes part of Fisheries and Oceans Canada, all Federal Government's civilian manned ships except for naval auxiliaries placed under the administration of one department.

2000 - 'V' Division established in new territory of Nunavit.

2003 - RCMP Marine Service administration to Assets & Procurement Branch, Corporate Management & Comptrollership.

APPENDIX 'E'

Assigned 'MP' Numbers to RCMP Vessels

MP 10 - COLONEL WHITE
MP 11 - FRENCH
MP 12 - HERCHMER
MP 13 - IRVINE
MP 14 - MACBRIEN
MP 15 - MACLEOD
MP 16 - PERRY
MP 17 - STARNES/WOOD
MP 20 - DUNCAN
MP 21 - HARVISON
MP 22 - MCCLELLAN
MP 23 - RIVETT CARNAC
MP 30 - FORT PITT
MP 31 - FORT SELKIRK (1)/VICTORIA
MP 32 - FORT STEELE (1)/BLUE HERON
MP 33 - FORT WALSH
MP 34 - FORT STEELE (2)
MP 35 - VALLEYFIELD II
MP 37 - OUTLOOK
MP 38 - DAWSON
MP 39 - WHITEHORSE
MP 40 - STANDOFF (2)
MP 41 - SLIDEOUT
MP 42 - BATTLEFORD
MP 43 - MOOSE JAW
MP 44 - LAC LA RONGE
MP 45 - DAUPHIN
MP 46 - BRULE (2)
MP 47 - RELIANCE
MP 48 - ATHABASKA
MP 49 - NICHOLSON
MP 50 - CAPTOR
MP 51 - TOFINO
MP 52 - ACADIAN
MP 53 - SIDNEY
MP 54 - FORT ERIE
MP 55 - SOREL
MP 56 - VALLEYFIELD
MP 57 - KENORA III
MP 58 - PORT ALICE
MP 59 - ADVANCE
MP 60 - AKLAVIK/STANDOFF (1)/FORT ST JAMES/REGINA
MP 61 - BRULE (1)/BEAVER
MP 62 - CARNDUFF
MP 63 - CHILCOOT (1)/YELLOWKNIFE
MP 64 - CUTKNIFE
MP 65 - FITZGERALD/BIG BEND
MP 66 - GRENFELL
MP 67 - LITTLE BOW
MP 68 - MOOSOMIN
MP 69 - SHAUNAVON
MP 70 - SLIDEOUT
MP 71 - TAGISH
MP 72 - YELLOWKNIFE/WILLOW BUNCH
MP 73 - PML 6/FORT MACLEOD
MP 74 - PML 9/DUFFERIN
MP 75 - MANYBERRIES
MP 76 - PML 15/CENTENNIAL
MP 77 - PML 16
MP 78 - PML 17
MP 79 - ML 1/WESTVIEW
MP 80 - ARRESTEUR/ML 2/TAHSIS
MP 81 - DETECTOR/CHILCOOT II
MP 82 - LAURIER/CUTKNIFE II
MP 83 - MACDONALD/INTERCEPTOR
MP 84 - MACKENZIE/BURIN
MP 85 - SHAUNAVON II
MP 86 - DETECTOR
MP 87 - NANAIMO
MP 88 - CARNDUFF II
MP 89 - TAGISH II
MP 90 - KENORA (1)/PEARKES
MP 91 - FORT FRANCES
MP 92 - FORT FRANCES II
MP 93 - MASSET
MP 94 - KENORA II/FRASER
MP 95 - LITTLE BOW II
MP 96 - MOOSOMIN II
MP 97 - GANGES
MP 98 - ALERT
MP 99 - ADVERSUS
MP 100 - CENTENNIAL

APPENDIX 'F'

RCMP Divisions

1873 - March West - 'Division' referred to a group of men and their horses

'A' Division - dark bay horses

'B' Division - dark brown horses

'C' Division - chestnut horses

'D' Division - grey horses

'E' Division - black horses

'F' Division - light bay horses

1881 -

'A' Division	Fort Walsh (28 men)
'B' Division	Fort Walsh (14 men)
	Qu'Appelle (47 men)
	Shoal Lake (4 men)
	Swan River (3 men)
'C' Division	Fort MacLeod (33 men)
	Blackfoot Crossing (15 men)
	Calgary (8 men)
	Macleod farm (5 men)
	Blood Indian Reserve (2 men)
'D' Division	Battleford (43 men)
	Saskatchewan (12 men)
	Prince Albert (2 men
	Fort Walsh (34 men)
'E' Division	Fort Walsh (34 men)
'F' Division	Fort Walsh (20 Men)
	Wood Mountain (20 men)

Total = 293 men

1884 -

HQ - Regina (1882)

'A' Division - Maple Creek (48 men)

'B' Division - Regina (129 men)

'C' Division - Fort MacLeod (68 men)

'D' Division - Battleford (200 men)

'E' Division - Calgary (112 men)

Total = 557 men

1885 -

HQ & Depot - Regina

'A' Division - Maple Creek, Medicine Hat, Swift Current

'B' Division - Regina

'C' Division - Fort MacLeod

'D' Division - Battleford

'E' Division - Calgary

'F' Division - Prince Albert

'G' Division - Edmonton, Fort Saskatchewan.

'H' Division - Fort MacLeod

'K' Division - Battleford, Lethbridge (1887)

1898 -

Yukon Territory split north and south

'B' Division - Dawson, Northern YT

'H' Division - Tagish, Southern YT

1899 -

'H' Division - Whitehorse, YT

1904 'N' Division - Athabaska

1905 -

'D' Division - Fort MacLeod

'M' Division - Fullerton, Hudson Bay

1910 -

'A' Division - Maple Creek

'B' Division - Yukon (1910)

'C' Division - Battleford

'D' Division - Macleod

'E' Division - Calgary

'F' Division - Prince Albert

'G' Division - Fort Saskatchewan

'K' Division - Lethbridge

'M' Division - Fort Churchill

'N' Division - Athabaska Landing

Depot Division - Regina

1914 -

'A' Division - Maple Creek

'B' Division - Yukon

'C' Division - Battleford

'D' Division - Macleod

'E' Division - Calgary

'F' Division - Prince Albert

'G' Division - Edmonton

'K' Division - Lethbridge

'M' Division - Fort Churchill

'N' Division - Athabaska Landing

Depot Division - Regina

1919 -
'A' Division - Maple Creek
'B' Division - Dawson, Yukon
'D' Division - Winnipeg
'E' Division - Victoria
'F' Division - Fullerton
'G' Division - Edmonton
'K' Division - Lethbridge
Depot Division - Regina

1920 -
'A' Division - Ottawa
'B' Division - Yukon
'C' Division - Brandon
'D' Division - Winnipeg
'E' Division - Vancouver
'F' Division - Prince Albert
'G' Division - Edmonton
'H' Division - Vancouver
'K' Division - Lethbridge
'M' Division - Macleod
'N' Division - Ottawa
Depot Division - Regina

1930 -
'A' Division - Ottawa, Ontario
'B' Division - Yukon
'C' Division - Brandon, Manitoba
'D' Division - Winnipeg, Manitoba
'E' Division - Vancouver, B.C.
'F' Division - Prince Albert, Sask.
'G' Division - Edmonton, Alta.
'H' Division - Vancouver, B.C.
'K' Division - Lethbridge, Alberta
'M' Division - Macleod, Alberta
'N' Division - Ottawa, Ontario
'O' Division - Ontario
Depot Division - Regina, Sask.

1932 -
'A' Division - Ottawa, Ontario
'B' Division - Yukon
'C' Division - Montreal, Quebec
'D' Division - Winnipeg, Manitoba
'E' Division - Vancouver, B.C.
'F' Division - Saskatchewan
'G' Division - Aklavik, N.W.T
'H' Division - Halifax, Nova Scotia
'J' Division - New Brunswick
'K' Division - Lethbridge, Alberta
'L' Division - Prince Edward Island
'M' Division - Macleod, Alberta
'N' Division - Ottawa, Ontario
'O' Division - Ontario
Depot Division - Regina, Sask.
Marine Section

1936 -
'A' Division - Ottawa, Ontario
'B' Division - Yukon
'C' Division - Quebec
'D' Division - Manitoba
'E' Division - British Columbia
'F' Division - Saskatchewan
'G' Division - N.W.T.
'H' Division - Nova Scotia
'J' Division - New Brunswick
'K' Division - Alberta
'L' Division - Prince Edward Island
'N' Division - Ontario
'O' Division - Ontario
Depot Division - Saskatchewan

1937 - Air Section
1946 - Aviation Section
1947 - Marine Division

2008 -
'A' Division - Ottawa, Ontario
'B' Division - St Johns, Newfoundland
'C' Division - Montreal, Quebec
'D' Division - Winnipeg, Manitoba
'E' Division - Vancouver, British Columbia
'F' Division - Regina, Saskatchewan
'G' Division - Yellowknife, N.W.T.
'H' Division - Halifax, Nova Scotia
'J' Division - Fredericton, New Brunswick
'K' Division - Edmonton, Alberta
'L' Division - Charlottetown, P.E.I.
'M' Division - Whitehorse, Yukon Territory (1974)
'N' Division - Rockcliffe, Ont. Training
'O' Division - London, Ontario
'V' Division - Iqaluit, Nunavut
Depot Division - Regina, Sask.
Air Division

Courtesy Gilles Gangne

APPENDIX 'G'

Harbour Defence Patrol Craft – HDPC

HMC HC6 - Willow Bunch
HMC HC11 - D1 then renamed HC36
HMC HC12 - D2
HMC HC13 - D10 then renamed HC180
HMC HC14 - D14
HMC HC15 - D15
HMC HC16 - D16
HMC HC17 - D17
HMC HC18 - Imperator
HMC HC19 - Cutknife
HMC HC20 - Brule
HMC HC24 - Tagish
HMC HC25 - Carnduff
HMC HC26 - Shaunavon
HMC HC27 - Advance/Big Bend
HMC HC29 - Arrow/Chilcoot
HMC HC30 - Slideout
HMC HC32 - Moosomin
HMC HC33 - Grenfell
HMC HC36 - Burma
HMC HC37 - Captor
HMC HC38 - Castor/Beaver
HMC HC39 - Standoff
HMC HC40 - Little Bow
HMC HC43 - Ellsworth
HMC HC46 - Fernand Rinfret
HMC HC47 - Guardian
HMC HC50 - Acadian/Invader
HMC HC51 - Islander
HMC HC63 - Protector
HMC HC88 - New Brunswicker
HMC HC104 - Vigil II

Courtesy RCMP Historical Collections Unit

Courtesy RCMP Historical Collections Unit

SOURCES

BOOKS:

Appleton, Thomas E., (1968), *Usque Ad Mare - A History of the Canadian Coast Guard and Marine Services,* Ottawa: Department of Transport.

Barr, William, (2005), *Red Serge and Polar Bear Pants,* Edmonton: University of Alberta Press.

Beahen, William and Horrall, Stan, (1998), *Red Coats on the Prairies,* Print West Publishing Services.

Boulton, James J., (1990), *Uniforms of the Canadian Mounted Police, Northbattleford:* Turner-Warwick Publications Inc.

Boulton, James J., (2000), *Head-Dress of the Canadian Mounted Police, 1873-2000,* Calgary: Bunker to Bunker Publishing.

Chambers, Captain Ernest J., (1972), *The North-West Mounted Police, A Corps History:* Coles Publishing Co. Reprint of the 1906 Mortimer Press edition.

Dobrowolsky, Helene, (1995), *Law of the Yukon: A Pictorial History of the Mounted Police in the Yukon:* Lost Moose Yukon Publishers.

Farrar, F.S., (1974), *Arctic Assignment, The Story of the St Roch,* Toronto: Macmillan of Canada.

Fetherstonhaugh, R.C., (1938), *The Royal Canadian Mounted Police,* N.Y: Carrick & Evans Inc.

Horrall, S.W., (1973). *The Pictorial History of the Royal Canadian Mounted Police,* Toronto: McGraw Hill Ryerson Limited, Canada.

Kelly, Nora and William, (1973), *The Royal Canadian Mounted Police, A Century of History 1873 - 1973,* Edmonton: Hurtig Publishers.

Knuckle, Robert, (1994), *In the Line of Duty–the Honour Roll of the RCMP since 1873,* Burnstown, Ontario: General Store Publishing House.

Larsen, Henry, (2000), *Reports and Other Papers Relating to the Two Voyages of the RCM Police Schooner 'St Roch',* Vancouver: Pierway Inc, and Vancouver Maritime Museum.

Lee, Herbert Patrick, (1928), *Policing the Top of the World,* London: John Lane.

MacDonald, Molly Anne, (1973), *The Royal Canadian Mounted Police*: Macmillan Press Ltd.

Macleod, R.C., (c1976), *The NWMP and Law Enforcement, 1873-1905,* Toronto: University of Toronto Press.

Macpherson, Ken and Burgess, John, (1981), *The Ships of Canada's Naval Forces 1910 -1985,* Toronto: Collins Publishers.

Maginley, Charles and Collin, Bernard, (2001), *The Ships of Canada's Marine Services:* Vanwell Publishing Limited.

Mills, John M., (1979), *Canadian Coastal and Inland Steam Vessels 1809 – 1930*: The Steamship Historical Society of America, Inc.

Morrison, William R., (1985), *Showing the Flag,* Vancouver: University of British Columbia Press.

Robertson, Douglas Sinclair, (1934), *To the Arctic with the Mounties,* Toronto: The Macmillan Company of Canada, Ltd.

RCMP Centennial Review, (1973), *Royal Canadian Mounted Police Centennial 1873 – 1973,* Ottawa: Rolph-McNally Limited.

RCMP Commissioner's' Annual Report for years 1903/1904, 1905/1906, 1907, 1908, 1910, 1913, 1914, 1917, 1918, 1920-1932 inclusive, 1934-1940 inclusive, 1946-1971 inclusive.

Privy Council, (1903), Annual Report of the Northwest Mounted Police, Sessional Paper No. 28. 1903, 9 Ottawa: Privy Council.
Privy Council, (1904), Annual Report of the Royal Northwest Mounted Police, Sessional Paper No. 28. 1904, 9 Ottawa: PrivyCouncil.
Privy Council, (1905), Annual Report of the Royal Northwest Mounted Police, Sessional Paper No. 28, 28A. 1905, 9 Ottawa: Privy Council.
Privy Council, (1906), Annual Report of the Royal Northwest Mounted Police, Sessional Paper No. 28. 1906, 9 Ottawa: Privy Council.
Privy Council, (1907), Annual Report of the Royal Northwest Mounted Police, Sessional Paper No. 28. 1907, 9 Ottawa: Privy Council.
Privy Council, (1905), Annual Report of the Royal Northwest Mounted Police, Sessional Paper No. 28. 1905, 9 Ottawa: Privy Council.

RCMP Quarterly Staff, *The Mounties As They Saw Themselves.*

RCMP 'G' Division Headquarters Ottawa (compiled by), (1961), *Royal Canadian Mounted Police in Canada's North.*

Steele, Harwood Elmes Robert, (1936), *Policing the Arctic,* London: Jarrod's.

Tucker, Gilbert Norman, Ph.D., (1952), *The Naval Service of Canada, Volume 1 and 2,* Ottawa: King's Printer.

Vancouver Maritime Museum, (2001), *Project Report – St Roch Preservation Campaign.*

INTERNET PUBLICATIONS

Appleton, Thomas E., (1968), *Usque Ad Mare–A History of the Canadian Coast Guard and Marine Services,* Ottawa: Department of Transport, retrieved from http://www.ccg-gcc.gc.ca/eng/CCG/USQUE_Table_Contents

Jarvis-Lowe, Bonnie, (1958, *The Loss Of The MP Fort Walsh,* retrieved from http://www.ourecho.com/story-925--THE-LOSS-OF-THE-MP-FORT-WALSH-.shtml

Roscoe, Spurgeon *G., Radio Stations Common? Not This Kind–Section 6*–Royal Canadian Mounted Police Marine Section, retrieved from http://www.coastalradio.org.uk/spud/spud/spud06.pdf

West Coast Marine Detachment Photo Gallery, retrieved from http://members.shaw.ca/rcmpwcmd/HistoricalPhotogallery.htm

Royal Canadian Mounted Police Marine Service Historical Review (2007) retrieved from http://members.shaw.ca/rcmpwcmd/Historical_Data.pdf

Royal Canadian Mounted Police History –
–Module I – North-West Mounted Police (NWMP) 1893-1904
–Module II – Royal Northwest Mounted Police (RNWMP) 1904-1920
–Module III – Royal Canadian Mounted Police (RCMP) 1920-1945
–Module IV – Royal Canadian Mounted Police (RCMP) 1945-2001, retrieved from http://www.rcmp-learning.org/history/history.htm

MacBride Museum, Whitehorse, Yukon in conjunction with Virtual Museum Canada and the Yukon RCMP Veterans Association, (2006), *The Force in the North.* Available from http://www.virtualmuseum.ca/Exhibitions/Force/en/home/

INTERNET DATABASES

Images Canada on-line database, found at http://www.imagescanada.ca/index-e.html

Royal BC Museum, BC Archives Visual Records on-line catalogue, found at the internet site: http://www.bcarchives.bc.ca/BC_Our_Collections/BC_Visual_Rrd_Collect.aspx

Transport Canada, Marine Safety Vessel Registration Query System, found at http://www.tc.gc.ca/ShipRegistry/advanced.asp?lang=e

The New Mills' List Database–compiled from Mills, John M, *Registered Canadian Steamships 1817-1930 over 75 feet.* Part of the Maritime Museum of the Great Lakes at Kingston databases found at http://db.library.queensu.ca/marmus/

North West Territories Archives on-line databases, found at http://pwnhc.learnnet.nt.ca/programs/archive.htm
NAVAL MUSEUM of Manitoba
National Archives of Canada – ArchiviaNet
Fisheries and Oceans Canada
Canadian War Museum
Government of Canada Military Heritage
Musee Naval de Quebec

PUBLICATIONS AND MAGAZINES

Arctic Magazine - Vol 56, No 1, March 2003.

CAHS Journal, v. XVII, 1979 Spring (Canadian Aviation Historical Society) by Air Commodore W.I. Clements.

DND Directorate of History on RCMP Marine History, ca. 1972, author update unknown.

Diver Magazine - September 1992.

Harbour and Shipping Magazine - February 1986, Sept 1991.

Mariner Life - July 2005.

Pacific Yachting Magazine - June 2006.

Resolution Magazine - Number 25, Spring 1992.

RCMP Quarterly Magazine - Jan 1959, July 1965.

RCMP Gazette - Vol. 53, No. 4, 1991.

SAR Scene Magazine - Vol. 4, No. 3, Oct 1994.

West Coast Mariner Magazine - June 1991, January 1993.

Attrell, Sgt P.A., Summer 1997, RCMP Marine Services. *Royal Canadian Mounted Police Quarterly,* Vol. 62-3, 30-32.

Baugh, Cpl V.R., Fall 1977. *Royal Canadian Mounted Police Quarterly,* Vol. 42-4, 39-40.

Bell, Cpl W.E.F., July 1946, The R.C.M.P. Marine Section in War. *Royal Canadian Mounted Police Quarterly,* Vol. 12-1, 54-62.

Bell, Cpl W.E.F., October 1948, Patrolling Canadian Inland Waters. *Royal Canadian Mounted Police Quarterly,* Vol. 14-2, 82-85.

Boutilier, Cpl B.G., April 1955, A Bit About Boats. *Royal Canadian Mounted Police Quarterly,* Vol. 20-4, 341-344.

Clark, Cst J.D.S., April 1954, Reliance. From The Old Fort (1883) to Present Day. *Royal Canadian Mounted Police Quarterly,* Vol. 19-4, 322-326.

Clements, Air Commodore W., Spring 1979, Preventive Operations by the RCAF for the RCMP 1932-36. *CAHS Journal (The)*, Vol. XVII, 3-10.

Coffin, Skipper Lieut H.W., April 1934, *From Rum Runner to Patrol Boat 4. Royal Canadian Mounted Police Quarterly,* Vol. 1-4, 184-186.

Dawe, S/Sgt G.H., Spring 1986, Wooden Ships, *Royal Canadian Mounted Police Quarterly,* Vol. 51-2, 8-12.

Gagne, Sgt O.G., July 1970, Patrol Boat Moosomin II. *Royal Canadian Mounted Police Quarterly,* Vol. 36-1, 14-15.

Gallant, Sgt G.S., Winter 1990, Centennial's Last Patrol. *Royal Canadian Mounted Police Quarterly,* Vol. 55-1, 15-16.

Gilbert, D., Fall 2005, Arctic Circle: Rediscovering the RCMP's Roots in the North. *Royal Canadian Mounted Police Quarterly,* Vol. 70-4, 26-32.

Hann, G.T., October 1940, The Cruise of the Chakawana. *Royal Canadian Mounted Police Quarterly,* Vol. 8-2, 193-198.

King, Sgt P, Winter 2002, Remembering the Mackenzie River Patrol of 1961. *Royal Canadian Mounted Police Quarterly,* Vol. 12-1, 54-62.

MacNeil, Skipper R.A.S., July 1938, The Marine Section of the Force. *Royal Canadian Mounted Police Quarterly,* Vol. 67-1, 36-40.

MacNeil, Sub-Inspr R.A.S., April 1946, The Marine Section of the Force. *Royal Canadian Mounted Police Quarterly,* Vol. 11-4, 192-200.

McKay, Cst M.R., July 1968, Marine Division at Expo. *Royal Canadian Mounted Police Quarterly,* Vol. 34-1, 36-38.

Milthorp, Skipper, P.R.F., October 1937, The Marine Section–Types of Vessels and Their Uses. *Royal Canadian Mounted Police Quarterly,* Vol. 5-2, 108-109.

Milthorp, First Officer, P.R.F., October 1939, Tropical Cruise, *Royal Canadian Mounted Police Quarterly,* Vol. 7-4, 153-156.

New RCMP Ships Commissioned, January 1959, *Royal Canadian Mounted Police Quarterly,* Vol. 24-3, 191-194.

Newman, Sgt R.O., January 1956, New RCMP Patrol Boats, *Royal Canadian Mounted Police Quarterly,* Vol. 21-3, 176-178.

Nevin, Sgt W.H., September 1945, Policing the Far North, *Beaver (The),* pp 6-10

"Of Things to Come" – 'Marine' Division, July 1955. *Royal Canadian Mounted Police Quarterly,* Vol. 21-1, 3-7.

Ouellette, R., Winter 2005, Patrolling Canada's West Coast. *Royal Canadian Mounted Police Quarterly,* Vol. 70-1, 8-12.

Palmer, Cst J.D., Fall 1983, Search and Rescue Aboard PV Pearkes. *Royal Canadian Mounted Police Quarterly,* Vol. 48-4, 8-13.

RCMP Eskimo Point, October 1956, *Royal Canadian Mounted Police Quarterly,* Vol. 22-2, 174-175.

RCMP Patrol Boat *Nanaimo*, July 1963, *Royal Canadian Mounted Police Quarterly,* Vol. 29-1, 22.

Royal Canadian Mounted Police Cruiser "Interceptor". July 1934, *Royal Canadian Mounted Police Quarterly,* Vol. 2-1, 4-5.

Roberts, Sub-Inspr G.C., January 1947, Mercy Missions at Sea. *Royal Canadian Mounted Police Quarterly,* Vol. 12-3, 216-217.

Roberts, Sgt N.C.C., April 1955, New RCMP Patrol Boat for the Great Lakes. *Royal Canadian Mounted Police Quarterly,* Vol. 20-4, 332-333.

Rogers, Cst I, Winter, 1990, The Reluctant Heron. *Royal Canadian Mounted Police Quarterly,* Vol. 55-1, 22-62.

Scott, Sgt E., April 1954, New RCMP Vessel for Pacific Coast. *Royal Canadian Mounted Police Quarterly,* Vol. 19-4, 314-315.

Scott, Sgt E., July 1958, Fangs of Ripple Rock, *Royal Canadian Mounted Police Quarterly,* Vol. 24-1, 5-10.

Some Preventive Service Cases. July 1944, *Royal Canadian Mounted Police Quarterly,* Vol. 2-1, 40-43.

Stanfield, Ruth, Fall 1982, The NWMP Launch *Gladys*. *Royal Canadian Mounted Police Quarterly,* Vol. 47-4, 30-32.

Thornily, PO J., July 1940, Our Marine Section. *Royal Canadian Mounted Police Quarterly,* Vol. 8-1, 58.

Van de Braak, Sgt W.A., Winter 1987, PV Stikine Commissioned. *Royal Canadian Mounted Police Quarterly,* Vol. 52-1, 24-27.

Wilson, Clifford, March 1945, Arctic Odyssey, *Beaver (The)*, pp 3-7

ARCHIVES:

Library and Archives Canada,

Library and Archives Canada. *Wrecks, Casualties and Salvage – Reported – Keewatin – On Lake Winnipeg*. (1890). RG 12, Vol. 1529, File 9708-K1.

(LAC) RCMP - *Collision between RCMP chartered boat Lincolin II and O.K. Service III* RG13 Series A-2 Vol. 401, File 1934-644.

(LAC) *Vessels built for or purchased by RNWMP between 1896 and 1911*. (1913). RG18, Vol. 424, File 35.

(LAC) *Motorboats (registered and unregistered) operated by RCMP.* (1923). RG18, Vol. 3177, File 1925.

(LAC) *List of Power and other Vessels in care of Police–Return to Dept of Marine and Fisheries.* (1924). RG18, Series F-1, Vol. 3177, File G945-4.

(LAC) *Annual Report, 1924 Parts 2*. (1924). RG18, Vol. 3177, File 855-3.

(LAC) *Scrapbook kept by Marine Division*. (1961-1969). RG18, Series F-1, Vol. 3562.

(LAC) *Boat Built by Major Walker to cross 'C' & 'D' Division, over Bow River–Boat at Calgary.* (1887). RG18, Series B-1, Vol. 1073, File 233-1887.

(LAC) *The History of Marine Division Parts: Supp A, Supp B, Supp C*. RG18, Series F-1, Vol. 4678, File 516-88.

(LAC) *The History of Marine Division Parts: Supp D*. RG18, Series F-1, Vol. 4679, File 516-88.

(LAC) *RCNVR- Proposal for RCMP Marine Section to be Unit of RCNVR for Training*. (1932-1939). RG24, Series D-1-a, Vol. 5678, File 112-1-34.

(LAC) *Shipbuilding – Work done for other Departments – Trial of motor launch for North West Mounted Police*. (1916-1926). RG42, Series C-1, Vol. 1069, File 138-3-4.

RG18, Acc. No. 1996-400,
Tracker No. 2000833002, Box No. 46.
RG18, Series A-1, Vol. 261. *Vessels under control of North West Mounted Police*.
RG18, Vol. 4592, File G1470-28, *Ship's Radio License RCMP Preventive Boats*.
RG24 Series D-1-a, Vol. 5676, *RCMP Boats – Construction of New Boats*.
RG24 Vol. 4919, File 1008-19-2, *RCMP Boat Classes*.
RG24 Vol. 5676, File 910701, Parts 1, 2 and 3, *Work Done for Police Dept*.
RG24 Vol. 5824, File 8000-298, *General Information RCMP Vessels*.
RG24 Vol. 6725, File 8000-470/27, *General Information* HMCS *Interceptor.*

OTHERS

L/Cdr Bryon Taylor, Ottawa

RCMP Marine Member

Robert F. Holtom, Reg #12551, retired
Doug Scattergood, Reg #28354, retired, B.C.
John Kerster, Reg #15481, retired, B.C.
Bernie Mason, Reg #24720, retired
Peter Attrell, Reg #33350
Omer Gilles Gagne, Reg #20138, retired
Insp Ken Burton, Reg #02623

RCMP Member

Don Klancher, Reg #22129, Officer #01552, retired.
Len Stratton, Reg #30433, retired, Newfoundland
Arnold Kay, Reg #21051, retired and Ottawa Archival Researcher

RCMP Historical Section, Ottawa
Daniel Somers and Sophie Chevalier-Forget

RCMP Historical Collections Unit, Regina
Carmen Harry
Vancouver Maritime Museum
Lisa Glandt

Canadian Coast Guard
Captain David Johns, CCG, retired

Others
Peter Caron, B.C.
Bonnie Jarvis-Lowe, Newfoundland
Mark Lowe, Newfoundland
Joe Parsons, Alberta
Pat King,
Jack Kruger, N.W.T.
William M. Pender, Alberta
Vancouver Maritime Museum
Lloyds of London Register

Right: Members of the RCMP West Coast Marine Detachment left to right: Cst Paul McIntosh, Cst Chris Caldwell, Cst John May, aboard the Nadon *in Spiller Channel after completion of a major log theft investigation.*

Overleaf: PV Lindsay *in the Strait of Georgia. Photo courtesy D.F.O. Richard Christianson.*

POLICE
POLICE
LINDSAY

Index

Cst Kenn Haycock was born in Woodstock, Ontario in 1951. His interest in historical research and genealogy was influenced by his grandparents. He joined the Canadian Armed Forces as a Radio Operator in 1970 and was transferred to the west coast of Canada to CFB Esquimalt and eventually to HMCS Terra Nova. He left the armed forces and in 1988 joined the Royal Canadian Mounted Police. He served mainly in the detachments of the lower mainland of B.C. In 1998 he had the opportunity to join the RCMP Patrol Vessel *Lindsay* in Vancouver and in 2000 was transferred to the newly organized RCMP Marine Services in Nanaimo, B.C. It was during some research into past vessels of the RCMP that it became apparent there was no single source of information for the huge and important contribution that Marine Services have made to the RCMP.

With the assistance of members of the Force and other Services, he compiled this history, list and details of vessels used by the RCMP since the March West. This compilation is as complete as possible but some records are very vague as to ownership, usage, and details. Every possible means has been exercised to ensure the information is accurate. It is hoped that the reader becomes more aware of the contributions made by the RCMP Marine Services to the coastal communities and people of Canada in the past and still today, as they patrol the waterways and oceans of this vast country.

PV Inkster *and a RCMP floatplane docked at Langara, Haida Gwaii, on the West Coast. Photograph courtesy of Cst Brian Kermer.*